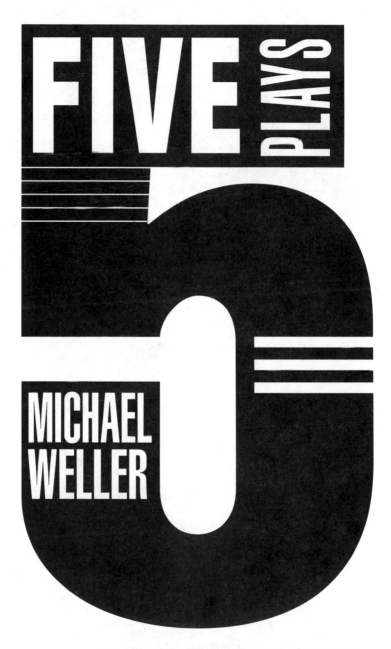

FIVE PLAYS

MICHAEL WELLER

THEATRE COMMUNICATIONS GROUP

This publication is made possible in part with public funds from the New York State Council on the Arts, a State Agency.

TCG books are exclusively distributed to the book trade by Consortium Book Sales and Distribution, 1045 Westgate Dr., St. Paul, MN 55114.

Library of Congress Cataloging in Publication Data
Weller, Michael, 1942-
Five plays / by Michael Weller; [introduction by Alan Schneider].
p. cm.
Contents: Moonchildren — Fishing — At home — Abroad — Loose ends.
ISBN-13: 978-1-55936-143-9
ISBN-10: 1-55936-143-3 (alk. paper)
I. Title.
PS3573.E457F58   1997
812'.54—dc21   97-40725 CIP

Cover design by Pentagram
Book design and composition by Lisa Govan

First TCG Edition, December 1997
Third Printing, June 2005

Contents

Foreword

by Michael Weller

Rereading these early plays for the first time in a decade and a half was a peculiar experience. As a rule, after something of mine is performed I close the door on it and clear my head for new work. I have *seen* these plays produced in the intervening years—some of them several times—but performance is an impersonal experience for a writer; more about actors and production than about the text. From time to time I entertained fleeting thoughts of looking over this or that early play but quashed them fast, afraid that a backward glance might make me cower with embarrassment or, worse, send me racing to my tool kit to fiddle and tinker away precious hours trying to improve upon the past instead of getting on with the principal business of a writer's life: today's pages.

So I set about revisiting these plays with a certain trepidation. As I read on, however, a mood of baffled amusement took hold, the sort of feeling you get when perusing old photos. "Were those *really* my friends back then?" "How did I ever *live* in that apartment?" "Where was that picture taken?" "*Who* is *she?*"

Entire encounters came as a surprise to me. I forgot I'd written them. I had in fact forgotten several small roles altogether, and in one case remembered character x being in play y, not play z (this *really* threw me). Some passages I recalled vividly enough, and certain scenes I recognized as embryonic attempts at things I would dramatize more fully (and better) in later plays, but in the main I felt as if I was listening to a stranger speak.

But not a *complete* stranger. Someone just different enough from who and what I know myself to be now that tampering with his words would be like invading another man's larynx. I'm obliged to commit more than enough sacrilege as a working screenwriter. As a playwright, never, dear god, never let it come to *that*!

Result: very little here is changed from the first edition. A word, a sentence, a line at most. I prefer to let the album stand as what it is: fond recollections of how the world struck me at certain times and places long gone.

As a writer, my concerns have naturally enough changed over the years. From being a solo act, with only myself to support and fret about, and with whole days free to write whenever the mood took me, I am now in my middle years and amply, happily, miraculously provided with all that implies . . . family, house, bills and days so full of things to do, that finding time to write for pleasure (plays) rather than profit (movies) is a constant juggling act. As a friend once observed, after forty years on earth, everything becomes maintenance.

I have come to see things more vertically, if you will—parents, children, generations of family—than horizontally; my contemporaries, our woes, our frolics. I am still chiefly concerned with my own generation's particular style of life, but I see it more in relation to the work we do, the partners we've chosen, the families we build or borrow, and the ideals we try to protect in the face of time, waning energy, increasing confusion and the hardening certainty of our appearance here being a limited engagement.

What seems to me unique and fascinating among those I know best (my generation) is how we've now lived to see the world change from one where we could plausibly (and with passion) believe that the efforts of a committed group of people like ourselves might alter a piece of history, to one where most if not all politics has become a subfunction (a rapidly diminishing subfunction) of global commerce. Our elected officials frantically tread water to create the illusion they are still necessary, while the important decisions of the day gravitate to the hands of international financiers accountable to neither voters, politicians nor mankind as a whole.

This is new. And to watch my generation sense the effects

of this power shift, with its attendant feeling of helplessness, is a fascinating enterprise. Some turn to religion, some turn cynical, others manage to invest themselves in something akin to traditional small-town volunteerism at a local level: their neighborhood, their block, their school, their gender group, their coworkers . . .

As a student, I recall furious debates with friends about the future disappearance of manual labor. It was assumed that in the foreseeable future, most of the dirty work would one day be done by machines. This would leave us free, said one side, to embellish our leisure time in unimaginable and wonderful ways (more theatre?!). The other side worried that it would leave a very large part of the human race with too much time on its hands and no good notion of what to do with it.

The latter group would seem to be winning the argument. And here, to me, is the deeper concern—there seems to be no compelling theory at hand to describe a course of action that might correct this trend or parlay it into a positive vision of the future we can invest in.

Both our political "parties" preach the same tired solutions to the same tired scenarios (cut the budget, cut expenses, cut taxes, tra-la, tra-la—for this we need office staff, not leadership). No one any longer believes these suggestions will solve the underlying problems. And in the midst of our disenchantment what is lost is hope. Whatever that rough beast may prove to be, we hear it slouching our way, but we don't know how to respond. We have no theory, no social agenda to arrest or resist its advance. We sit and wait. We look away. We get on with fixing the doorknob, planning the holiday, going to the movies. We splinter into smaller and smaller interest groups that seem less real than a neighborhood and less inspiring that a "nationhood." To what do we belong? To what do we owe allegiance? To what thing bigger than our own well-being can we assign value?

However, I digress. America, history, theatre, my plays—that's it, I was talking about . . .

In one respect my playwriting has changed very little over the years, and, reading the work in this volume again, it was instructive to see a clear continuity between my earliest and my latest output. Most of the plays herein are profligate, huge, impractically so; lots of actors; lots of sets. If I wrote them today they'd never be done professionally, at least not readily. I managed to sneak in just under the Wire of Time, before public and corporate abandonment of the arts shifted into high merry gear and, among other things, shaved the average size of a producible new play to something in the neighborhood of five actors.

But I *still* write large cast plays. It's what I like to write, it's what brought me into the theatre to begin with—the idea that I could put on stage a canvas, a gallery, a portrait of a time and place. My early excitement with theatre came from nights at the Royal Shakespeare Company and the National Theatre under Laurence Olivier, the T.N.P. in Paris, the Berliner Ensemble and, later, when I returned to live in New York, watching the phenomenal work of Andre Gregory's Manhattan Project, whose *Alice in Wonderland* I saw no less than six times. Big plays. Big sets. Big visions. Bustle. Movement. Dramatic daring, imagination, abundance.

This is still what I want to see when I go to the theatre. And I believe audiences do, too. They *crave* something on a scale reflecting the fact of many people assembled in one space to watch a story enacted, to see imitations of themselves striving, erring, achieving, failing and reaching the greatest of all moments in drama: recognition of their moral selves.

So rereading these plays presented me with a disquieting question. If I started out writing large plays when large plays were often produced, and I find myself 16 years (and 10 plays) later still writing large plays when productions are harder to come by and will perhaps one day soon be all but *impossible*, why continue writing for theatre?

This question any playwright of my generation is bound to face sooner or later, even that lucky devil whose Muse inspires him to pen only exquisite miniatures for a casts of two actors and a duck. Why continue? Why?

And, sadly, some of our most gifted writers, unable to find an answer, have vacated the old shop to work exclusively in the gilded precincts of movieland. This is a loss both to them and to us. To us, because fine writing is rare at any time, and writers who speak with authority in a distinctive voice are more necessary now than ever—and to *them* because a steady diet of film writing in this day of creation-by-committee *always* seems to dull the cutting blade of originality and to leave an author with too little he can point at and call his own, for which he can take full credit and derive full satisfaction.

Happily, we have some inspiring examples of dramatists who have managed to weather long and difficult careers in theatre and continue to write for it against all odds—Edward Albee, Arthur Miller, Horton Foote . . .

What keeps them going? What keeps *any* dramatist going? What keeps *me* going?

Love of theatre, obviously. Memories of past triumphs we can dream of seeing repeated one day? Habit? Routine? An insane optimism, an irrational hope that some unforeseen twist of human evolution will cause audiences to max out on electronically delivered stories and crave a new experience of live actors impersonating life events before a live gathering?

Maybe it's a compulsion to achieve that most elusive of creatures, the perfect play—"*this* time, if I have an idea perfectly suited to my gifts, and if I work hard enough, and if I have time, luck, inspiration and whatever else it takes, maybe *this* time I'll reach my apotheosis."

Sure, it's all those things. I even have a personal favorite suggested by my first teacher of playwriting, the great John Matthews, who offered, "the only reason to write a play is so you can see exactly what you want to in theatre once in a while."

But for me the reason above all that I keep going on with this impossible endeavor—and I offer it in response to Alan Schneider's anecdote in his introduction to the original publication of these plays, where he has me asking how anyone stays sane in this business after the age of fifty. I don't remember the incident, but according to Alan's retelling, he offered no answer. And here I am, over fifty and still going at it with, by and large, immense pleasure. So . . .

What keeps *me* sane, and the reason I go on, is that every new play is the first time out. And because it is always the first time, it is always the next one that might prove to be *the* experience of a lifetime, the one which to miss would diminish me, the one everything before was aiming at, the quintessence, the top of the mountain. If this feeling ever abandoned me, I would walk away from theatre without a glance back.

This hope, this *vision* of a perfect experience, has little if anything to do with dreams of success or failure commercially. I've done enough theatre to know that the magic, small, large and larger, can happen in a black-box theatre with only a dozen people watching. Or it can happen in a two-thousand-seat auditorium full to bursting. But when it does there is something inside that tells you unequivocally, "this is it."

And then . . .

How do you *know* for sure? Maybe there's better ahead. If it can still be this good after thirty years, maybe it can be even better next time, and the time after . . .

Here's a story with a happy end. *Loose Ends* (included here, cast of eleven) was accepted for production six days after I sent it to the Arena Stage in Washington, D.C., in 1979. My most recent produced play, *Buying Time* (not included, cast of thirteen), took five years to get from page to stage. It was announced several times and canceled several times for lack of funds. And then, finally, it was performed in February 1996 at the Seattle Repertory Theatre. You would think after thirty-odd produced plays my excitement threshold would be lower than that of a novice, but everything about the show *felt* like the first time: the cast, the set, the direction—I even had, for the first time in my career, useful suggestions from, of all things, a *dramaturg*!!!

And in the end it was hands down the best experience of my career. To watch audiences swept along by a story I wrote, roused to shouting aloud at several turns of event, and to reach the curtain with a rare sense of having exposed and explored a segment of society (lawyers) in the company of a living, breathing audience eager to hear, to see, to participate in the journey . . . Okay, five years is a while, but the moment was, is and always will be worth waiting for.

And repeating. Right up to the eve of Armageddon when, as Goethe imagined he'd do, some playwright will hear the approaching hoofbeats, kneel and plant an apple tree.

New York
September 1996

Introduction

by Alan Schneider

Writing any kind of suitable preamble to a collection of Michael Weller's plays, especially when that collection happens to contain two with which I have been associated as director and another for which I served as a sort of minor catalyst, turns out to be much more difficult than directing them. I'm too prejudiced about what I consider the obvious virtues of Mike's writing, as well as too fond of him personally, to be objective. Besides, he's one of the few playwrights I have ever known who has gone on speaking to me the morning after, when some of the reviews weren't good. Nor am I unaware of his own basic generosity and good humor toward other playwrights, toward the actors and directors who help shape his plays, even toward that mad, impossible and unpredictable universe of the American theatre, which he alternately hates and loves.

Yet appreciating Mike's plays (and presence among us) as much as I do shouldn't entirely disqualify me from talking about them (and him). A reporter observing us together once said that we might somehow be related—"father and son—two soft-spoken, gentle people keenly alert to life's possibilities for joy and pain." Apart from the thought that no one else in my extremely lengthy career has ever described me as either "soft-spoken" or "gentle," I tend to concur, at least in that final phrase. Mike's plays (as well as Mike himself) are eminently attuned to both joy and pain. I have several manu-

scripts on my bookshelves, as well as a flock of personal letters tucked away in various drawers, which furnish ample
proof of that.

In one of John Osborne's early plays, his unhappily under-
rated *Epitaph for George Dillon,* the title character, a strug-
gling actor, says of himself that he always plays "scornful"
parts. I've remembered that description, and it comes in
handy now, when I'm thinking about how best to describe
Mike's plays. These plays are fun, fundamentally decent (in
spite of their profusion of four-letter words), deliciously
actable—and actors love playing in them. They are also, I
sometimes find myself thinking, not exactly "scornful" but
"irreverent." Not irrelevant, perish the thought—irreverent.
Comedically irreverent, lovingly irreverent, perceptively irreverent. Reverent, with irreverent vibrations.

For Mike is himself, I think, quite reverent about life's
deeper pains and joys. What he is irreverent about is its silli-
ness, its stupidities, its pretensions. He is reverent about the
weak, of both sexes, but skeptical about the excuses and
deceptions the successful and strong provide to justify their
dominance. If life is indeed a comedy for those who think and
a tragedy for those who feel, Mike somehow succeeds in both
thinking about and feeling for his characters at the same time,
making us chuckle at his constant irreverences. And, concur-
rently, with his persistent reverence for what really is important, he brings responses from our all too jaundiced contemporary tear ducts.

In the third scene of *Moonchildren,* the play with which
Mike first greeted us, the landlord, Mr. Willis, visits his collection of youthful collegiate renters, who baffle but clearly fas-
cinate him. "You decided whatya gonna do when you get out
of college?" he asks them. The answer comes back without a
blink from an ambitious and articulate young fellow who is
somehow named Cootie: "I'm gonna be a homosexual." It isn't
precisely the answer Mr. Willis, or the audience, expects. The
audience loves it, even if Mr. Willis isn't sure.

If one looks for two lines to epitomize the particular brand
of irreverence, the special sensibility, humor and bright out-
rageousness of Mike's writing ear, his sense of how we really

talk and think, this brief pass-by will do as well as any. (There are hundreds more.) In the space of a few simple and unadorned syllables, Mike manages to sum up the attitude of a generation: social, political, sexual—and comedic. Without any visible effort and with great economy of language, he succeeds in being simultaneously funny and moving, ironic and truthful, clear and ambiguous. It is no small feat for a writer still on the sunny side of forty.

As a playwright, Mike has been compared, variously and not always to his advantage, with such other contemporary American writers as David Mamet, David Rabe, Edward Albee and Sam Shepard (with whom he happens to share a love of music and greyhound racing)—as well as with such non-American figures as the aforementioned John Osborne, Noël Coward and even (!) George Bernard Shaw, although in this latter case, I think the comparers had one specific play, *Heartbreak House,* in mind.

To my understanding and observation, the playwright whom Mike most calls to mind—in his sympathy for frailty, his bittersweet compassion, the gentleness of his intensity, and his keen awareness of time's fragile evanescence—is none other than Anton Chekhov. I remember vividly that the very first time I read *Moonchildren*—it was then still called *Cancer,* a title which had successfully confused and put off its English audiences—I thought of it at once as a kind of American cousin of *The Cherry Orchard.* At least, Mike's writing was equally indirect and equally ruminative, funny-sad and sad-funny, with lots of subtext and plenty of pastel-colored insights into the passing of time, that great robber who steals equally from us all.

For in Mike, as in Anton Pavlovich, what is important is not always or at all what is spoken; what is important is what is thought and, even more, what is felt, including what the characters themselves do not even know they are thinking or feeling. This is especially true in the big scenes. With Mike, as with Chekhov, it is the music—inner and outer—which counts as much as the actual words. Small wonder that he started out as a musician; after all, that other fellow was a doctor.

Not everyone who has been listening out there these past ten years of Mike's visibility has accepted that music—although it

is clear that the audience for his special tonality is now growing, both here and abroad; and his appearance on our stages,
of all sizes and shapes, is more and more continuous.
Surprisingly enough, a decade or so after our first awareness,
Mike remains not nearly so well known or rewarded with
official honor as are some of his contemporaries. (He may,
indeed, be becoming more recognized as the screenwriter of
Hair and *Ragtime*.) He has never taken the "Tony" for a season's best play or been granted the dubious distinction of the
Pulitzer Prize. But in retrospect, two of the plays included in
this volume, *Moonchildren* and *Loose Ends,* are now generally accepted as two of our past theatrical decade's most significant contributions.

What remains clear in my mind is that on the basis of the
five plays included in this, the first putting together of his
plays, Mike's work is as likely to endure as that of any other
living American playwright. But I doubt that he ever gets very
reverent about that possibility.

Mike's achievement, which one of his most understanding
critics, Mel Gussow of *The New York Times,* described as
that of a "perceptive, humane playwright who has something
to say about his contemporaries," has come, of course, to be
recognized by many others. When *Moonchildren* first opened
at the Arena Stage in Washington in 1971, after a short run
at the Royal Court in London, where Mike was then living,
The Washington Post's longtime reviewer, Richard L. Coe,
declared, "Welcome, loud and clear to a fine new American
play." When the play moved on to New York, many of that
city's critics were, surprisingly enough, equally favorable.
Even Walter Kerr, with whom I hardly ever seem to agree,
called it "the most moving play in New York at the moment,
and one of the funniest." And Clive Barnes, who has caused
me anguish on other occasions, said that it was "the most
amusing, articulate, and witty comedy to emerge on Broad-
way in some seasons." In spite of all this, the production, for
various reasons, all of them still not clear, never found its
audience; and *Moonchildren* and Mike had to wait for a later
off-Broadway version—which I (of course) didn't like as
much—to make an impression.

The critics have also gone on telling us how well and profoundly Mike's plays have succeeded in reflecting the particular periods in which they were placed. *Moonchildren* was "a lament for a generation," "an epitaph for its time." And in *Loose Ends,* he was the "dramatic spokesman of his changing generation." But Mike did not sit down specifically to write *the* play of "the '60s" or, a few years later, another one for "the '70s." "I don't want to summarize my generation," he once told a too-persistent interviewer. "My plays just come out of the things I'm wondering about, or that I see my friends going through." Nor is he just writing diluted autobiography, as many of his contemporaries have so often tended to do. It's just that Mike sees—and hears—so well what he and his friends have gone through, and shapes the results so skillfully and accurately, that his characters generally wind up being people we know very well—including ourselves. His people behave and think and talk exactly the way we remember and recognize. And his situations and scenes manage to be so special and yet so truthful that they somehow catch the essence of their particular time. As Thornton Wilder let us know—and Mike is a great fan of Wilder's—the universe lies in each passing moment, as well as in each individual grain of sand.

Mike has also told us that he likes to write about people "who are living by accident." But there is, to the careful onlooker or reader, certainly no accident about the texture of his writing, or at least about his control of that writing, spontaneous and free as it appears. His plays seem loosely woven and yet are deceptively well made. And, as critic Robert Brustein once noted about Chekhov's construction of his plays, beneath their gentle, seemingly drifting surfaces, there is always "the tensile strength of a steel girder, the construction being so subtle that it is almost invisible. While his characters seem to exist in isolated pockets of vacancy, they are all integral parts of a close network of interlocking motives and effects." So it is, I think, with Mike's work: the careful putting together of accident, the bittersweet and the brash intertwined, pranks and profundity, the sense that life is so impossible that the only solution is to laugh at it.

One of the great virtues of a full-length play, Mike once

said to somebody somewhere, "is the amount of time and space available in the middle of the event to create inner resonances and to relax the dramatic texture and show people in partial repose in the eye of the hurricane." This is a pretty good description of the manner of his own work. For the repose of his characters, whatever it appears to be on the surface, is certainly only partial; and the hurricanes, of various sizes and natures, are clearly out there in the wings. I would consider that each of his plays in this volume, long or not so long, can properly be characterized, basically, as "reaction shots" to the swirling currents of their particular life-contexts. (No wonder that he has gotten interested in writing screenplays.)

Moonchildren, as by now everyone, including those who have never read it or seen it, must know, is about the college generation of what we have come to call, at this remove, "the '60s." It is not about their hair or their clothes or even about their sex or drug habits. (Drugs are never mentioned, by the way, though occasionally directors take certain liberties, as Mike will remember.) Rather, it is about their insides, the painful ways in which these young people, the kids of Mike's own generation, face their very uncertain futures, face and cover up their very definite fears of going out and getting older or killed or both. Each moment of pain is hidden under bright responses and even brighter laughter; and there is a lot of each, pain as well as laughter. As Walter Kerr put it early on, the play is "an antic needle pointing north to the chill."

Mike himself said it somewhat differently (and I hope he will forgive me for reminding him). In a letter written before our first rehearsals at Arena, he gave us a startling and revealing metaphor for his new play: "It is perhaps a description of a puzzle . . . a group of people who, for one reason or another, are compelled to make a journey by foot across a desert strewn with patches of quicksand. Aware of the nature of the danger, but not of its several locations, they have evolved, prior to the journey, a pattern of travel, a set of warning signals, a complex shorthand to alert each other of possible danger ahead . . ."

"On the other hand," he added just so we wouldn't take

him too seriously or grimly, "it's just this old play with a few technical problems but basically straightforward enough and with some good chuckles along the way." (The technical problems include about a million glass milk bottles, now virtually unobtainable anywhere, which also have to be gotten on and off stage in the twinkling of Mike's eye.)

What's eminently clear in all this is that *Moonchildren* is not "just this old play." It's really about the passing of an age, personal and political. Once all too relevant and too close for comfort, it has with time receded into something safer, though not necessarily slighter or less meaningful. Certainly, in its seemingly quiet, uncharted, even meandering way, it still serves to make us both wonder and care, still helps us to understand the way we were in those dim, distant, mysterious days, and still makes us smile. Perhaps, with allowances for detail, that's the way some of us still are—as any group of about-to-be-graduates can still tell you if they would choose to talk.

Whatever, it still seems to me, as it did originally, immensely honest, immensely perceptive and real, and marvelously funny. In other words, vintage Weller. And I will always recall and treasure those all-too-brief weeks I spent in Washington pretending to be young again with Bob and Mike and Kathy and Cootie and Shelly and all those other lovely and impossible moonchildren.

Fishing (produced first at the Public Theater in 1975 and again last season off-Broadway) forms the second phase of Mike's original plan for a trilogy about growing up in America. Never as successful in its acceptance as the other two (*Moonchildren* and the later *Loose Ends*), the play deals with another group of the time's "children," somewhat older, tougher perhaps, certainly more disillusioned, who have drifted off into the wilds of the Pacific Northwest and the drug culture to find themselves. Once more, the play blends humor and compassion for individual weakness. Like *Moonchildren*, it is about several sets of relationships. Perhaps in itself, in some measure, it is as incomplete and undefined as some of those relationships turn out to be. But, as Frank Rich of *The New York*

Times wrote on the occasion of its most recent production in New York, "The writing is magical; with the utmost economy and grace, Mr. Weller has captured both the whimsy and pain of the drug experience, even as he exposes the longings and fears of two complicated people." Less obvious, perhaps, on its surface, and more difficult to read, *Fishing* has, in the theatre, an effect greater than the sum of its parts.

One of the first constructive steps I took when I succeeded John Houseman as director of the Juilliard's Theatre Center in 1976 was to commission Mike to take a contemporary subject and write for us a short play, which we could then tour with our upper-division students. Every season, under the auspices of Lincoln Center, of which Juilliard is a component part, our students did a short journey around New York's high schools with some classic play—which sometimes provoked a considerable quantity of boredom, as well as pennies thrown up on stage. I figured that Mike, more than any other playwright I knew, could make use of the youthfulness and energies of our young students in some way that would be interesting and significant to them as well as to their equally young audiences. Perhaps they would then not be quite so bored.

Unfortunately—or fortunately, as matters turned out—Lincoln Center's slightly older powers-that-be decided, when they read the finished script—now called *Abroad (Split, Part 2)*—with its sexual complications and its emphasis on switching and breaking off relationships, that the play would be too "mature" for the New York City school system's tender inhabitants. They were thus denied the experience. Undaunted, as is his usual wont, Mike laughed and proceeded to extend and deepen his original one-act piece into a full-length exploration of the same subject. Eventually, he invited me to direct the longer version, now called *Loose Ends*, in both Washington and New York. Juilliard's loss was to become the rest of the American theatre's gain.

The original one-acter, as well as its later added "first" part, *At Home (Split, Part 1)*, have both had a variety of presentations, off-off-Broadway, off-Broadway, and in the regional theatre. Their double demonstration of the ultimate sadness of that merry-go-round ride through the labyrinths of American marriage and American divorce, which we had all been taking, seems not to have shattered the moral fabric of the Republic beyond what other forces have succeeded in doing—even though I'm sure that by now, plenty of those same high-school students have been observing it at firsthand.

If *Moonchildren* made us aware of the outer defenses and inner emptiness of so many of those college kids of what now seems several generations past, the aptly titled *Loose Ends* really tells us how it was—and is—for some of those kids after they grew up and got into "the real world" to face the shifting quicksands of a decade later: the sexual revolution, women's liberation, and the fun-and-terror games of the "Me Decade," with all its multiple-choice questions without proper or prepared-for answers.

Moonchildren is, or at least might be, considered to be about the shedding of innocence. *Loose Ends* is about what happens to two well-intentioned young people for whom "commitment" is an old-fashioned idea, yet to whom lack of commitment does not bring either fulfillment or happiness. "Unfaithful" is a word both Susan and Paul had hoped to discard. They found instead that though the rules and the labels may have changed, the fundamental sense of what a relationship is and does has not. Mike wanted to write a play, as he said, with the texture of a Japanese print or a haiku, which dealt with stages of a relationship and yet managed to invoke all the "in-between time." The flow of American life in those fast-changing American '70s gave him a suitable context and a suitable theme: coming apart.

His tone alternately rueful or brooding, Mike, again in this play, holds us up to his special inner vision and tells us once more about ourselves as we really are right now—comfortably uncertain, unhappy amid all our material goodies, lonely in all our crowds, hemmed in in the midst of greater and greater freedom, unsuccessfully groping for an answer to all the paradoxes so much choice has opened up before us.

Once more it is Chekhov whom I feel shimmering out there somewhere. But on stage it is Mike himself—as always, honest, flavorful and funny—with not a dry eye in the house at the end. There's hardly a hint of either 'Nam or Watergate, yet I cannot think of a recent American play which so accurately catches the tone and flavor of what we were doing and feeling around the time of those two great man-made catastrophes, whose fallout we are still feeling in all of our pores.

Gently, and with his usual understanding and intelligence, Mike tells us the story of two young people who wanted and needed each other but who somehow could not connect. That story, told in a succession of locales and year-apart scenes, sums up the changing values and attitudes of the decade past but not forgotten as well as any play I know. And those scenes rise like a musical climax to culminate in as shattering and explosive a confrontation as anything I've read or worked on since *Who's Afraid of Virginia Woolf?* With this play of his, Mike has, it seems to me, brought to our stage the ethical and esthetic equivalent of such films as *Annie Hall, An Unmarried Woman, Kramer Versus Kramer* and *Ordinary People* and has effectively competed with them. In so doing, he has reasserted the theatre's age-old power to deal effectively and powerfully with enduring human themes and with the larger social issues which continue to greet and challenge our society. For this, and for the chance to work on the play with him, I shall be eternally grateful.

After a rather tense and too-vocal production "conference" at the Circle-in-the-Square during rehearsals of *Loose Ends*, as the two of us were walking dispiritedly out the door of the theatre, Mike turned to me and asked me how it was physically or emotionally possible for anyone to survive in the American theatre past the age of fifty. I suggested to him that although I didn't know the answer, I had myself already passed that number by at least a decade and intended to go on a while longer—at least as long as he went on writing plays for me to direct.

With that same amount of time on the other side for him

yet to cover, Michael Weller is, I am sure, just hitting his stride and making his mark as a playwright in the American theatre. With a little luck, and a few less production conferences, he might even go on beyond—that is, if Hollywood doesn't get him permanently (knowing him as well as I do, I don't believe it will). And if the five plays which follow these rambling impressions are any indication, the American theatre will be glad to hear from him for a long time to come.

La Jolla, California,
November 1981

MOONCHILDREN

The play premiered under the title *Cancer* at the Royal Court Theatre, London, England (William Gaskill, Artistic Director) on September 14, 1970. Roger Hendricks Simon and Peter Gill directed the following cast:

MIKE	Seth Allen
RUTH	Karen Ludwig
COOTIE	Davis Hall
NORMAN	Chuck Jones
DICK	Richard Portnow
KATHY	Mari Gorman
BOB	Martin Shaw
RALPH	Chris Malcolm
WILLIS	George Margo
LUCKY	Andrew Neil
SHELLY	Cara Duff-MacCormick
BREAM	David Healy
EFFING	Chris Malcolm
MURRAY	Al Mancini
SANTA CLAUS	Ann Way
COOTIE'S FATHER	Hal Jeayes
PLUMBER	Al Mancini
MILKMAN	David Healy

The American premiere was presented by the Arena Stage, Washington, D.C. (Zelda Fichandler, Producing Director; Thomas C. Fichandler, Executive Director), in November 1971. Alan Schneider directed the following cast:

MIKE	Kevin Conway
RUTH	Maureen Anderman
COOTIE	Edward Herrmann
NORMAN	Christopher Guest
DICK	Stephen Collins
KATHY	Jill Eikenberry
BOB	James Woods
RALPH	Donegan Smith
WILLIS	Robert Prosky
LUCKY	Ronald McLarty
SHELLY	Cara Duff-MacCormick
BREAM	Howard Witt
EFFING	Ted Hannan
MURRAY	Ben Kaplan
COOTIE'S FATHER	Russell Carr
MILKMAN	Mark Robinson
*PLUMBER	Richard David
*SANTA CLAUS	Jean Schertler

*The asterisked roles were cut during rehearsal.

This production then moved to New York, where it opened at the Royale Theatre in February 1972 with the following cast changes:

BREAM	Louis Zorich
EFFING	Peter Alzado
MURRAY	Salem Ludwig
COOTIE'S FATHER	George Curley
MILKMAN	Michael Tucker

Characters

MIKE	WILLIS
RUTH	LUCKY
COOTIE	SHELLY
NORMAN	BREAM
DICK	EFFING
KATHY	MURRAY
BOB	COOTIE'S FATHER
RALPH	MILKMAN

Time

1965–1966

Place

A student apartment in
an American university town.

Scene 1

The stage is dark. You can't see anything.

MIKE: I heard something. She definitely made a noise.

RUTH: Shut up.

MIKE: I'm telling you, I know the noise they make. That was it.

RUTH: For chrissakes, be quiet. You keep talking and she'll know we're here.

COOTIE: I was just thinking. I read somewhere about how they can see in the dark.

RUTH: I never read that.

COOTIE: No shit, I read they got these hundreds of thousands of millions of tiny, submicroscopic, photosensitive cells in each eyeball, so when it gets dark they can just turn on these cells and see like it was daytime.

MIKE: He's right, Ruth. Hey, Cootie, you're right. I remember reading that in a back issue of the *Vertebrate Review.*

COOTIE: That's it, that's the one. Special eyeball issue.

MIKE: Yeah, yeah. July.

RUTH: You guys must be pretty stupid if you believe that. What do you think they have whiskers for? The whole point of whiskers in the first place is so you can get around in the dark. That's why they stick out so far, so you don't bump into things. Chairs and refrigerators and that.

MIKE: Hey, shhhh. I think she's starting.

RUTH: Well, you're the one that got me going about whiskers in the first place, so don't tell me shhhh.

MIKE: O.K., O.K., I'm sorry, O.K.?

RUTH: So shut up if she's starting.

COOTIE *(Pause)*: How many kittens can they have at any one session?

MIKE: There's a recorded case of thirty-eight.

RUTH: Shhhh, for chrissakes.

COOTIE: What I want to know is how are we gonna see her when she starts giving birth?

RUTH: Jesus, how stupid can you get? We'll turn on the light.

COOTIE: Yeah, but the whole thing is how do we know when to turn on the light? Like, what if we're too early?

MIKE: Or too late?

COOTIE: Yeah, what if we're too late?

MIKE: Or right in the middle . . .

COOTIE: Holy shit, yeah, what if we flip on the old lights when she's halfway through a severe uterine contraction? She'll go apeshit and clamp up and kill the kitten. And if the kitty gets really lucky and wriggles free, it'll grow up into a pretty fucked-up animal.

MIKE: We're sowing the seeds of a neurotic adult cathood . . .

COOTIE: . . . doo-wah, doo-wah . . .

RUTH: Hey, shut up, you guys, willya? Willya shut up?

COOTIE: We're just pointing out that's a shitty way to start life.

RUTH: I know the noise, all right?

MIKE: I think there's probably a more scientific way to watch a cat give birth.

RUTH: Everybody shut the fuck up.

(A long pause.)

NORMAN: How much longer are you guys gonna have the lights out?

COOTIE: Jesus Christ, Norman, why do you have to go creeping up like that? We forgot you were even in here.

NORMAN: I'm not creeping up. I'm just sitting here. Maybe you didn't notice when you came in, but I was reading this book. I mean, I thought you were only gonna have the lights out for maybe a few minutes or something, but you've already been in here for about an hour and . . . and I really can't read very well with the lights off. I mean . . . you know . . .

COOTIE: Norman, you can't rush a cat when it's giving birth. You try to rush a cat in those circumstances and you come smack up against nature.

MIKE: Norman . . .

NORMAN: What?

MIKE: Don't fight nature, Norman.

NORMAN: I'm not. I'm just trying to read this book.

COOTIE *(Pause)*: Is it a good book?

RUTH: For chrissakes, what's the matter with everyone?

NORMAN: I don't know. It's a pretty good book. I don't follow all of it. It's written in a funny kind of way, so you forget a lot of it right after you've read it. A lot of guys in the mathematics department say it's pretty good. I don't know though.

RUTH: Hey, Norman, can't you go to your room if you want to read?

NORMAN: I don't want to.

MIKE: Why not, Norman?

COOTIE: Yeah, why do you want to creep around in here being all spooky and everything when you could just go to your room and read, huh?

NORMAN: I don't know.

COOTIE: We may be in here for hours and hours, Norman. Maybe even all night. The whole operation from initial labor to the biting off of the umbilical cord could very easily take an entire night. *(Pause)* Norman?

NORMAN: All night, huh?

COOTIE: You never know.

RUTH: Brother, you try to get a few guys to shut up for a little while. . .

MIKE *(Loud)*: C'mon, c'mon, hey, everybody, let's have a little quiet around here. I don't want to see anyone panic and lose their heads and start running in all different directions knocking down passersby and trampling on innocent women and children.

RUTH: I swear to Christ, Mike, if you don't shut up I'll kill you.
MIKE: O.K.

(At this point, the hall door opens and the kitchen is lit up a little. Dick is standing in the doorway trying to see into the dark, where Norman is sitting at a round kitchen table with a book by him, and Ruth, Mike and Cootie are crouched around a cardboard carton with a hole in it. Norman grabs up his book to take advantage of the crack of light. Dick just stands there. Ruth and Cootie speak on top of each other.)

RUTH: Hey, c'mon, shut the door, Dick.
COOTIE: Shut the fucking door.
MIKE *(After a pause)*: We'd really like you to shut the door, Richard.

(Dick shuts the door and everything goes black. A moment later it all lights up again because Dick has just opened the icebox and it's the kind that has an automatic light inside. So now we see Dick squatting in front of the icebox while the others watch him, except for Norman, who's really trying like mad to read. You can see the kitchen pretty clearly now. The icebox is very old, dating from the time when electricity was replacing the iceman. It's just a box on legs with one of those barrel-shaped coolers with vents on top. You maybe can't see it yet, but on the door of the icebox there's a large inscription that reads "GOD IS COOL." Stacked neatly against one wall are eight hundred sixteen empty two-quart milk bottles, layer upon layer with planks between each level. It's a deliberate construction. There's a huge copper stack heater in one corner by the sink, and it has a safety valve at the top with a copper tube coming out of it and snaking into the sink. The floor is vinyl, in imitation cork, alternating light and dark, but the conspicuous thing about this floor is that it's only half-finished. Where the cork tiles end there is a border of black tar, by now hard, and then wooden floor in broad plank. Around the

kitchen table are six chairs, all from different sets. Various posters on the wall, but none as conspicuous as a map of Europe near where the telephone hangs. The sink is full of dirty dishes. There is a pad hanging by the icebox, and a pencil. Everyone uses the kitchen in a special way. So Dick is squatting in front of the open icebox.)

RUTH: That's very cute, Richard.

MIKE: C'mon, shut the fucking icebox. We were in here first.

NORMAN: I was reading when you guys came in

(Dick turns to them, looks, then turns back to the icebox.)

COOTIE: Dick, in my humble opinion you're a miserable cunt and a party pooper.

DICK *(Standing)*: All right, now listen. This afternoon I went down to the Star Supermarket and got myself four dozen frozen hamburgers. Now that's forty-eight hamburgers, and I only had two of them for dinner tonight.

RUTH: And you never washed up.

MIKE: Hey, Dick, are those Star hamburgers any good?

DICK: Listen, I should have forty-six hamburgers, and when I counted just now there was only forty-three. Three hamburgers in one night. And for your information I've been keeping track of my hamburgers since the beginning of the semester. There's almost fifty hamburgers I can't account for.

COOTIE: Jesus, Dick, you should have said something before this.

MIKE: Yeah, Dick, you had all them hamburger thefts on your mind, you should have let it out. It's no good keeping quiet about something like that.

DICK: Look, I'm not about to make a stink about a couple of hamburgers here and there, but, Jesus Christ, almost sixty of them. I'm putting it down on common stock and we're gonna all pay for it. *(He turns on the light)*

RUTH: Dick, willya turn out the light, please?

DICK: I'm sorry, but I've lost too many hamburgers. I'm putting down for four dozen. *(He goes to the pad on the wall and makes an entry)*

RUTH: Now willya turn the light out?

DICK *(Examining list)*: Shit, who put peanut butter down on common stock?

MIKE: I did. I got a jar of chunky last Thursday and when I opened it on Saturday somebody'd already been in there. I didn't eat all that chunky myself.

DICK: Well, I never had your peanut butter. I'm not paying for it.

MIKE: Well, I never had any of your goddamn sixty hamburgers either.

COOTIE: I think I may have had some of that chunky peanut butter. Could you describe your jar of chunky in detail?

MIKE: Elegant little glass jar, beige interior . . .

(Kathy enters through the front door, as opposed to the hall door. The hall door leads to everyone's rooms.)

KATHY: Oh, boy, look out for Bob. *(She starts across the kitchen to the hall door. She carries lots of books in a green canvas waterproof book bag slung over her shoulder)*

RUTH: What's wrong with Bob?

KATHY: He's in a really shitty mood. I've seen the guy act weird before. This is, I don't know, pretty bad, I guess.

MIKE: Where is he?

COOTIE: Yeah, where's Bob?

MIKE: Good old Bob.

COOTIE: Where's good old Bob?

KATHY: And fuck you too. I'm serious.

NORMAN *(Looking up from his book)*: Boy, I really can't absorb very much with everyone talking.

KATHY: We were just sitting there, you know, in Hum 105, and that prick Johnson started in about the old cosmic equation again.

NORMAN: What's the cosmic equation?

RUTH: So why'd that upset Bob?

KATHY: I don't know. That's the thing . . .

DICK: I bet Bob's responsible for some of my hamburgers. I notice you and him never go shopping for dinner.

KATHY: It's really weird the way he sort of . . . well, like today, you know . . . I'm not kidding, he might be cracking up or something.

(Bob enters through the front door, carrying his books. He looks all right. Everyone stares at him.)

RUTH: Hi, Bob.

MIKE: Hi, Bob.

COOTIE: Hi, Bob.

NORMAN: Hello, Bob.

BOB *(Pause)*: Hi, Mike, hi, Ruth, hi, Cootie; hello, Norman. *(Pause)* Hi, Dick.

DICK: Listen, do you know anything about . . . ?

BOB: No, I haven't touched your fucking hamburgers.

DICK: Well, someone has.

MIKE: How you been, good old Bob?

COOTIE: How's the old liver and the old pancreas and the old pituitary and the . . .

BOB: Is there any mail?

COOTIE: There's this really big package from Beirut. It took four guys to get it up the stairs.

MIKE: We think it's a harp.

RUTH: There's a letter in your room.

(Bob looks at them quizzically, then goes down the hall. Kathy follows him.)

RUTH: I think Kathy's right. There's definitely something wrong with Bob.

DICK: Yeah, he's out of his fucking mind, that's what's wrong with him.

RUTH: You can talk.

MIKE: Hey, c'mon, c'mon, let's have a little order around here . . .

RUTH: Stop fucking around. You heard what Kathy said. Something's troubling Bob.

MIKE: So what?

COOTIE: Yeah, fuck Bob.

MIKE: Fuck good old Bob.

NORMAN: Maybe he's worried about the future. *(All look at him)* I mean, you know, maybe he's worried about it. I mean, I don't know him all that well. Just, you know, maybe he's worried about what he's gonna do when, you know, after he graduates and everything.

DICK: He ought to be worried.

MIKE: You bet your ass he oughta be. Same goes for all of you guys. You oughta be worried, Dick. Cootie, you oughta be worried. I oughta be worried. I am. I'm fucking petrified. You watch what happens at the graduation ceremony. There's gonna be this line of green military buses two miles long parked on the road outside and they're gonna pick us up and take us to Vietnam and we'll be walking around one day in the depths of the rain forest looking out for wily enemy snipers and carnivorous insects and tropical snakes that can eat a whole moose in one gulp and earthworms sixteen feet long and then one day when we least expect it this wily sniper'll leap out from behind a blade of grass and powie. Right in the head. I'm worried.

DICK: Anyone that can spell can get out of Vietnam.

NORMAN: I'm in graduate school. They can't get me.

DICK: Norman, you couldn't buy your way into the army.

NORMAN: I wouldn't go.

MIKE: Why wouldn't you go, Norman?

NORMAN: Huh?

COOTIE: Yeah, think of the army. What about them? They need good mathematics graduate students out there in the marshes of Quac Thop Chew Hoy Ben Van Pho Quay Gup Trin.

NORMAN: I don't agree with the war.

MIKE: Well, for God sakes, then, let's stop it.

NORMAN: I had my medical and everything. I passed. I could've pretended I was insane or something.

DICK: Pretended?

RUTH: Hey, doesn't anyone here give a shit about Bob?

MIKE: Hey, c'mon, everyone that gives a shit raise your hand. *(Cootie, Mike, Dick and Norman raise their hands)* See, we all give a shit. So what should we do?

RUTH: Well, I don't know. Maybe we ought to try and find out what's troubling him.

DICK: Maybe he doesn't want us to know. Just maybe.

COOTIE: Yeah, what if he's teetering on the brink of a complete schizophrenic withdrawal and the only thing keeping him sane is knowing we don't know what's troubling him.

MIKE: It's our duty as classmates and favorite turds to leave him alone.

RUTH: Maybe something's wrong between him and Kathy.

DICK: Like what?

RUTH: I don't know. That's what I'm asking.

DICK: He doesn't give a shit about her. Not really. She's just a good lay, that's all.

RUTH: How would you know, Dick?

NORMAN: I thought they were in love.

DICK: Jesus, Norman, where the hell is your head at?

NORMAN: Huh?

MIKE: Define the problem, then solve it.

COOTIE: Yeah, what's troubling good old Bob?

MIKE: I think we oughta all go to bed tonight with notebooks under our pillows, and when we get a well-focused and comprehensive idea about the central dilemma of Bob's existence we oughta write it down in clear, concise sentences, with particular attention to grammar and punctuation.

COOTIE: Yeah, then we can meet in here tomorrow and pool our insights.

MIKE: That's a really great plan.

RUTH: I'd really like to know what's troubling him.

DICK: I'd really like to know who the fuck is eating my hamburgers.

NORMAN: Why don't you talk to him?

RUTH: What?

NORMAN: I mean, you know—Bob. If you want to find out what's troubling him, probably the best thing to do is talk to him and say, What's troubling you, or something like that, and then if he wants to tell you he can and if he doesn't feel like talking about it . . . then . . . well, you know . . .

RUTH: Yeah, maybe I'll do that.

NORMAN *(Pause)*: Yeah, that's what I'd do if I wanted to know. I mean, I'm not saying I wouldn't like to know what's troubling him. I'd really like to know if you find out, but I . . .

(Mike has been kneeling by the cat box and peering into it.)

MIKE: Jesus Christ. Jesus H. fucking Christ.

NORMAN: What's wrong?

MIKE: She wasn't even in there.

COOTIE: What! All that time we were looking at an empty box and she wasn't even in there?

MIKE: She must've slipped out while we had our backs turned.

COOTIE: Sneaky little beastie.

MIKE: Cootie, you don't understand. She might be out there in the road right now.

COOTIE: Right now.

MIKE: With all the traffic.

COOTIE: Oh, Christ, and all those architects driving home drunk from seeing their mistresses . . .

MIKE: And trying to figure out what to tell the little woman. I mean, she's been waiting up all night in a chartreuse quilted sleeping gown with curlers in her hair . . .

COOTIE: Worrying about the kiddies. Three boys, twenty-seven girls. They all got appendicitis . . .

MIKE: Simultaneously. And when she called the kindly family doctor he was away in Cuba . . .

COOTIE: Doing research for his forthcoming book . . .

MIKE: "Chapter Eight: Peritonitis and Social Democracy."

COOTIE: Jesus, I hope we're not too late. *(He and Mike rush off down the hall)*

DICK: Hey, Norman, are these your bananas?

NORMAN: You can have one. I don't mind.

(Dick takes one and puts the others back in the icebox. Cootie sticks his head in around the hall door.)

COOTIE: You coming, Ruth?

RUTH: No.

COOTIE: Your heart is full of bitterness and hate, Ruth. *(His head disappears again)*

DICK: You done the essay for Phil 720?

RUTH: No.

DICK: It's due tomorrow.

RUTH: Yeah?

DICK: Yeah.

NORMAN: Is that a good course, Philosophy 720?

RUTH: Nope. Professor Quinn is an albino dwarf queer with halitosis and he smokes too much.

DICK: He does not.

RUTH: Three packs of Pall Mall a day is too much. He's gonna die of cancer.

DICK: He's a genius.

RUTH: You have a thing about queers.

DICK: Fuck off, Ruth.

RUTH: You started it. *(She goes into hall. Dick stands and eats his banana, chewing slowly. Norman tries to read but Dick's presence distracts him)*

DICK: How come you're reading that book?

NORMAN: I don't know. It's supposed to be pretty good.

DICK: What are you gonna do when you finish it?

NORMAN *(Thinks)*: I'll start another one.

DICK: Yeah, but what happens when you forget this one. I mean, it'll be as if you hadn't even read it, so what's the point?

NORMAN: Oh, I don't know. I happen to believe you learn things even when you don't know it. Like, if you're reading something right now . . . I mean, I am reading something right now and maybe I'll forget it in a while . . . I mean, I'm forgetting a lot of it already, but I happen to believe I'm being altered in lots of ways I may not be aware of because of . . . well, you know, books and experiences. *(Pause)* Life.

DICK: That's what you believe, huh?

NORMAN: Um, yes, I believe that.

(Mike and Cootie enter, wearing heavy winter parkas and boots. They look like trappers.)

COOTIE: Boy, if we're too late I hate to think of all the dead cats we'll have on our conscience.

MIKE: You gonna help, Dick?

DICK: Fuck off.

MIKE: How about you, Norman, aren't you gonna do your bit for the world of cats?

NORMAN: I'm just in the middle of this chapter. *(Mike and Cootie shake their heads in disapproval and rush out. Norman tries to read again as Dick eats the banana, watching him)* Hey, it's really hard to read, you know, when someone's watching you and everything.

DICK: Don't you ever get the feeling you're really irrelevant?

NORMAN: I don't think so.

DICK *(In one breath)*: I mean, you go into the mathematics department every day and sit there looking out the window and thinking about cars and women and every now and then a couple of numbers come into your head and there's all these Chinese guys running around solving all the problems worth solving while you sit there wondering what the hell you're doing.

NORMAN: No, it's not like that. Well, you know, it's not that simple. I mean . . . *(Pause)* I guess it's a lot like that. Are you doing anything relevant?

DICK: You can't get more relevant than Far Eastern studies. Ask me anything about the Far East and I'll tell you the answer. That's where everything's happening. China, Vietnam, Japan, Korea. You name it.

NORMAN: I guess I ought to know more about those things. I don't know, I keep thinking there's a lot of things I should know about.

DICK: The thing is, Norman, the way I see it, you're already deeply committed to the system. You take away black ghettos, stop the war in Vietnam, distribute the wealth equally throughout the country, and you wouldn't be in graduate school.

NORMAN: How come?

DICK: You see, you don't know anything about what makes it all work, do you? *(He throws the banana peel into the cat box)*

NORMAN: Hey, you shouldn't throw that in there.

DICK: Why not?

NORMAN: Well, I mean, that's the box for the cat. Maybe she won't want to have kittens on a banana peel.

DICK: Norman, how long have you been living here?

NORMAN: Well, you know, about three months. A little longer maybe. About three months and two weeks altogether.

DICK: Have you ever seen a cat around here?

NORMAN: Well, I don't know. I'm out a lot of the time.

DICK: Norman, there is no fucking cat. We haven't got a cat Boy, for a graduate student you got a lot to learn. *(He starts out but turns to look Norman over a last time)* Jesus. *(Then he's gone down the hall. Norman kneels by the cat box and examines it as some muffled piano chords fill the silence. It's Bob playing a lazy, rich, drifting progression, moody–Bill Evans–style. Kathy walks through the kitchen in a man's robe, carrying a towel. She lights the stack heater. From inside the hall we hear Dick's voice yelling)*

DICK: STOP PLAYING THAT FUCKING NOISE. I'M TRYING TO READ. HEY, BOB.

KATHY *(Goes to the hall door and yells down)*: Mind your own goddamn business, Richard. *(A door slams, and the music, which had stopped momentarily, starts again, but louder. She turns)* Hey, listen, Norman. If you're gonna be in here for a while could you do me a favor and make sure no one turns off the water heater, 'cause I'm just taking a shower. And if you get a chance, could you put on some coffee, 'cause I'll be coming out in about ten minutes and I'd like a cup when I come out. O.K.?

NORMAN: Do you have any books on Vietnam?

KATHY *(Pause)*: Yeah. A few.

NORMAN: Are they good books?

KATHY: Well, you know, some are, some aren't. Why?

NORMAN: I just, you know, wondered, that's all. *(Kathy watches Norman go to the stove and fumble around with the coffee percolator. She shrugs and goes out. We hear the bathroom door close and, moments later, the sound of a shower running)* Actually, I've been thinking I'd like to read some books about Vietnam. I mean it's been going on all this time. I don't know, though. I've never read any books about it. Maybe if I could read one book, then I'd know a little more about it and I could decide if I wanted to read another. Would it be O.K. if I borrowed one of your books to start with? I'd give it back as soon as I finished it. *(He looks around and sees he's alone. He goes out the door. We hear the bathroom door opening and a yell)*

KATHY *(Offstage)*: Goddamnit, Norman, what are you doing in here?

NORMAN *(Offstage)*: I was wondering if you'd lend me . . .

KATHY *(Offstage)*: Hey, get the hell out of here, I'm taking a shower.

(A door slams.)

NORMAN *(Offstage)*: I just wanted to know if it was O.K. for me to borrow one of those books about Vietnam.

KATHY *(Offstage)*: Well, Jesus Christ, can't you wait till I'm done?

NORMAN *(Offstage)*: Oh . . . yeah, I'm sorry. *(Pause)* Is that all right with you?

KATHY *(Offstage)*: Hey, don't stand around out there. You can borrow as many goddamn books as you want, only get away from the door, 'cause it just so happens I don't like a lot of people standing around outside the bathroom door while I'm washing.

(Norman comes back into the kitchen. He fixes a little more of the coffee, then goes to the hall door and yells down the hallway.)

NORMAN: I'll just make the coffee first, and when you're finished in there I'll come down to your room with you and get the book. Hey, listen, if you decide to have your coffee in here, could you go down to your room first and bring the book in with you? Yes, that's probably better. Hey, is that O.K.? *(Pause)* Hey, is that O.K.?

(No answer. Norman is left baffled, as the lights dim and Bob's piano chords keep going and going.)

Scene 2

It's a few days later. Norman is reading. Ruth is making sandwiches, and Cootie and Mike are rolling up a banner.

COOTIE: I don't know about the wording.

MIKE: I think it's pretty good wording.

COOTIE: I'm not too happy about it.

MIKE: You're unhappy about the wording.

COOTIE: Well, I'm not, you know, cut up about it or anything, but I'm definitely not as happy as I could be about it.

MIKE: Ruthie, we need an impartial third voice over here.

RUTH: Who wants orange marmalade?

MIKE: I'd like an orange marmalade.

COOTIE: I want two orange marmalade and one chunky peanut butter, please.

RUTH: How 'bout you, Norman?

COOTIE: And I wouldn't mind a chunky peanut butter and orange marmalade mixed.

RUTH: Hey, Norman, do you want sandwiches or not?

COOTIE: You gotta have sandwiches handy if you're coming, Norman. On your average march you'll find you get through a good two peanut butter and jellies before you even get to where you're supposed to demonstrate, and then after circling round and yelling militant slogans at the monument or park or poison-gas plant or nuclear-missile establishment for a couple hours, you're just about ready for another peanut butter and jelly.

MIKE: Or cream cheese and olives.

COOTIE: Bacon, lettuce and tomato. I mean, I know you meet a lotta pretty groovy people at these marches, but you can't count on them having extra sandwiches for a new acquaintance.

RUTH: Hey, Norman, willya please tell me if you're coming with us or not?

NORMAN *(Unfriendly)*: I'm going with Dick.

COOTIE: You're lucky there. You'll get hamburger on toasted roll if you go with Dick. He takes sterno and cooks right out there in the middle of lines of charging cops and tear gas and mace and everything.

(Dick enters.)

MIKE: Hey, Dick, you better hurry up and get dressed for the march.

COOTIE: Yeah, Dick, you don't want to be late or all the best ass'll be grabbed up.

DICK *(Indicating banner)*: What's it say?

COOTIE: "Buy Government Bonds."

RUTH: You want some of our peanut butter and marmalade?

MIKE: What's this about giving away all our peanut butter and marmalade all of a sudden? He wouldn't give us any of his lousy hamburgers. We had to pay for those hamburgers on common stock.

DICK: Where's Kathy and Bob?

MIKE: Yeah, where's good old Bob? *(Yells)* HEY, YOU GUYS, ARE YOU COMING?

KATHY *(Inside)*: Yeah, hold on a minute, willya?

MIKE: They're coming.

COOTIE: Hey, Norman, I been watching you pretty closely for the last few days and I have this definite impression you've been displaying hostility toward me, Mike and Ruth, in that order.

NORMAN: I'm just reading this book . . .

COOTIE: Don't be negative, Norman. You're trying to pretend I hadn't noticed your emotions. You happen to be up against a disciple of Freud, Jung, Adler, Pavlov, Skinner and the honorable L. Ron Hubbard, to mention but a few. It just so happens I can detect subatomic trace particles of hostility within a six-mile radius of anywhere I am.

MIKE: It's no use contradicting him, Norman. If he says he can feel hostility, that's it. I mean, even I can feel it and I'm only moderately sensitive to hostility up to about a hundred eighty yards.

NORMAN: I'm not feeling hostile . . .

COOTIE: You're not only feeling it, you're dying to tell us about it. That's a basic axiom of hostility.

NORMAN: Oh, boy, you guys.

DICK: Leave him alone.

COOTIE: Dick, that's the worst thing you can do. I know you think you're being a good shit and everything, but if the guy is riddled with hostility and he doesn't get it out of his system, it's gonna go haywire and zing all around inside his body till he's twenty-eight years old and then he'll get cancer.

RUTH: You know, we're gonna be really late if those guys don't hurry up . . .

MIKE: That reminds me of a guy I was reading about. He got so pent up with hostility his head fell right down inside his body, no shit, that's what I was reading, right down between his shoulders.

COOTIE: Fell?

MIKE: Yeah, straight down till all you could see was these two little eyeballs peeping out over his collarbone.

COOTIE: Mike.

MIKE: What, Mel?

COOTIE *(Pause)*: Fell?

MIKE *(Pause)*: Sank?

COOTIE: Subsided.

MIKE: Right.

COOTIE: In fact, as I remember it, his head eventually disappeared completely.

MIKE: Don't rush me, I'm coming to that. Now, Norman, I want you to pay very close attention because this case is a lesson in itself. You see, everybody used to warn this particular guy to loosen up and maybe see an analyst, but the guy refused on the grounds that it would cost too much, and that turned out to be really stupid economy, because with his head inside him like that he couldn't see anything and he had to hire a guy, full time, seven days a week, to lead him around. The guy was so tight with his money he tried to solve the problem by rigging up this ingenious system of mirrors, like a periscope, but the natural movements of his body kept knocking the mirrors out of alignment, so in addition to the guy that led him around, he had to hire another guy, full time, seven days a week, to keep readjusting the mirrors. You can imagine the expense involved.

COOTIE: There was a very fine article about that guy in the *Hostility Journal*, spring number. Did you happen to catch that article, Norman?

MIKE: Did it tell about what happened to him?

COOTIE: Well, it was one of those stories in two parts, and wouldn't you know it, that's just when my subscription ran out.

MIKE: Oh, well, you missed the best part. You see, when his head got down as . . . *subsided* as far as his stomach . . .

COOTIE: . . . thank you . . .

MIKE: . . . he went and hired a top-notch transplant surgeon to replace his belly button with a flexible, clear plastic window so he could see where he was going.

COOTIE: Jumpin' Jehoshaphat!

MIKE: And I'm happy to announce, the operation was a complete success.

COOTIE: Fantastic! No problems with rejection or anything?

MIKE: Nope. The Dow Chemical Company set up a ten-man, two-woman research team and they developed a type of clear plastic window that matched the guy's antibodies perfectly. In a matter of weeks, the guy was able to live a completely normal life again, skin diving, stamp collecting, a lot of political work. He could even go to the movies when he felt like it, but he had to sit up on the back of the seat and it caused a lot of hard feelings with the people sitting directly behind him. But that's the great thing about the average moviegoing audience; they respected his infirmity.

COOTIE: Fuck a duck!

MIKE: Shut up, sonny boy, I ain't finished yet.

COOTIE: There's more?

MIKE: Yeah, you see, the really incredible thing was when the guy woke up one morning and realized his head was still sinking . . .

COOTIE: . . . subsiding . . .

MIKE: . . . and he went to this doctor to check it out. He was just walking along, you know, and when he got to this corner to stop for a red light a dog peed on his leg, and when he bent forward to see what was making his pants wet a guy on some scaffolding right behind dropped a pipe wrench on his back, and the impact of this wrench, plus the slightly inclined position of the guy's upper body, knocked his head back into place.

COOTIE: Hot diggity!

MIKE: Well, the guy went apeshit, jumping all over the place, singing songs right out there on the streets . . . and that's just when it all had to happen. This poor guy, after all his suffering, was finally looking forward to a happy and productive life . . .

COOTIE: Oh, shit, yeah, I remember now. The poor son of a bitch.

MIKE: Yeah, you 'member, he was just standing out there in the street stopping traffic in both directions, tears of humble gratitude streaming down his cheeks and some stupid . . . (He sees Kathy and Bob standing in the hallway door ready for the march) . . . oh, hi, Bob, hi, Kathy.

RUTH: Hey, do you guys want some of our peanut butter and marmalade?

BOB: I've got an announcement.

COOTIE: We used to have a nearsighted canary . . .

RUTH: Listen, I gotta make these sandwiches and we're gonna end up short if I don't get some cooperation around here.

COOTIE: Hey, Norman hasn't even got a banner. Norman, aren't you gonna bring a banner?

BOB: Mel, willya please shut up? I'm trying to tell you guys something.

COOTIE: Well, fuck you, I'm talking to Norman. You want him to get all the way down to the demonstration and they disqualify him 'cause he doesn't have a banner.

RUTH: Everyone is gonna fucking well eat whatever I make.

DICK: You want some help?

RUTH: Look, it's not like I don't know how to make sandwiches . . .

MIKE: Hey, everyone, c'mon, c'mon, let's have a little order around here. Everybody stay where you are and don't panic. O.K., Bob, I think we got everything under control now.

BOB: Thank you.

MIKE: That's O.K., Bob.

BOB: I've just got this . . .

MIKE: Bob?

BOB: What?

MIKE: Anytime.

BOB: What?

MIKE: Anytime you want a little peace and quiet so you can make an announcement without a lot of people talking over you, just ask me and I'll do what I can for you.

BOB: Thank you, Mike.

MIKE: That's O.K., Bob, you're a good shit.

BOB *(Hesitates, trying to find words to frame his vague thoughts. When he speaks, it is halting)*: Look . . . I just thought maybe it was about time somebody around here . . .

MIKE: Do you want some water or anything?

RUTH: Oh, for chrissake, shut up, Mike.

COOTIE *(Cooling things)*: Yeah, shut yer mouth, sonny boy, yer creatin' a public nuisance.

RUTH: Go on, Bob.

BOB: No, no, look, all I want to say is . . . Norman, if there is one way to remain irrelevant and ineffective it's to sit with your nose buried in a book while life is raging all around you. *(Norman looks up and closes his book)* Thank you. O.K. Announcement . . . *(He walks around the room, again trying to think of how to put it. As he starts to speak . . .)*

MIKE: Earthquakes in Singapore . . . ?

RUTH *(Incredible rage)*: SHUT UP!

BOB: Never mind.

MIKE: Sorry. I'm sorry.

KATHY: What's wrong, Bob?

BOB: Really, nothing, nothing at all. I just had this stupid thought the other day in humanities. Johnson was saying something idiotic, as usual, and I just started to watch him carefully for the first time talking to us, you know, thirty kids who think he's a prick, and I realized that he probably thinks all of us are pricks . . . and I just started to wonder what we're all doing. You know what I mean? What the fuck are we all doing, seriously, tell me, I'd really like to know . . . in twenty-five words or less . . . No, no, sorry, come on, carnival time. Let's go marching.

KATHY: I found the letter, Bob.

BOB: What letter? *(Kathy takes an official letter out of her bag)* Kathy, where did you get that? Come on, give it here.

KATHY: We're supposed to be like all together in here. If you can't say it yourself, I'll say it for you.

(Bob is momentarily confused, then realizes that Kathy thinks he was trying to tell everyone about the letter. He finds the situation absurd, annoying and funny.)

BOB: Kathy, that letter has nothing to do with anything and it's none of your business and would you please give it back?

(Kathy hands the letter to Ruth. Ruth reads.)

RUTH: Oh, fuck.

(Ruth hands the letter on. Each reads in turn. It ends in Mike's hands. Bob waits impatiently as the letter makes its round. He's embarrassed and then begins to find it funny that everyone, especially Kathy, has construed the letter as his problem. Mike is by now looking quite seriously at him.)

BOB *(Laughing it off)*: It's just for the physical. I mean, I'm not dead yet.

(As Bob says this, something amusing passes through his mind and he stops talking. Mike is looking at the letter again. The others watch Bob.)

MIKE: They misspelled your name?

BOB *(Comes out of his brief daydream)*: Huh?

MIKE: Jobert.

BOB *(Amused)*: Oh, yeah.

MIKE: Jobert Rettie. Dear Jobert Rettie. Hi, Jobert.

BOB: Hi, Jike.

MIKE: Good old Jobert.

COOTIE: How ya feelin', good old Jobert?

BOB: Dead, how 'bout you?

MIKE *(Sees what's happening and comes to the rescue. Pause)*: Hi, Jel.

COOTIE: Hi, Jike.

MIKE: Hi, Jorman.

NORMAN: Huh?

MIKE: Hi, Jorman.

NORMAN: Oh, hi.

MIKE: Hi, Jathy, hi Jick.

DICK: Fuck off.

MIKE: Juck off? Why should I juck off, Jick?

(The doorbell rings. Cootie rushes over and answers it. At the door, a young man in a suit and tie and horn-rimmed glasses, with an attaché case, which he has concealed just out of sight behind the doorframe.)

COOTIE: Hi, Jister.

MIKE: Ask him his name, Jel.

COOTIE: What's your name?

RALPH: Ralph.

COOTIE: Hi, Jalph, I'm Jel and that's Jathy, Jorman, Jike, Jick, and Job, and we're just on our way down to City Hall to beat the shit out of some cops. Wanna come?

RALPH *(Pauses momentarily, then launches his pitch)*: I'm from the University of Buffalo and I'm in the neighborhood doing market research. You don't mind my asking you a few questions, do you? *(As he says this last, he reaches down, takes up his concealed attaché case, bends his head like making ready for a dive, and advances swiftly but deliberately into the middle of the room. This swift movement, plus the running patter, is designed to force the average housewife to back away and give ground, but since Cootie merely steps aside when Ralph bends down for his attaché case, we are treated to the entire technique out of context. Ralph ends up in the middle of the room still bent over, motionless. He looks up and around and straightens himself, laughing nervously at everyone watching him)* Do all you people live here?

MIKE: No, we're just using the place for a few days. This is a fantastic coincidence because the guy that lives here just went away for a few days to do a series of special guest lectures at the University of Buffalo.

RALPH: Really? No kidding? That's some coincidence, huh? That's really a fantastic coincidence. Well, ahhh, here's what I'd like to do. I'd like to interview one of you people. I'll choose one of you at random and everybody else can listen and if the guy I choose has a particular opinion that differs significantly from what the rest of you believe, we'll just stop and take a consensus, O.K.? Hey, you guys all work, don't you? I mean, you're not students or anything?

COOTIE: We mostly hold various government jobs.

RALPH: I see. Are any of you married?

RUTH: I'm married to him *(Mike)* and she's married to him *(Bob and Kathy)*.

BOB: Actually, we're getting a divorce.

RALPH: Oh, I'm very sorry.

BOB *(Very sincerely to Ralph)*: No, please. It's just, I've been dying for a while, nothing serious, you know, but now I've decided I'm definitely dead, you see, so I'll have to change my name. It's a legal technicality. We'll marry again under my new name. Jobert. *(Pause)* Job.

RALPH: Oh . . . well . . . that's certainly very unusual. Now this is going to get a little difficult, really. I've got to improvise some of these questions because the standard form is pretty rigid, like, you know, it asks things about your children's opinions and that would hardly apply in a case like . . .

MIKE: I have several kids by a former marriage.

RUTH: Hey, how come you never told me about that?

MIKE: If you remember, dear, we did discuss it.

RALPH: Can I just edge in here, I mean, ha-ha, I don't want to interrupt a little marital tiff or anything, but, ha-ha, you know. *(To Norman)* And how about you sir, do you have any children?

NORMAN: I don't have any children. I'm not married.

RALPH: Well, sir, I would guess, am I right, I would guess that you are the oldest person staying here. I only mean that in the sense of responsibility. Am I right?

MIKE: The guy that actually lives here is older, but he's not here right now.

RALPH: No, he's lecturing, right? I remember, ha-ha. Now I'd just like to ask you the following question. Have you ever heard of a teaching program called the World Volumes Encyclopedia?

DICK: Hey, are you selling encyclopedias?

RUTH: Hey, yeah, are you trying to sell us a set of encyclopedias?

RALPH: I'd like to make it very clear that I am not authorized to sell any product, I'm merely doing market research.

MIKE: Jesus Christ, he's not even selling the fucking things. You go and write to the central offices and you wait for a whole year to hear from them and when they finally decide to send a guy around he's not even authorized to sell you a set. I'm not hanging around here listening to a guy that isn't even authorized to sell the World Volumes Encyclopedia while millions of women and children are dying out there in Vietnam. *(He grabs the banner and starts huzzahing as everyone follows him out of the door. Dick and Norman stay behind with Ralph, who is yelling after them)*

RALPH: Hey, hey, listen, I can sell you a set if you want one. *(He turns to Dick and Norman)* Hey, do you guys really want to buy a set of encyclopedias? I can sell you a set. I got a number of deals and there's a special discount for government employees.

DICK *(To Norman)*: You going?

NORMAN: Yes, I've been reading a lot about it lately.

DICK: You want to come with me?

NORMAN: Well, yeah, if you don't have any other plans.

DICK: O.K., hold on a minute. *(He goes out the hall door)*

RALPH: Hey, who are all you people?

NORMAN: We just live here.

RALPH: I go to college. I don't really come from Buffalo. I live in town. I'm trying to earn some money in my spare time. Are you guys really government employees?

NORMAN: I'm a graduate student.

RALPH: Yeah, well, I didn't want to say anything, but I didn't really think you guys were government employees. What are you studying?

NORMAN: Mathematics.

RALPH: I wanted to study mathematics. My father said he wouldn't pay so I'm studying law. Boy, do I hate law. I'm living at home. Do you guys all live here together?

NORMAN: Yes.

RALPH: And . . . and the girls too?

NORMAN: Yes.

RALPH: Oh, boy, what a life, huh? I'm gonna get me a car pretty soon. I'm saving up. The thing is, I'm not really doing too well selling encyclopedias. I can't pull it off. I wish I could figure out why. I've been thinking about it and I think maybe it's because I can't give the sales pitch credibility. That's pretty bad if I'm gonna be a lawyer because a lot of the time you have to defend people you know are guilty. The thing is, these encyclopedias are really shitty. *(He blushes)* Sorry. I mean, you know, they're not very good.

(Dick reenters. He is carefully groomed, dressed in a pea jacket and well-laundered jeans. He wears a large, orange Day-Glo peace button.)

DICK: You ready?

RALPH: You going out?

DICK: Listen, if you're gonna eat anything, lay off the hamburgers O.K.?

(Dick and Norman start out.)

NORMAN: I don't see why he has to go saying he's dead. I mean, that's only for him to have a physical. It's pretty easy to fail a physical. I've heard of guys that pretend . . .

(They are gone.)

RALPH *(Alone, looks at the open door)*: Hey!

(Blackout.)

Scene 3

A few hours later. Kathy is sitting in the kitchen, upset. Ruth comes in the front door. She has just returned from the march.

RUTH: Bob here?

KATHY: No.

RUTH: Hey, what's wrong. You want some coffee?

KATHY: Please. *(Ruth takes off her coat and starts making coffee)* How was it?

RUTH: Weren't you there?

KATHY: No.

RUTH: I thought you and Bob were coming. You were on the bus and everything. I got lost when the cops charged. Boy, they really got some of those guys. Fucking pigs.

KATHY: When we got there he said he didn't feel like marching.

RUTH: Why not?

KATHY: Oh, Ruthie, I don't know. I don't know anything anymore. You devote two years to a guy and what does he give you? He never even told me about the letter. Drafted, and he didn't even tell me.

RUTH: He's not drafted. The letter's for the physical. All he has to do is act queer. They're not gonna take a queer musician.

KATHY: That's what I told him on the bus. He wouldn't even listen until I called him Job.

RUTH: What?

KATHY: He said he was dead. "Bob is dead."

RUTH: He's putting you on.

KATHY: That's what I mean. Me. He's even putting me on. Ungrateful bastard. The things I've done for him, Ruthie. Shit, I sound just like my mother. You know what I mean. I'm not complaining, but you know, you get tired of giving all the time and nothing's coming back. You know what I told him? I said he was the first guy I ever had an orgasm with. I mean, it really made him feel good. Now I gotta live with it. How can you explain something like that.

RUTH: Hey, no shitting around, did he really say he was gonna join?

KATHY: You know what he told me? He thinks the whole antiwar movement is a goddamn farce. I mean, Jesus, I really thought we were relating on that one. It's not like I'm asking the guy to go burn himself or anything but, I mean, he knows how I feel about the war and he's just doing it to be shitty. There's something behind it, I know that. He's like reaching out, trying to relate to me on the personal level by rejecting me but, like, I don't know how to break through. He says he's gonna study engineering in the army and then when he gets out he's gonna get some kind of plastic job and marry a plastic wife and live in a plastic house in some plastic suburb and have two point seven children. Oh, shit, Ruth, it's all too much. He went to a cowboy film.

RUTH: Well, you know, that's how it is.

KATHY: But Ruth, it's not like a fantasy scene. I know the guy. He'll go through with it. I mean, he really thinks he's serious. He doesn't see it's all part of a communication thing between him and me.

RUTH: I don't know. Like, maybe he's really serious. Mike's got this thing about physics. His tutor says he's a genius. O.K., maybe he is, like what do I know about physics? The thing is, he's gonna end up working for his old man in the lumber business. It's all laid out from the start. You have to fit in.

KATHY: You don't want him to do that, do you? If the guy is into physics you've gotta really stand behind him and make it all happen for him.

RUTH: I don't know. You have some kids and everything. I mean it's not like you can't have a meaningful life if you get married and have kids.

KATHY: Wow, I don't believe you really mean that.

RUTH: Look, Kathy, I don't want Mike to saw wood for the

rest of his life, but what can I do about it? Why shouldn't he get into wood? Like, what if he does physics for the rest of his life and he's a genius and ends up head of department at some asshole university; you find out one day he's being financed by the C.I.A.

KATHY: These guys. They think they don't need you, so you go away and they freak out. Mike is a really brilliant guy. I mean, we all know that. You could really do things for him if you tried. You should've seen Bob when I first met him.

RUTH: I did.

KATHY: He used to compose all this really shitty music and like when he did something good he didn't even know it. You had to keep telling him yes, it's good, it's really great. A whole year it took for him to believe it. He's writing some fantastic stuff now, ever since, you know, I told him he was the first guy.

RUTH: Yeah, and look at him now.

KATHY *(Upset again)*: You think you're really relating like crazy and then, I don't know, it's a whole new scene. It's like you don't even know him anymore.

RUTH: Maybe you ought to stop relating so hard.

KATHY: You don't know him, Ruth. I really know the guy and he needs me.

RUTH: Yeah, but maybe you ought to lay off for a while.

(Mike bursts in through the front door.)

MIKE: Holy shit, where were you?

RUTH: I got lost and came home.

MIKE: Christ, it was horrible. We got stopped by this line of cops. Me and Cootie were right up front so I told him we should get everyone to join hands and stand still. We're standing there and this one pig starts running toward Cootie and you know how he gets when he sees pigs and he always gets diarrhea. I don't know, he should have said something, but he got the urge so bad he started to run, you know, trying to find a toilet, and this dumb pig thought he was trying to resist arrest.

KATHY: Is he all right?

MIKE: They took him to the hospital. He's, I don't know, they said he'll be all right. He got it in the back.

(Cootie walks in.)

COOTIE: Boy, what a shitty march. You had to go and get separated with all the eats. I could've really used a marmalade and chunky peanut butter.

RUTH: Hey, did you know, Bob really wants to join the army? He's not even gonna try and get out. He didn't even go to the march.

COOTIE: He didn't miss much.

KATHY: He went to a goddamn cowboy film.

COOTIE: Hey, is that the one with Kirk Douglas and Gina Lollobrigida and Curt Jurgens and Orson Welles and Tom Courtenay and . . .

KATHY: You guys are really something. You don't give a shit what happens to him. I thought we were, like, all together here. Smug bastards. I'll tell you something.

COOTIE: What's that, Kathy?

KATHY: You're no better than the people fighting this war. *(She storms out of the room down the hall)*

MIKE: She's pretty cut up, huh?

RUTH: She thinks he's serious.

MIKE: Isn't he?

(Cootie starts jumping and singing, punctuating each note with a leap. He snarls the song.)

COOTIE: We shall over cu—u—um,
  We shall over cu—u—um,
  We shall overcome some day—ay-ay-ay-ay
  Oh, oh, oh, deep in my heart
  I do believe.
  We shall over . . .

MIKE: Shut up, Mel.

COOTIE: If Bob's really serious, we gotta stop the war quick so he doesn't get sent over there to get killed by an antipersonnel bullet.

(Dick comes in, livid.)

DICK: Fucking Norman is fucking out of his fucking mind.
That's the last time I ever take him with me. *(Dick takes
a bottle of milk from the icebox, kills it, and places it on
the stack)*

MIKE: Hey, what's the matter, Dick, didn't you get yourself
some left-wing ass?

COOTIE: Don't be ashamed, sonny. If she's waiting out there
in the hallway, bring her in and show us the goods.

DICK: Norman had a fucking gun with him. He took a fucking revolver to the march.

MIKE: Is he a good shot?

DICK: I'm not shitting around. We're sitting on the bus and
he's telling me he's reading Ho Chi Minh on guerrilla war
and he doesn't think marches are effective. So he says he's
gonna use the marchers like an indigenous population
and start a guerrilla war against the cops. I mean, I
thought he was just fucking around. You know Norman.
Then he pulls out this fucking revolver right there on the
bus, people looking and everything, and he says he's
gonna get a few cops and would I help him create a diver-
sion. He's out of his fucking mind.

MIKE: How many'd he get?

DICK: Fuck you.

COOTIE: He got the girl, huh?

DICK: Where's Kathy and Bob?

RUTH: Bob's not here.

DICK: Kathy here?

RUTH: Leave her alone. She's upset.

COOTIE: Yeah, I wouldn't try to lay her just yet, 'cause she's
still going with Bob.

(Dick walks out down the hall.)

MIKE: That was a pretty stupid thing to say.

COOTIE: Just came out.

RUTH: Who cares? Everyone knows what dirty Dicky's up to.
Except maybe Bob.

MIKE: And maybe Kathy.

RUTH: Kathy knows.

COOTIE: Do you think a guy could become a homosexual just by willpower? Could someone learn to like guys?

(A knock on the front door.)

RUTH: It's open.

(In walks Lucky, the downstairs neighbor, led by Mr. Willis, the landlord.)

WILLIS: Lucky tells me there's been a lotta noise up here. Is that right?

MIKE: Sorry, Mr. Willis, we had a little outburst up here. It's my fault. I just got a letter my sister had a baby.

COOTIE: We were celebrating.

WILLIS: That's all right, but keep it down. Lucky here was saying how you woke his wife up. She's a very ill person. I don't want any more complaints.

MIKE: Don't you worry about that, Mr. Willis, I'll take it on myself to keep this place really quiet.

LUCKY: Listen, I told you kids once before, and I'm not telling you again. You gotta get rid of those galvanized aluminum garbage cans in the yard and get plastic ones like everyone else.

RUTH *(Angry)*: I don't see why we can't keep the ones . . .

MIKE: Ruth, now calm down, Ruth. I'm sorry, Lucky, but Ruth's pretty upset. Her father's fallen ill and they don't know for sure if it's . . . you know.

LUCKY: You got the galvanized aluminum ones out there. You'll have to get rid of the galvanized aluminum ones and get plastic.

WILLIS: I'll take care of the rest, Lucky. Thank you for bringing this particular grievance to my attention.

LUCKY: I'll give you till Monday, then I want to see plastic out there. *(He leaves through front door)*

WILLIS: Whew, I hope I seen the last of that loony today. Nothin' but complaints day and night. The guy was born with a hair across his ass. So who's gonna give the land-lord a little coffee?

(Ruth makes a move to get it.)

WILLIS: Thanks, sweetheart. Brother, what a day, what a stinker of a day. Where's Bobby?

MIKE: He's dead.

WILLIS: Dead? He's dead? You guys really kill me, you guys. You got a whole sense of humor like nothin' else. Dead, huh? Smart kid, Bobby. Hey, you been to the march?

COOTIE: Yep.

WILLIS: Great march. I watched it on Channel 8 in color. Brother, clothes you guys wear come out really good on color TV. You know, that guy Lucky can be a lotta trou-ble. He got a mind, like, you know, the size of a pinhead, you know what I mean? Just one sugar, sweetheart.

MIKE: You want the rent?

WILLIS: Rent, schment. I come to see how you guys are get-ting along and you talk to me about rent. How many landlords care, tell me that? One in a million, I can tellya. Hey, you decided whatya gonna do when you get out of college?

COOTIE: I'm gonna be a homosexual.

WILLIS: A homo . . . You guys really slay me, you guys. What a sense of humor. You know, I'd give ten'a my other ten-ants for any one of you guys. You kids are the future of America, I mean that deeply, not too much milk, beauti-ful. Yeah, you kids live a great life up here. I got tenants complaining all the time about the way you kids carry on, and I'll tell ya something, you wanna know why they complain? 'Cause they'd give the last piece of hair on their heads to live like you kids are living.

RUTH: How's Mrs. Willis?

WILLIS: Huh? Oh, yeah, great, just great. Well, just between you and me and the wall she's gettin' to be a pain in the ass. She wants me to get rid of you, too. Why? I ask her. She don't like the way you live. O.K., I say, if you know so much, how do they live? She don't know and she don't wanna know. I try to tell her, you know, about the wild parties and stuff and taking drugs to have all new sensations in the body and the orgies with six or seven of you all at once. You should see her eyes light up. Same thing with all the tenants. When they hear what it's really like up here they go all funny. They'd pay me a hunnerd dollars to hear more, but they ain't got the nerve to ask. "Get rid of them." That's all I hear. Wamme to tell you something?

MIKE: If you got something to say you didn't ought to hold back.

WILLIS: Tremendous. You kids are tremendous. Listen. When the neighbors try to tellya about when they was young don't believe it. It's a lotta bull, and I should know. When we was young it was so boring you fell asleep when you was twenty and you never woke up again. You hear them stories Lucky tells about the war? Crap. He's sittin' down there holdin' his dick watchin' Doris Day on television. He'd give his left nut to know what's happenin' up here. This is the best cup of coffee I've had all day. I got a theory about it. It's when the head and the stomach don't talk to each other no more. That's when everything goes to hell. I'm gettin' so I don't know what I want half the time. I got these dreams, really crazy dreams. I got this one where I'm in a clearing, you know, it's right in the middle of the jungle and there's this tribe of Africans, I mean, like I don't know if they're Africans but they're livin' in the jungle and they're black so I figure they must be Africans. They got this skin. It's, you know, black, but really black. This maybe sounds kinda screwy, but it's really beautiful this skin. It's a dream, remember. I'm not sayin' black skin is beautiful, if you see what I mean. I'm in charge of the whole works in this jungle and I got it all organized so the men live in one hut and the women live in another hut and there's a big sort of square in between where nobody's allowed after lights-out. They live like this all their life. There's no marryin' or anything. I'm a kind of witch doctor and I got this tribe believing . . . well, you know, they're just, like, Africans, and they don't know you gotta have a man and a woman to make babies, and I got 'em thinkin' you get babies when the moon shines down a girl's thing and hits the inside of her womb. And I got this whole ceremony where a girl comes to me when she wants a baby and I tell her she gotta wait until it gets dark and the moon comes up. Then I tie her to a plank, face up, and tilt the plank so her thing is facing the moon and then I go to the hut with the guys inside and get one of them to jerk off on a leaf, you know, one of them tropical leafs that's really big. Then I roll this leaf up like it's a tube and I sneak across the square holding this leaf in my hand all rolled up, until I get to the girl. She's lying there in the moonlight all black and shiny and her thing is opened right up 'cause she thinks . . . and I got this tube full of jis in my hand, and I'm coming closer so I can smell everything and . . . *(Comes out of it)* Jesus, what am I saying? I'm going crazy. It's just a dream, what I'm telling you.

RUTH: That's the most beautiful thing I ever heard.

WILLIS: Listen, I got carried away. I didn't mean none of that.

MIKE: Mr. Willis, if you'd've had the opportunities we've had you'd've probably ended up one of the great poets of the century, and I mean that includes Rimbaud, Rilke, Williams, Pasternak and Ginsberg.

COOTIE: And Whitman.

MIKE: Yes, Whitman included.

WILLIS: Oh, Jesus, you kids, you kids. I feel like I can tell you anything. Somebody could've thought I was pretty screwy if I told them some of them things.

RUTH: How many landlords have poetry in their soul?

WILLIS: Yeah, yeah. Hey, I gotta run now. Listen, it's really great having you guys around. If I could get some of them other tenants to come up here and listen to you, the world would be a better place to live in, you know what I mean?

MIKE: It would be a much better place.

COOTIE: A hundred percent better, at least.

RUTH: You're a beautiful person, Mr. Willis. Never be ashamed of it.

WILLIS: No, I ain't. I ain't ashamed of myself. Hey, you know what I was sayin' before about all them complaints. I lost a lotta tenants on account of you. I can't afford any more, so keep it quiet or I'll have to get rid of you. Wonderful coffee, sweetheart. Seeya. *(He leaves through front door)*

RUTH: I wonder how long before they put him away?

(Kathy, clothes a bit messed up, flounces into the kitchen and gets a glass of water. Dick follows her as far as the kitchen, as if he was trying to stop her, but when he gets to the doorframe he stops, feeling the tension in the room. He tries to button his shirt casually, not sure whether he wants the others to know what just happened between him and Kathy.)

COOTIE: Hi, Dick, how's it hanging?

(Kathy stiffens at the sink. Dick turns and goes down the hall out of sight.)

MIKE: I still can't figure out what to get good old Bob for Christmas.

(Before Kathy can reply, the doorbell rings. No one moves.)

COOTIE: Whose turn is it?
KATHY: You're a miserable bastard.
COOTIE: What'd I say? We're just playing a chess tournament.
KATHY: Listen, this is my scene, mine. You guys stay out of it. O.K., Ruth!
RUTH: It's her scene, guys, you stay out of it.
COOTIE: Roger.
MIKE: Sam.
COOTIE: Larry.
MIKE: Richard.
COOTIE: What's Richard getting Bob for Christmas?

(The doorbell rings again, and Mike jumps up to get it. Shelly's standing there.)

MIKE: Hello there, I don't know you.

SHELLY: Hi. Does Norman live here?

MIKE: Does anyone here know a Norman?

SHELLY: He said he lived here. I met him at the march today. He said to come here and wait for him. I been standing out in the hall 'cause, like, I heard someone talking and I didn't want to disturb anyone and then this guy just came out so I figured, well, it's now-or-never kind of thing. I'm Shelly.

RUTH: Come on in. I'm Ruth.

SHELLY: Oh, good, then Norman does live here because I wasn't sure when he gave me the address. Sometimes you meet a guy at a march and he'll like give you an address and you end up waiting for a few days and he never shows. Did that ever happen to you? It's happened to me a lot of times.

KATHY: Listen everyone, I'm serious, I don't want him to know. I'll tell him when the time's right.

RUTH: It's your scene.

(Kathy exits down hall. Shelly, meanwhile, goes under the table and sits down on the floor.)

SHELLY: I'm sorry about this. If you want to laugh go ahead, I'm used to it. It's just I've got this thing at the moment where I keep sitting under tables and I figured I'd better do it right away instead of pretending for a while I didn't sit under tables. I mean, sitting under the table is "me" at the moment, so why hide it? Have you ever done it?

RUTH: Want some coffee, Shelly?

SHELLY: I'm a vegetarian.

MIKE: Coffee's made from vegetables.

SHELLY: I don't drink coffee, thanks. I'll just wait for Norman.

COOTIE: Where's Norman?

SHELLY: Well, he was arrested for carrying a concealed weapon, but he said it's O.K. because he has a permit. He's really a total-action freak, and he's very committed to the whole peace thing.

COOTIE: Oh.

MIKE: Well now . . .
COOTIE: How about that?

(Fade out.)

Scene 4

Norman is trying to read. Shelly is under the table blowing bubbles. Mike and Cootie are playing chess.

MIKE: I still think you should've said something, Norman. I mean it's got nothing to do with putting you on. If Dick said we didn't have a cat, all right, I mean he's got a right to think that but, I mean, it's really irresponsible of him to go running all over the place saying we don't.
NORMAN: Well, you turned off the lights that time when you came in. I was trying to read.
MIKE: Yeah, but that was the nitty-gritty, no-nonsense, down-to-earth needs of the moment because a cat just won't give birth with the lights on.
NORMAN: Dick says you don't have a cat.
MIKE: Will you listen to what I'm trying to tell you?
COOTIE: You can't move there.
MIKE: Why not?
COOTIE: Mate in thirty-four.
MIKE: Shit, I didn't see that. O.K., your game. *(Mike and Cootie start rearranging the pieces)*
COOTIE: Yeah, you see, Dick gets these things and he'll tell you, like, we don't have a cat or something like that. We would've explained if you'd just come out and asked instead of getting all hostile and paranoid and thinking we were putting you on.
SHELLY: Wow, bubbles are really something else. I think they're maybe divine.
MIKE: Bubbles are divine, Shelly.
COOTIE: So's Bogart.
SHELLY: Oh, Bogart, wow.

COOTIE: You're pretty happy, aren't you, Shelly?

SHELLY: Oh . . . yeah. Like, it's the right foods. And being under the table.

MIKE: You gotta watch the paranoid thing, Norman.

NORMAN: You were putting me on about the cat.

MIKE: See, you got this very paranoid thing about the cat.

NORMAN: I have not . . .

COOTIE: And the worst thing is how you get all defensive about it every time we bring it up. We're not denying your validity to doubt, Norman. We're not rejecting you as a human being. It's just you have a very paranoid personality because your father's a cop and that means you grew up in a very paranoid atmosphere.

SHELLY: Wow, your father's a cop?

NORMAN: Well, you know . . .

SHELLY: You never told me that. I think that's really great. My brother always wanted to be a cop.

COOTIE: My uncle's a cop.

MIKE: Yeah, that's right, our uncle's a cop.

NORMAN: That's what I mean, you see . . .

MIKE: What do you mean?

NORMAN: Well, I mean, you've got to go making fun of my father being a cop.

MIKE: Look, Norman, it just so happens our uncle is a cop and why the hell should you be the only one around here with a cop in the family. You see, you got paranoid again, thinking we're putting you on. I mean, we could do the same thing. How do we know your father's a cop? We don't. We trust you.

COOTIE: Yeah, and if you'd've been more outer-directed maybe you'd've seen you have a lot in common with us. A lot more than you ever expected.

MIKE: Then maybe we could've prevented that whole tragic episode with the gun.

NORMAN: Yeah, well, I don't know about you guys.

MIKE: You're not trying to say it wasn't a tragic episode?

COOTIE: It was an abortion of academic freedom, pure and simple.

MIKE: Hear! Hear!

COOTIE: I mean, when they can kick mathematics graduate students out of school just for trying to murder a few cops . . . And, by the way, Norman, I've heard that your being kicked out of school was the doing of the Dean of Admissions, a man who is known far and wide to be cornholing his widowed sister in the eye-sockets regularly . . .

MIKE: And without love.

COOTIE: And when the moon comes up he ties her to this plank . . .

MIKE: Mel . . .

COOTIE: So put that in yer pipe and smoke it. And don't try to tell us you enjoy having to schlepp down to the Hays Bick every night to wash dishes for a dollar ten an hour.

NORMAN: Oh, I don't know.

SHELLY: Hey, are you guys brothers?

MIKE: Now there, look at that, Norman. Shelly's wondering about the relationship between Mel and me, and instead of being all paranoid about it and going crazy wondering, she comes right out and asks.

SHELLY: Hey, are you?

COOTIE: Yeah, we're brothers.

SHELLY: Wow, I didn't know that either. I keep learning all these things about you guys.

MIKE: See, everything's cool now. Everybody trusts each other. That's what it's all about.

NORMAN: Well, I mean, with washing dishes I get more time to read. I've been thinking a lot and I guess it's like Dick said. I was pretty irrelevant before. Mathematics is pretty irrelevant no matter how you look at it, and bad mathematics is about as irrelevant as you can get.

SHELLY: I left school after the first month. I'm not saying I'm really relevant, yet, but like, some of my friends in school are really into bad scenes. School is evil. You can't find out where it's at when you're studying all the time to fit your head into exams. I'm getting to where I can read recipes all day and really get something out of it.

NORMAN: Yeah. I'm learning all this stuff about Vietnam. It's really something. I mean, I'm getting to the point where maybe I can do something really relevant about it.

MIKE: I wouldn't call the gun business relevant.

NORMAN: I was still in school when I thought of that.

SHELLY: Norman's got this fantastic idea.

NORMAN: Well, I haven't thought it all out yet . . .

SHELLY: No, Norman-baby, don't like close all up. It's the most relevant thing I ever heard of.

COOTIE: Jesus, Norman, how long have you been walking around with this idea all locked up inside you?

NORMAN: I didn't get it all at once. It sort of came in stages, but I think it's about right.

COOTIE: Man, you're gonna go crazy if you keep everything inside like that.

SHELLY: Tell them the idea, Norman.

NORMAN: Well, you see . . . *(Pause)* I'm gonna set myself on fire as a protest against the war. *(Cootie and Mike look at him and exchange brief glances)* I've thought about it a lot. I mean, I've read I guess about a hundred books about the war and the more you read the more you see it's no one thing you can put your finger on. It's right in the middle of the whole system, like Dick said. I shouldn't've tried to kill those policemen, but I didn't know then they were part of the system like everything else. No one's got the right to take anyone else's life, that's what I've decided. But I've still got the right to take my own life for something I believe in.

SHELLY: I'm gonna burn with Norman. We're gonna burn together. We've thought it all through and, like, if he burns himself alone that's just one person. Everyone'll say he's insane, but if two of us do it . . . wow. Two people. What are they gonna say if two of us do it?

MIKE *(Pause)*: Three of us.

COOTIE: Four of us.

MIKE: You, too, huh?

COOTIE: It's the only way.

NORMAN: Hey, wait a minute. I've read a lot about the whole subject and I really know why I'm gonna do it. I'm not just doing it for fun or anything. You can't just jump into it.

MIKE: Listen, Norman, you don't have to believe this if you don't want to but it's the truth, on my honor. Me and

Cootie talked about the exact same thing a year ago. We were all ready to burn ourselves . . .

COOTIE: It was more than a year ago.

MIKE: More than a year?

COOTIE: Almost a year and a half.

MIKE: That's right, a year and a half, boy, time really goes quick . . .

COOTIE: It sure does . . .

MIKE: The thing is, we decided against it because we figured two isn't enough.

COOTIE: You know how the papers can lie. "Brothers Burn!"

MIKE: Yeah, "Hippie Brothers in Suicide Pact." That kind of shit.

COOTIE: But think of it. With four of us!

NORMAN: You really want to do it?

MIKE: It's the only way.

NORMAN: I mean, I wasn't sure yet. I hadn't made up my mind definitely. I was still looking for another way.

SHELLY: No, Norman-baby, it's the only relevant gesture. Like you said.

(A long pause while Norman thinks.)

NORMAN: O.K.!

COOTIE: After the Christmas vacation.

MIKE: No, no, after graduation. We'll study like mad and get fantastic grades and graduate with honors so they can't say we were cracking up or anything.

COOTIE: Yeah, we'll get Phi Beta Kappa. I'd like to see them say we're insane when two Phi Beta Kappas go up in flames with the son of a policeman and the daughter of a . . . Hey, what does your father do?

SHELLY: Well, it's kind of funny. I mean, he's a pretty weird head in his way. He's got, like, six or seven jobs at any one time.

COOTIE: That's O.K. Daughter of a weird head with six or seven jobs at any given time. That covers the whole spectrum.

NORMAN: What does your father do? I mean, I know your uncle's a policeman because I trust you, but you never said what your father did. I was curious. Like if they bring our fathers into it what'll they say about you?

COOTIE: He's a trapper.

SHELLY: Wow, that's really something else. Like a fur trapper?

MIKE: Furs and hides, you know. Rabbit and mink and muskrat and beaver and elk and reindeer and seal. Some otter. Penguin.

SHELLY: Wow, penguin.

COOTIE: Well, you know, he works the Great Northwest Territory up to the mouth of the St. Lawrence Seaway and over to the Aleutians.

SHELLY: Boy, this'll really blow everyone's mind.

MIKE: Yeah, this'll make everyone think twice, all right.

COOTIE: You know, we can't tell anyone about this. If word gets out they'll send squads of police around here and we'll get arrested and put under psychiatric observation and subjected to a battery of tests that make you look nuts no matter how you answer.

NORMAN: I won't say anything.

SHELLY: Oh, wow, like you don't even have to worry about me.

NORMAN: I didn't even know there were any trappers left.

(A knock on the door.)

MIKE: Come in.

VOICE: C'mon, c'mon, open up in there.

(Mike opens the door and finds two cops standing there. Bream is elderly and Effing is young.)

BREAM: You live here?

MIKE: Yes, sir.

BREAM: Look, you know what I mean, you and who else.

MIKE: Well, there's me and my brother Cootie . . . um, Mel, and there's Norman, Dick, Bob, Kathy and Ruth.

BREAM: Kathy and Ruth, huh? Those are girls' names.

MIKE: Kathy and Ruth are both girls, sir.

BREAM: Don't block the doorway. *(Mike stands aside as Bream and Effing enter. Effing wanders around the room, inspect-*

ing. Bream indicates Shelly) Which one's she? You Kathy or Ruth?

SHELLY: I'm Shelly.

BREAM: Shelly, huh? You didn't say nothin' about no Shelly.

MIKE: She doesn't live here, sir.

BREAM: Visiting?

SHELLY: I'm with Norman.

BREAM: You're Norman, huh?

NORMAN: She's my girlfriend.

BREAM: Good, we got that straight.

EFFING: Hey, Bream, this here's a map of Europe.

BREAM: Yeah. Now listen. There's been a complaint from the people across there. I know you kids are students and you probably think you own the goddamn country, but I got some news for you. There's laws around here and you gotta obey them just like everyone else.

MIKE: We appreciate that, sir.

EFFING: Hey, Bream, look at all them milk bottles.

BREAM: Yeah. Now listen. I don't want to hear any more complaints about you guys. I'm a reasonable man, which is something you can get verified by askin' anyone on the force, but when I gotta put up with a lotta stupid complaints I can cause trouble and I mean real trouble, with a capital T.

EFFING: Hey, look at all them dishes in the sink, Bream.

BREAM: Yeah.

NORMAN: What was the complaint?

BREAM: What do you mean, what was the complaint? The complaint was guys and girls parading around in here bare-ass. Now look, I'm not the kind of dumb cop that goes around throwing his weight everywhere to prove he's some kind of big shot. I don't need to, you follow me. I know what I know and I know what I don't know, and one of the things I know I don't know is what the hell the kids are up to nowadays, but O.K. That's my problem. If you wanna run around naked that's O.K. by me, and I hope you kids take note of the fact that I'm winking one eye when it comes to the law about cohabitation.

MIKE: We appreciate that fact, sir. It was the first thing we noticed.

COOTIE: I sure appreciate it. I think I can speak for Norman and Shelly, and if any of the other guys were here they'd appreciate it a lot.

MIKE: I mean it's not as if we underestimate the life of a cop. For chrissakes, I mean, our uncle's a cop. His father's a cop. A lot of us around here are pretty close to the world of cops.

BREAM: You got cops in the family?

EFFING: Hey, Bream, look at this heater.

BREAM: Yeah.

MIKE: It's not like we don't know what you guys have to put up with. It can be pretty crappy job.

BREAM: I don't know . . .

MIKE: I'm not saying it doesn't have its rewards. My uncle's life is full of rewards. His father's life is very meaningful.

BREAM: Yeah, that's what I mean.

(Cootie gets up and starts to leave the room.)

EFFING: Hey, Bream, the kid's leaving the room.

COOTIE: I got a call from nature.

BREAM: That's legit. You go ahead, kid.

(Cootie goes out the front door.)

EFFING: Hey, Bream, the kid says he's going to the euphemism and what if he's got some stuff on him or something. He can flush it down and come back clean.

BREAM: He's O.K.

EFFING: Jesus, Bream. Sir.

BREAM: The guy's new on the job. He don't know the score yet.

MIKE: You know how some people exaggerate. I mean, look what they say in the papers about you guys. Maybe, like after a shower we'll come in here to get an anchovy snack or chocolate milk or something, and we forget to put something on . . .

EFFING: Look at that, Bream, the girl keeps sitting under there . . .

BREAM: Goddamnit, Effing, who's in charge around here?

EFFING: But she's sitting under there . . .

BREAM: Did we come here to investigate a complaint about a girl sitting under the table?

EFFING: No, sir, but . . .

BREAM: The girl happens to be well within her rights as a tax-paying citizen of the community to sit under any table she wants, and until we get complaints about her sitting under there, we leave her alone. Understand?

EFFING: Yeah, yeah, yeah . . .

SHELLY: Thanks.

BREAM: That's O.K., lady. The kid's a rookie. They give us pros a bad name. Now let me tell you something about the people complaining about you. They look in here and see you guys bare-assed and they're complaining because they're so sick of looking at each other they gotta go spying on you. We know about them people. They're strict Roman Catholics. Twelve kids in four rooms. The old man can't keep it in his pants for ten minutes running. So they got troubles, right, and everyone that's got troubles wants to give troubles to someone else. So they make a complaint, and that's well within their rights as law-abiding citizens of this community. I got enough troubles without their goddamn complaints. I got enough to do watching the Vietnam freaks and the niggers and the loonies going up on buildings with high-power rifles picking off everyone down below. Let me give you some good advice. Get curtains. They got some fiberglass curtains at Woolworth's, you can't tell them from real cotton. Twelve dollars and fifty cents a pair and they come in eight colors, plain and patterned. You get some curtain rods for a dollar sixty-nine apiece and for a total of twenty-eight dollars and thirty-eight cents you save yourself from a lot of crazy neighbors. If you can't afford twenty-eight dollars and thirty-eight cents, get some gingham, thirty-nine cents a yard at Penney's. Measure your windows and allow a foot extra at each end. All you gotta do is take up a three-inch hem at each end, fold it over once, and hand-stitch. A couple of curtain rings and you're in business. Can you remember that, or d'you want me to write it down?

SHELLY: Hey, yeah, would you do that?

(Bream takes out a notebook and starts to write. Effing is nervous.)

EFFING: The kid's been gone a long time.

BREAM: I got eyes, Effing.

EFFING: Yeah, yeah, yeah, O.K.

BREAM *(Writing)*: So, what are you kids gonna do with your-selves? *(Pause)* Am I being nosy or something?

MIKE: No, I mean, there's a lot of opportunities all over the place. We're not jumping into anything without we've looked the whole thing over.

BREAM: Smart kids. Boy, that's really something. Cop sending his kid to college. They must pay him pretty good, huh?

NORMAN: I guess so.

BREAM: Yeah, what's he a sergeant . . . lieutenant or some-thing?

NORMAN: He's Chief of Police for Erie County.

BREAM *(Whistles)*: Whew! Pretty good. That shut me up O.K. Chief of Police. Oh, boy, that's really something.

NORMAN: It's just his job, you know.

BREAM: Look, ah, here's your instructions. I want them up by Wednesday. Any complaints after that and all of you guys'll be in court, father or no father, you understand me? This ain't Erie County.

MIKE: Yes, sir.

NORMAN: O.K.

COOTIE *(Returns and stands in the door. There's a pause)*: That's better.

Scene 5

Ruth is scraping some cat food into a bowl. A cat comes in and eats. Ruth keeps glancing at her watch.

RUTH: Kitty-kitty-kitty-kitty-kitty. Chomp, chomp. Good girl. Make a lot of milk for the kitties.

(Kathy comes in from the hall and throws herself down on a chair.)

KATHY: Oh, Jesus, Ruth, how am I ever gonna tell him?
RUTH: Who?
KATHY: Bob, for chrissakes. Who else?
RUTH: Well, how should I know?
KATHY: I never slept with Dick. I know you got the idea I did, but it's not true. He never got all the way . . .
RUTH: . . . O.K. . . .
KATHY: . . . Yet. *(Pause)* I'm not saying I wouldn't like to.
RUTH: So go ahead.
KATHY: Well, don't try to pretend it doesn't mean anything to you. You know as well as I do it'll kill Bob if he ever finds out I'm even thinking of sleeping with Dick.
RUTH: That's how it goes.
KATHY: Ruthie, look, we've known each other since freshman year. I can tell when you're thinking something. This is really a big decision I've gotta make. What am I gonna do about Bob? I mean, it feels like maybe we're you know, finished, but I like the guy. I really like him a lot and I respect his music. But I know he could never relate to me as a friend. It's gotta be tied up with sex. I mean, Richard really seems to dig me, but I don't know. He's pretty together. He's not the kind of guy you could really do something big for. Not like Bob.
RUTH: Oh, for shit's sake, Kathy, Dick is a fucking parasite.
KATHY: That's not fair, Ruth.
RUTH: Fair! Do you know what that guy's doing to get into graduate school? You ever heard of Professor Roper in the Eastern Studies department?
KATHY: He's Dick's adviser.
RUTH: Yeah, and he also happens to be queer as a three-dollar bill, and Dick is fucking his wife to keep her quiet so good old Roper can suck cock with all those graduate students from Thailand or Malaya, or whatever the hell they are.

KATHY: Who said?

RUTH: Who said? For chrissakes, Kathy, the whole goddamn school knows about it. "Dirty Dicky."

KATHY: That's why?

RUTH: Yeah, what else? I mean, the guy washes eight times a day.

KATHY: Oh, man, how long have you guys known about this? I mean, why didn't anyone ever tell me? You can't just let him screw up his future like that. Hasn't anyone tried to do anything about it?

RUTH: Like tell him Mrs. Roper's got clap?

KATHY: Ruthie, the guy must be really suffering.

RUTH: Oh, shit, Kathy, let's not have the big savior thing.

KATHY: That's not very funny.

RUTH: Look, we're all gonna graduate pretty soon, and we're all gonna go away, and probably we'll never see each other again except maybe like at Christmas or something. So why don't you worry about yourself and never mind about Dick and Bob. They'll be O.K.

KATHY: Boy, you sure have changed, Ruth. I don't know. You sure have changed.

(Bob comes through front door carrying books.)

BOB: I don't believe it. It's incredible. You know what happened today in counterpoint class? Remember I was telling you about Eric Shatz?

RUTH: . . . three armpits . . . ?

BOB: The very one.

KATHY *(Nicely)*: Bob . . .

(Bob, who has gone to the icebox to steal some of Dick's hamburgers, stops short in whatever gesture he is holding, only for a moment though, just long enough to cut Kathy. When he resumes his story, he is talking only to Ruth, who is wrapping a Christmas present.)

BOB: Today Shatz turned in this perfect, spotless, clean counterpoint exercise. I mean, for someone as filthy as Shatz, that's a miracle. They say his high-school yearbook voted him "The Most Likely to Attract Infectious Disease." *(Bob has the hamburgers out by now. Kathy, being all nice, takes the hamburgers from him, indicating that she'll cook. Bob goes away from her and sits with Ruth)* He picks his nose and squeezes his pimples right there in class, and his counterpoint exercises have to be seen to be believed. He writes them in pencil, and if he makes a mistake or something, he spits on his eraser and rubs the paper about a hundred times . . . per note, so by the time he hands it to Professor Bolin, it's just this gray sludge with lots of little black things swimming around on it. Anyway, about a week ago, when Shatz handed over his work, Professor Bolin put on a pair of gloves before he'd take it, so Shatz must've got the message and this week when Bolin called for homework, Shatz set this beautiful, clean exercise down on the piano. We couldn't believe it. Bolin just sat there staring at it, and we all sat staring at Bolin, and after about ten minutes, no shit, it took that long, Bolin turned to us and said, "Free will is an illusion." Isn't that too much?

KATHY: Bob, can I talk to you . . . ?

BOB *(Ignores her)*: The thing is, Bolin's got a Ph.D. He's also written two books and a couple of hundred symphonies and string quartets and they say he taught himself twenty-two languages in four hours or something . . .

KATHY: Please, Bob, I want to talk to you . . .

BOB: And another thing, Bolin's wife got drunk at a faculty party for the music department last year and she yelled, "Fuck Schönberg, I wanna dance," and then she went and laid the only black professor in the school, which all goes to show that when Bolin tells you free will is an illusion . . . you better believe it.

KATHY *(Pointed)*: Bob, I would like to talk to you . . .

BOB: Hey, Ruth, did I ever tell you the one about the guy that died and came back to life as Job?

KATHY: Oh, don't start that shit again.

BOB: Again? It started over a month ago. I mean, even Bolin caught on after two lessons. Of course, he still makes me walk around the music building every time I put down parallel fifths, but that's how it goes, life is trying at the best of times, every cloud has a silver lining, a stitch in time saves nine . . .

RUTH *(Looks at her watch)*: I've gotta go.

BOB: Did I say something?

RUTH: No. Kathy wants to talk to you about sleeping with Dick.

KATHY: Ruth . . . bitch!

(Ruth goes out the front door, grabbing her coat on the way.)

BOB *(Pause)*: Meanwhile, back at the ranch . . . You'll never believe this, but when I came in just now, I didn't expect that. Bedbugs, maybe. Thermonuclear war . . .

KATHY: She had no right.

BOB: I'm trying to think of something appropriate to say, like "Name the first one after me." That's Job. J-O-B. Job.

KATHY: Please, Bob, can I say something . . . ?

BOB: Do you have trouble pronouncing the name Job?

KATHY: Jesus Christ, you're impossible.

BOB: Ah, yes, but I exist, nonetheless.

KATHY: You've just cut me right out. You're not even trying to relate to me anymore. *(Pause)* Well, you're not.

BOB: No, Kathy. The fact is, I like you a lot. I, um, sort of love you, if you know what I mean.

KATHY: I don't really want to sleep with Dick.

BOB: Then don't.

KATHY: It's just, he tried to get me that night after the demonstration.

BOB: I know. He told me.

KATHY: That shit.

BOB: I thought it was pretty good of him.

KATHY: He never got into me, you know.

BOB: That's nice.

KATHY: Oh, Bob. I'm sorry.

BOB: If Bob were around I'm sure he'd forgive you.

KATHY: What'll we do?

BOB: What do you mean? Like study or something?

KATHY: Bob, how does it stand? Is it . . . it's over, isn't it?

BOB: Between us, you mean?

KATHY: Yes.

BOB: If that's what you want.

KATHY: Of course I don't want it. I love you a lot.

BOB: O.K., so let's study for Phil 720.

KATHY: Oh, for chrissakes, show some emotion. I don't know where I'm at with you half the time.

BOB: Look, what's the big hang-up? If you want to stay with me, O.K. If you want to move into Dick's room, go ahead. If you don't know for sure, stay one night with me and one night with him till you start feeling a definite preference for one of us . . .

KATHY: Jesus Christ, Bob, what's the matter with you?

BOB: I'm Job. Bob's dead.

KATHY *(Is in a furious slow burn. She stands and goes toward the hall door)*: All right . . . all right . . .

(Before she can exit a knock on the door stops her. A game. Who's going to open the door? Bob picks up a book and starts reading. Another knock. Kathy sighs. She's above these silly games. She opens the door on a middle-aged man in well-cut coat. A businessman from head to foot. This is Murray, Bob's uncle.)

MURRAY: Hi. Does Bob Rettie live here?

BOB *(Looks up from his book)*: Murray!!

MURRAY: Can I come in?

BOB: What the hell are you doing here?

MURRAY: Guy flies a couple thousand miles to see his nephew, maybe he can come in, huh?

BOB: Yeah, yeah. Come in, come in . . . sit down . . .

MURRAY: Hey, I bet you're surprised to see me, huh? Maybe a little happy.

BOB: Yeah, I mean I haven't seen you for a couple thousand years or something.

MURRAY *(To Kathy)*: It's longer than that since he wrote.

BOB: Oh, ah, that's Kathy. My uncle.

MURRAY: How do you do.

KATHY: Hi.

MURRAY: You drink a lot of milk, huh?

BOB: Yeah.

(They laugh.)

MURRAY: Where'd you get that goddamn icebox?

BOB: Oh, you know . . .

MURRAY: Is this the way you been living? Bobby boy, why didn't you tell me. Write a letter, say Murray I need a little cash, I'd've sent you some money for a decent refrigerator.

BOB: Murray, we're living O.K.

MURRAY: So. I'm sorry for breathing. Did I interrupt something?

BOB: No. Nothing at all.

MURRAY: Are you two . . . ah . . .

BOB: Yeah—Murray, look, sit down, take your coat off . . .

MURRAY: Hey, Bobby, Bobby-boy. You got long hair . . .

BOB: Yeah, it keeps growing.

MURRAY: Still proud, huh? *(To Kathy)* Just like his mother . . . *(Murray looks at the two of them and shrugs)* Well what can I say . . . ?

KATHY: Look, I think I'll . . .

BOB: How long you in town for?

MURRAY: Oh, you know. Business.

KATHY: Excuse me, I'm gonna . . .

BOB: How's the kids?

MURRAY: Oh, fine, fine, keep asking about you.

BOB: Auntie Stella?

MURRAY: Oh. You know. We got a new house . . .

BOB: Great. Where you going, Kathy . . . ?

KATHY *(Has been edging toward the door. Quietly)*: I'll be in Dick's room if you want me. *(She exits)*

MURRAY: Is she O.K.?

BOB *(Flat)*: Yeah. It's her time of the month, you know.

MURRAY: Say no more. You don't have to tell me about that. Nice girl. Very nice. *(Laughs)* So . . .

BOB: Come through New York?

MURRAY: Yeah, you know, passed through.

BOB: You passed through New York, huh?

MURRAY *(Uneasy)*: Yeah, sure, you know . . .

BOB: D'you see Mom?

MURRAY: Yeah, yeah, sure. She'd maybe like a letter every now and then. Your own mother.

BOB: It's not like that, Murray. When I see her, I see her.

MURRAY *(Shiver)*: Jesus Christ. *(He removes a shiny metal hip flask and drinks)*

BOB: You O.K.?

MURRAY: Sit down, Bobby boy.

BOB: I'm O.K. like this.

MURRAY: I got something to tell you, you should maybe be sitting down when I tell you.

(Bob sits. Murray pulls his chair close and takes Bob's head in his hands. Bob is stiff.)

MURRAY: Bobby-boy, oh, Bobby. I'd like to see more of you. Me and the family. You maybe come out and visit, huh?

BOB *(Flat)*: What's happened, Murray?

MURRAY: How am I supposed to tell you?

(Pause.)

BOB *(Long pause)*: Cancer? *(Murray nods)* How long's she got?

MURRAY: A week, two weeks. I don't know. Any time now.

BOB: Those operations . . . kidney trouble. Oh, shit, why didn't someone tell me?

MURRAY: You got your studies, we should worry you to death?

BOB *(Flat)*: Fuck you all.

MURRAY: I thought . . . I thought maybe you and me fly to New York tonight.

BOB: Yeah, get in there quick for the payoff. That'll be just great.

MURRAY: She doesn't know yet.

BOB: Yeah. "Hi, Mom, I just came flying in with Murray a couple of weeks before Christmas vacation to see you for no good reason." You think she won't guess?

MURRAY: We can always tell her something.

BOB: You planning to keep it from her, too? I bet it's the first thing she thought of. Two years. She had that first operation two years ago. She's been dying for two years and I didn't even fucking know it.

MURRAY: I don't want to hurt anybody.

BOB *(Pause)*: I'll pack some stuff. No, you stay here. I want to be alone.

(Bob goes down the hall. Murray sits. Very short pause, then Mike and Cootie burst in through the front door, laden with Christmas presents. They see Murray, cross the kitchen to the hall door, exit, and start arguing loudly just outside in the hallway. After a moment they reenter, Mike leading. Deferential.)

MIKE: Me and my friend were wondering if you could settle a little argument for us.

MURRAY: What?

MIKE: Were you or weren't you the guy behind the bar in *Key Largo,* starring Humphrey Bogart and Edward G. Robinson?

MURRAY: I'm Bob's uncle.

MIKE *(To Cootie)*: He's Bob's uncle.

COOTIE: Are you a for-real uncle?

MURRAY *(Confused)*: Yeah, yeah, I'm his uncle.

COOTIE: Maternal or paternal.

MURRAY: I'm related to Bob through his mother. She was . . . she's my sister.

MIKE: That means you and him have different names.

MURRAY: Yeah, he's a Rettie, I'm a Golden.

MIKE: That's a pretty convincing story, mister.

COOTIE: Most of the pieces fit pretty good.

(Mike and Cootie start toward the hall. Shelly comes in the front door.)

SHELLY: Hi, everyone.

MIKE: Hiya, Shelly.

COOTIE: Good old Shelly, hiya.

(Mike and Cootie are gone down the hall.)

SHELLY: Hey . . . excuse me, do you know if Norman's here?

MURRAY: I don't know who Norman is.

SHELLY: One of the guys here. I mean, like he lives here. You someone's father?

MURRAY: I'm Bob's uncle.

SHELLY: Bob? Oh, yeah, Job. *(She sits under the table)* I'm waiting for Norman. Hey, are you, like, a for-real uncle?

MURRAY: You kids keep asking that.

SHELLY: You don't think of him with relatives.

MURRAY: Look, if you don't want me to stay in here, I'll go and help Bob.

SHELLY: No, you stay here. Like, I enjoy company. Hey, is he here?

MURRAY: I'm afraid I don't know your friend Norman.

SHELLY: I mean Job. Your nephew.

MURRAY: Yes, he's here. I'm waiting for him.

SHELLY: He's, like, in here somewhere? Inside the apartment?

MURRAY: Yes. Look, you want to go down and ask him about Norman, go ahead.

SHELLY: Is he in the toilet?

MURRAY: He's in his room.

SHELLY: Wow, that's like really weird.

MURRAY: He's just packing, that's all.

SHELLY: Yeah, but I mean, if you're his for-real uncle, how come you're like sitting in here when he's down there?

MURRAY: Look, he . . . *(Weeping softly)* . . . I don't know.

SHELLY: Hey, you're really crying like crazy. What's the matter? I thought you were, like, waiting for him to come back here, you know, to the apartment or something. I just wanted to know because I'm waiting for Norman to come back so I thought we could maybe sit here together waiting and that would be something we had in common, then you told me he was in his room packing and everything and I thought that was sorta weird 'cause if you're like his for-real uncle you could just go down there and be with him. Why's he packing?

BOB *(Entering with bag)*: O.K. I'm ready.

SHELLY: Hey, Job, you going away?

BOB: I'll be back in a few days.

SHELLY: Like, you mean, you're not just going home early for Christmas vacation.

BOB: No.

SHELLY: Oh. O.K. Hey, Merry Christmas, you guys.

BOB: Merry Christmas.

MURRAY: Merry Christmas.

(Dick comes in through the front door. Bob and Murray start out. Dick is baffled.)

DICK: Hey, you going?

BOB: Yeah. Kathy's in your room. *(Pause)* She doesn't like it from behind.

(Bob and Murray are gone.)

DICK: Where's he going?

SHELLY: I don't know, but the guy with him is his for-real uncle and he's a weird head.

(Kathy comes into the kitchen.)

KATHY: Hey, did Bob just go out?

SHELLY: Wow, he didn't even tell you?

DICK: He left with his uncle.

KATHY: Uncle?

SHELLY: Yeah, like it's his for-real uncle, I'm pretty sure.

KATHY: Jesus, why didn't he say something? I mean, I been waiting for him down there . . .

SHELLY: Well, the uncle said Job went down to his room to pack, and I mean, like if you were in there with him and he started putting a lot of socks and underwear and toilet stuff in a suitcase you should've got suspicious and asked him something, like where's he going.

KATHY: Look, I went to the bathroom, O.K.?

SHELLY: Ya didn't flush.

KATHY: Mind your own business, Shelly. What does he expect me to do? How can I make plans for the Christmas vacation if he just . . . shit, he could've said something. *(Dick in a feeble attempt to avoid Kathy's rage, tries to sneak out down the hallway)* And listen, you, you have a lot of nerve telling him about that night.

DICK: I didn't say anything.

KATHY: He said you told him.

DICK: Honest, Kathy, I never did.

KATHY *(Vague)*: I'm really getting to hate this place. *(She starts down the hall. Dick starts after her)*

DICK: Kathy!

(Before Dick can get down the hall, Ruth rushes in through the front door, breathless.)

RUTH: Oh, wow, have I ever had the most fantastic experience! *(Dick goes down the hall, slamming the door. She yells)* You're a shit, Dick.

SHELLY: You seen Norman?

RUTH: Oh, hi, Shelly. Hey, let me tell you about what just happened to me. It really blew my mind.

(From down the hall, we hear voices singing.)

MIKE AND COOTIE *(Singing, offstage)*:
WE WISH YOU A MERRY CHRISTMAS
WE WISH YOU A MERRY CHRISTMAS
WE WISH YOU A MERRY CHRISTMAS
WE WISH YOU A MERRY CHRISTMAS
WE WISH YOU A MERRY CHRISTMAS
WE WISH YOU A MERRY CHRISTMAS
WE WISH YOU A MERRY CHRISTMAS
WE WISH YOU A MERRY CHRISTMAS
AND . . . *(Mike and Cootie rush in from the hall dressed in Santa Claus costumes and end the song)*
A HAPPY NEW YEAR.

MIKE: We got a present for you, Ruth.

SHELLY: Hey, where'd you get those?

COOTIE: We're doing collections this year. Yep.

MIKE: You want to see the great old present we got ya?

RUTH: I was just gonna tell Shelly what happened when I went to see Quinn. You know Quinn, the albino dwarf . . .

MIKE: Oh, yeah, old Quinn.

COOTIE: Good old Quinn.

RUTH: Yeah, right. Well, I had to see him about homework for the Christmas vacation and, I mean, like, he was the last person I wanted to see. I always thought he was a vicious little bastard. I mean, he can be pretty shitty.

MIKE: They say he shot a man in Abilene.

COOTIE: In the back.

RUTH: Listen, willya? I went into his office and he's standing by the window, you know, three feet high and everything. I thought he was probably gonna ask why I wasn't doing any homework, and I had this whole speech worked out about how I thought he was a pretentious little snot and how I frankly didn't give a shit about philosophy and even less of a shit about him, if that's possible and . . . oh, you know, I was really going to kill him. Anyway, he told me to come over to the window, so I came over and we both stood there looking out. Snow everywhere, like, white wherever you looked and a lot of snow coming down like in those paperweights you shake up, and there's all these kids down below coming out of the building, all little lumps moving across the white in slow motion, and we're looking at them, just the two of us for, I don't know, about a minute or two, and then he just turns to me, like without any warning, and says this incredibly beautiful thing . . .

MIKE: Hey, don't you want to see the nifty present we got ya?

RUTH: Let me tell you what the guy said, willya?

MIKE: Right, you tell us what Quinn said, then we'll show you the present.

RUTH: Yeah.

MIKE: Will you look at the present first, then tell us what Quinn said?

RUTH: For Christ sake, stop fucking around and listen.

MIKE: All right, what did Quinn say?

COOTIE: I'd like to hear what Quinn said.

(As Ruth is about to speak, Kathy runs through from the hall and out the front door with a valise in hand. Dick shouts from offstage down the hall.)

DICK *(Offstage)*: Kathy. *(He enters and on his way across the room and out the front door, buttons his overcoat)* Kathy!

(Ruth's face shows worry as she watches this. Seconds after Dick exits, she takes her coat and follows, leaving Mike, Cootie and Shelly alone. There is a pause.)

COOTIE: What was that all about?
MIKE: Things around here are getting a little out of control, Cootie.
COOTIE: You feel that way, huh?
MIKE: I do.
COOTIE: Well, what are we gonna do about it, movies or roller-skating?
MIKE: Cootie, sometimes you're really a dumb asshole.
COOTIE: But then again sometimes I'm not. *(Gets up and walks down the hall slowly)*
SHELLY: Hey!

(Mike exits after Cootie, leaving Shelly alone.)

(Slow fade.)

Scene 6

Most of the posters are down. A bare feeling. Around graduation. There's some letters on the table. Ruth, alone, is reading her letter. Dick comes in from outside, dressed for warm weather, perhaps carrying a box. He opens the icebox.

DICK: Shit, nothing left.
RUTH: We cleaned it.
DICK: Anyone gone yet?

RUTH: No. Why don't you look at your grades?

DICK *(Opens letter)*: Jesus.

RUTH: Bad?

DICK: Fucking awful.

RUTH: Do you graduate?

DICK: Yeah, just.

RUTH: They sent Kathy's grades here.

DICK: That was tactful.

RUTH: Maybe she'll be around to pick them up. I got into graduate school.

DICK: Great.

RUTH: Philosophy.

DICK: Philosophy?

RUTH: Yeah! *(Pause)* I mean, you know, why not? *(Dick starts toward the hall)* Hey, Dick, I don't get it. You know that day she left, just before Christmas . . . did you get into her?

DICK: How low can you stoop, Ruth?

RUTH: No, I mean, you know, just, she must've done something to fuck you up this bad.

DICK: Kathy did not fuck me up.

RUTH: Yeah, well, ever since she left you've been looking like really terrible. You never even studied for finals. I mean, you were the academic head around here. Hey, you did get her, didn't you, and I bet she told you you were the first guy that ever turned her on. *(Dick starts out again)* Did she? Oh, come off it, Dick, I just . . . I thought we were friends.

DICK: You know what that goddamn fucking little cunt told me? Just before she left? She told me I was screwing Roper's wife. Me, screwing Roper's wife.

RUTH: Well, you know Kathy.

DICK: She said everybody in the whole fucking school knew about it. It got back to Roper.

RUTH: Wow, I bet he was pretty pissed off, huh?

DICK: He was pretty good about it, considering. He pulled me in after a tutorial and gave me the old "Richard, my boy" speech. He thought I started the rumor. Me. Shit. "Richard, my boy, it's said you're doing unenviable things to my wife. My boy, that particular assignment has already been well seen to. It's not like you to claim credit for someone else's work." You ever tried to do a paper for someone who thinks you've been saying you're screwing his wife? Shit. Poor old fairy. Boy, what a fucking mess.

(Bob comes in the front door.)

RUTH: Hey, Bob, you got your grades.
BOB. Oh, yeah. *(He looks)*
RUTH: How'd you do?
BOB: O.K. This for Kathy?
RUTH: Yeah. *(Bob starts to open Kathy's letter)* Hey, that's private property.
BOB: What the fuck's gotten into you all of a sudden. *(Reads)* A, A, A, A . . . B minus. B minus in Poetry 210. Man, she really went to pieces without us. I hope she hasn't had a nervous breakdown or anything. Whew, B minus.

(A knock on the door. Dick opens it. It's Lucky.)

LUCKY: Listen. I just seen Mr. Willis. He wants you out by tomorrow night.
BOB: How ya been, Lucky?
LUCKY: What? Oh, yeah. Well, if you want a hand, you know where to find me.
RUTH: Thanks a lot, buddy.
LUCKY: Don't get fresh, girlie, don't give me lip. You can talk how you want when you're with your own kind, but you show some respect when you're with Lucky. Smart alecks. Think you know everything. You don't . . . you don't know . . . you don't know what it's like living downstairs. That's something I know about. I know about living downstairs. I live downstairs. You seen me . . . you seen me out there, sitting out there. Well, you seen me . . .
BOB: Yeah, yeah, lots of times.
LUCKY: All right. That's what I mean. I sit out there. I'm out there. I got my Budweiser. I got my pretzels. Oh, yeah . . .

I'm not just sitting out there, you know. I'm watching. I'm keeping my eyes open. *(He's slowly going into a trance)* I see them cars go by, all them cars. Fords. I see Fords out there. Chevies. Lincolns. Oldsmobiles. Plymouths. I see the odd Cadillac, oh, yeah, don't worry about that. It's all up here. You think I'm just sitting there with my Budweiser and pretzels. Think you know it all, oh, yeah.

DICK: Don't worry, we took care of it.

LUCKY: Huh?

DICK: We did like you said. Got rid of those plastic garbage cans and got some galvanized aluminum.

LUCKY: All right, that's what I mean. Now, if you want any help, I'll tell you what you do. You come downstairs. O.K.? *(As Lucky goes, we see him look around and call "Kitty-kitty")*

RUTH: Guess I'll pack. *(Gets up to leave. Dick starts taking down one of his posters)*

BOB: Where's everyone?

RUTH: Mike and Mel went out with Norman. They're meeting Shelly at the flicks. *Casablanca.* You should see the marks they got. They're both magna cum.

DICK: Magna cum. Sneaky bastards.

RUTH: Yep. *(She goes out down hall)*

DICK: You staying for graduation?

BOB: No, you?

DICK *(Shakes head no)*: Hey, you really going into the army?

BOB: Yeah, as a hostage. I don't know. What are you doing?

DICK: Shit, I don't know.

BOB: Anything lined up for the summer?

DICK: Yeah, delivering milk. It's your friendly college graduate, Mrs. Miller. "Such a shame, the boy went to college." Maybe I'll get sterilized, save any kids having to go through all this. She really was a bitch, you know.

BOB: I guess so.

DICK: Guess so, shit, I hope she gets cancer of the tits and suffers like crazy while she's dying. Honest to Christ, she's the first person I ever met I could really kill.

BOB: Yeah.

DICK: Oh, great humility scene.

BOB: No, it's just, you know, that's how it goes.

DICK: You know something, Bob? You know what's wrong with you?

BOB: I been waiting all this time for someone to tell me. What's wrong with me, Dick?

DICK: You let her get your balls, Bob.

BOB: That was pretty careless, wasn't it?

DICK: No shit, Bob. I remember when you got stung by that bee in the humanities quadrangle. I always wondered about that. I mean, you're supposed to yell when something like that happens. You don't stand there wondering if you should say something. You really are dead, you know.

BOB: Yeah, well, that's what I was trying to tell everyone right before Christmas. I thought I might just try it out, you know, being dead. Didn't feel any different.

DICK: I don't get it.

BOB: No, it's a pretty weird thing.

DICK: I gotta pack.

BOB: Yeah.

(Dick leaves the room. Mike and Cootie burst in through the front door, panting heavily.)

MIKE: Oh, shit, man, we've really had it. Christ, how could the guy do it? I thought he was kidding.

RUTH *(Comes in with a small suitcase)*: Hey, you guys better hurry up and pack. We gotta be out of here tomorrow.

COOTIE: Ruth, sit down, huh? Something pretty bad just happened. Seriously, no shitting around.

RUTH: Where's Norman?

COOTIE: Norman's . . . he just . . . oh, shit.

MIKE: He set himself on fire.

BOB: He what?

MIKE: All that stuff he was reading. He just . . . I don't know. He got this idea. Oh, fuck, how could the stupid bastard ever . . . shit.

RUTH: I thought you guys were going to see *Casablanca*.

MIKE: No, we had to tell you that. He had this plan. Honest to shit, we didn't know he was serious. Him and Shelly. We thought he's just . . . we went to the common and he took all his clothes off and poured gasoline all over himself.

COOTIE: We were just shitting around, Ruth. Honest. If we thought he was serious we'd've stopped him.

MIKE: It was that fucking Shelly.

RUTH: You fucking stupid . . .

MIKE: I'm telling you, it wasn't our fault. He wouldn't have lit the match. I know he poured the gasoline, but he'd never've lit the match.

BOB: He's . . .

MIKE: Oh, shit, it was awful. He just sat there turning black. I didn't want to look, but I couldn't turn away. His skin just, Christ, it just fell away from his face and his blood . . . *(Puts head in hand)*

RUTH: Stupid fucking guys. You should've known Where's Shelly?

COOTIE: She went crazy, Ruth. She just cracked up. We had to practically knock her out. She's O.K. now.

(Shelly comes in the front door. Her eyes are closed and her fists clenched. Ruth runs to her, doesn't know what to do.)

RUTH: Shelly, oh, Shelly, Jesus . . .

SHELLY *(Teeth clenched)*: Fucking guys.

(Norman comes in. He's soaking wet and carries a gasoline can. Mike and Cootie rise.)

MIKE: See, everything's cool now. Everybody trusts each other. That's what it's all about.

(Mike smiles oddly at the others.)

COOTIE *(Registering it all)*: Holy shit!

SHELLY *(Yells)*: Creeps. *(To Ruth)* You got any first-aid stuff?

RUTH: Yeah. *(She gets a box from the pantry. It's a huge white box with a red cross on it, obviously stolen)*

BOB: Hey, what happened?

NORMAN *(Sits)*: I'm all right.

SHELLY. Don't talk, Norman. Would you make him some coffee?

RUTH: Yeah. Those guys said you burned yourself.

NORMAN: I'm O.K.

(Ruth makes coffee while Shelly ties a bandage around Norman's wrist.)

SHELLY: Sorry if this hurts. Hey, Ruth, those guys are really bastards. They gotta learn you don't joke around sometimes.

BOB: Hey, were you really gonna burn yourself?

NORMAN: Well, you know . . .

SHELLY: We were all supposed to do it. All four of us. We waited all this time for them to graduate with good grades and everything. Six months almost. I mean, like, the war could've ended. Fucking creeps. They went and put water in the gasoline can.

NORMAN: I think I might be getting a cold.

SHELLY: We're making coffee, Norman. Keep cool.

BOB: Hey, were you really serious?

NORMAN: Well, I thought, you know, with the war and everything.

SHELLY: Water, shit.

NORMAN: Well, there was some gas in that can.

SHELLY: Fucking creeps.

NORMAN: I definitely smelled gas when I poured it over me.

SHELLY: Hold still, Norman.

NORMAN: I mean, I knew there was something wrong when I kept holding the match to my wrist and nothing happened.

SHELLY: What do you mean, nothing happened? What's wrong with you, Norman? You call that burn on your wrist nothing? It's the worst burn I ever saw. We're lucky we didn't get arrested.

NORMAN: I've seen movies of the Buddhist monks setting themselves on fire. They usually go up pretty quick in the movies. I bet it hurts a lot. My wrist really hurts.

RUTH *(Brings Norman some coffee)*: Listen, we have to be out of here by tomorrow.

NORMAN: All right.

RUTH: Well, what are you gonna do?

NORMAN: I haven't thought about it too much. I thought I was going to be dead by now. I hadn't planned beyond that.

RUTH: You got a place to stay?

SHELLY: He'll stay with me.

NORMAN: Yeah, O.K.

RUTH: We'll have to have a big cleanup in case Willis comes around.

NORMAN: I was thinking maybe I'll try to get back into graduate school. I'm getting sick of washing dishes.

(Bob has been taking down his map of Europe from the wall.)

BOB: I think I'll go to Europe.

NORMAN: I'm not really angry at Mel and Mike. In a way I'm kind of glad I'm not dead.

SHELLY: I think those two guys are really evil.

(Ruth goes down the hall.)

BOB: You ever been to France?

SHELLY: I went last summer.

BOB: What's it like?

SHELLY: Shitty. They're really uptight in France. I got busted in Calais. Two weeks in prison with the runs. That's no joke.

BOB: Maybe England.

NORMAN: I was in England once.

BOB: What's it like?

NORMAN: I went on a bicycle trip with the Youth Hostel Organization. My father sent me.

BOB: How was it?

NORMAN: It was O.K.

SHELLY: England's a lousy place.

NORMAN: I don't know. I met some nice people. I saw Buckingham Palace. The food's not very good, but it didn't rain much. I guess it was a pretty valuable experience. I remember thinking at the time my horizons were a lot wider after that trip. I don't remember why I thought that. Maybe I'll go back there one day.

BOB: Oh, well, there's always Italy or Greece.

SHELLY: If you go over there, check out Algeria. Algeria's really something else . . .

(Mr. Willis opens the door.)

WILLIS: O.K. if I step in? Hey, what have you done to your hand?

NORMAN: It's just a burn.

WILLIS: Too bad, huh? Look, how's about if I see everyone for a minute? Everybody here?

BOB *(Yelling)*: DICK, RUTH, MIKE, COOTIE, C'MERE A MINUTE. MR. WILLIS WANTS US.

WILLIS: Hey, hey, hey, you don't have to do that. You don't have to yell on account of me. *(All come in)* Hi, how's everybody? Gettin' ready for the big day? You gonna wear them long robes and everything, hey? All that fancy ceremony. Pretty good, huh? Listen, I just wanna give the place a quick once-over because I'll tell you why. I got this tenant moving in pretty soon, so I gotta be sure everything's shipshape. Get rid of them milk bottles, that's the first thing, and I'll pick up the rent for this month, O.K.? How 'bout this floor, huh? You gonna finish it? Hey, I asked a question, who's supposed to be doing this floor?

BOB: I am, Mr. Willis.

WILLIS: So how come you leave it half-finished?

BOB: Sorry, I never got the time.

WILLIS: Well, you get it. I give you good money for them tiles, put me back a hunnerd bucks. How many landlords you find'll do that?

BOB: Yeah, O.K.

WILLIS: By tomorrow night, understand? Now, let's have a little look round the place. *(He goes down the hall followed by Bob, Ruth, Cootie and Mike)*

NORMAN: Mike. *(Mike turns)* Listen, I just want to tell you. I'm not angry about what happened.

MIKE: What do you mean?

SHELLY: You're a real creep pulling a trick like that.

MIKE: That's what I get for saving his life?

SHELLY: It's none of your business. It's the existential right of every living person to take his own life.

MIKE: No one's stopping you now.

NORMAN: What I wanted to say is, if you and Mel are coming back next year to go to graduate school, maybe we can share a place. I mean, you know, I could come down here early and look around.

MIKE: You going home for the summer?

SHELLY: He's staying with me.

NORMAN: Yeah, well I might go home for a few weeks. Visit my folks. The best way is you write to my father, care of the Police Department, Erie County, and if I'm not at home he'll know where to forward it.

MIKE: Right. Me and Cootie'll be up in the great Northwest Territory helping Dad with the furs. If you don't hear from us, just go ahead and find a place for all of us, 'cause sometimes the mail gets delayed.

NORMAN: Don't worry, I'll get a place.

MIKE: Commissioner of Police, Erie County.

NORMAN: That's right.

(Mike smiles at him, not without warmth. In come Cootie, Ruth, Bob, Dick and Mr. Willis.)

WILLIS: Not bad. I'll tellya what I'll do. I'll keep the fifty-dollar deposit for holes in the plaster and the broken window.

COOTIE: Hey, we didn't break that window. That was broken when we moved in.

WILLIS: That's not my problem, Cootie. I keep the fifty and if any of you guys got an objection, you want to take it up with me, let's have it. Look, I got a living to make like everybody else in town. Maybe you think I'm being a rotten guy, but you wait. You go out there in the world and you're gonna see things, you'll think old Willis was Snow White and the Seven Dwarfs all rolled into one. You're gonna see dishonesty, you're gonna see mean people, you see swindlers, killers, queers, you see guys trying to double-park on Saturday morning, you take my word. The thing I love about you kids is you're honest, you're direct. There's no shitting around with you. Yeah, I know it sounds corny, but I'm gonna miss having you guys around. You gotta save this poor fuckin' country, and excuse my language. There was a time, I can remember, when you paid your taxes and you knew your money was goin' into the right things. Good, wholesome things. Look at it nowadays. Two blocks away there's a house full of guys known all over the neighborhood to practice open homosexuality. Open homosexuality two blocks away, and there's kids playing right outside that house every day. I don't know. I'd go jump in the lake if it wasn't for you kids. I never knew anyone like you, and I been around, let me tellya. You know where you are, you know where you're going, and you know how to get there. That's never happened before in the history of this whole fucking country. God bless you kids, and good luck. I'll take a check for the rent.

COOTIE *(Sings)*: For he's a jolly good fellow.
OTHERS *(Joining in)*: For he's a jolly good fellow,
For he's a jolly good fellow,
That nobody can deny.
That nobody can deny.
That nobody can deny.

(Etc., all the way through. Willis beams, entirely unaware of the spoof.)

Scene 7

The next afternoon. The kitchen is bare of furniture. The icebox is gone, only a few milk bottles left. Only one chair left. Bob is laying the vinyl tiles. Cootie comes into the room with his Father. He grabs the last valise by the front door.

COOTIE: Hey, Bob, I'm going.
BOB: Yeah, we'll see you.

COOTIE: Yeah.

MIKE *(Comes into the kitchen from the hall door)*: You going?

COOTIE: Yeah. Oh, this is my father. That's Mike, that's Bob.

BOB: Hi.

MIKE: Hi.

FATHER: A pleasure.

MIKE: What?

FATHER: It's a pleasure meeting you.

MIKE: Oh, yeah, right.

COOTIE: Well, see you guys. Hey, what you doing next year?

BOB: Oh, I got a job in a department store.

COOTIE: Playing piano?

BOB: Harp.

COOTIE: Great. Well, see ya.

BOB: See ya.

MIKE: Yeah, see ya, Cootie.

FATHER: Nice meeting you boys.

(Cootie leaves with his Father.)

MIKE: They don't look like each other. Good old Cootie. Where's Norman?

BOB: He left about an hour ago.

MIKE: Never said good-bye or anything.

BOB: You should've seen it, putting all his stuff in the back of a police car.

MIKE: What?

BOB: Yeah, his old man's Commissioner of Police, or something.

MIKE: I'll be fucked.

(Ruth comes in from the hall with two suitcases and sets them down by some other suitcases near the door.)

RUTH: I guess that's it. Where's Cootie?

MIKE: He just left with his dad.

RUTH: Some friend. No good-bye or anything.

MIKE: We'll see him next year.

RUTH: No we won't.

(Mike and Ruth go down the hall for their last luggage. Dick and the Milkman enter through the front door with empty cartons. They load the remaining bottles.)

DICK: Hey, I wouldn't mind a little help here. I gotta catch a train.

MILKMAN: I don't understand you guys. You're supposed to be college graduates. Eight hundred and fifty-seven two-quart milk bottles. That's not the kind of thing a grown-up person does. You're supposed to be grown-ups. I don't get it.

(The phone is ringing.)

DICK: That's the last one.

MILKMAN: O.K. I just hope you guys don't think you can go through life hoarding milk bottles like this. I got enough to do without this. I got a regular route. *(To Dick)* Look, if you want to pick up a lot of bottles, put your fingers right down inside, you get more that way.

DICK: O.K. Hey, you guys, you're a lot of help.

(Milkman and Dick go out with their cartons.)

BOB *(Answering phone)*: Hello, oh, yes, how are you? No, this is Bob. Bob Rettie. No, music. Yes, of course I remember you. No, he's not in right now.

(Mike and Ruth have reentered, motioning Bob that they have to go. He motions back that it's O.K. He waves good-bye as they pick up their suitcases and begin to leave.)

RUTH: Hey, good luck.

BOB: Yeah, yeah, you too. See ya, Mike.

MIKE: See ya.

(Ruth and Mike exit through front door.)

BOB *(Back to phone)*: Sorry, Mrs. Roper, I was just saying good-bye to some people I . . . some friends of mine. I don't know if he'll be back or not. Can I leave a message? *(Pause)* Look, Mrs. Roper, I'm very sorry about that but there's nothing I can do if he's gone. I can tell him to call you if he comes back. Mrs. Roper, look, calm down. Listen, I'm hanging up now, all right? I gotta hang up now. Good-bye, Mrs. Roper.

(Bob hangs up and returns to the floor tiles. Dick comes in alone through the front door.)

DICK: Boy, that guy was sure pissed off about the bottles. You should've seen the look on his face.

BOB: Hey, you know that guy you studied with, Professor Roper?

DICK *(Pause)*: Yes.

BOB: His wife just called.

DICK: What'd she want?

BOB: She just . . . I don't know. Nothing, I guess. Pretty weird.

DICK: Yeah, pretty weird. *(He puts on his coat and takes up his bags)*

BOB: Hey, Dick.

DICK: What?

(They look at each other.)

BOB: I don't know. See ya.

DICK: Yeah. *(As Dick is leaving, he sees Kathy, who is standing in the doorway)*

KATHY: Hi. Can I come in? *(Dick moves aside. He and Bob stare at Kathy. This makes her a little nervous)* Everyone gone?

DICK AND BOB *(Together)*: Yeah . . . *(They exchange a nervous glance)*

BOB: Except for me and Dick. We're still here. We're right in front of you, as a matter of fact . . .

DICK: That's a nice coat she's wearing. That's a very nice coat, Kathy.

KATHY *(Knows something is going on but doesn't know what)*: Thanks.

BOB: Hey, Dick. *(Dick leaves)* See ya. *(To himself)*

KATHY: Finishing the floor?

BOB: Evidently.

KATHY: Kind of late, isn't it? *(Pause)* Did they send my grades here?

BOB: Right there. You did really shitty.

KATHY *(Gets the letter)*: Bob, listen . . . I'm sorry about . . . sounds pretty silly.

BOB: No, I accept your apology for whatever you think you did.

KATHY: I saw Ruth the other day. She said you've been . . . well, pretty bad this semester.

BOB: Did she say that?

KATHY: I wish I'd known . . . couldn't you have . . . you should have told me to stay.

BOB: Well, it slipped my mind. Sorry.

KATHY: You shouldn't be so ashamed of your feelings.

BOB: O.K.

KATHY: I'm serious. You've gotta learn to let go. Like your music. It's all squenched and tidy.

BOB: O.K. I'll work on that.

KATHY: Oh, Bob.

BOB: What?

KATHY: I really wish you'd've told me. I'd've come back. I never really related to Richard.

BOB: I'll tell him when I see him.

KATHY: Yeah, you're right. Why the hell should you be nice? Oh, well, good luck . . . and, you know, when you see your mother say hello for me.

BOB: O.K.

KATHY: How is she?

BOB: She's okay. Sort of dead.

KATHY: I like her, Bob. You're lucky. She's, you know, she's a real person.

BOB: No, she's you know, a real corpse.

KATHY: All right, have it your way.

BOB: No, it's not what I wanted particularly. No, taken all in all, from various different angles, I'd've preferred it if she lived. I'm pretty sure of that.

KATHY *(Pause)*: She's not really . . . ?

BOB: School's over.

KATHY: Bob, do you know what you're saying?

BOB: Kathy, please get the fuck out of here.

KATHY: But, I mean, Ruth never told me . . . Didn't you tell anyone?

BOB: Yeah, I just told you.

KATHY: But, I mean . . . when . . . when did . . .

BOB: Christmas. No, no, it was the day after.

KATHY *(Sits)*: Jesus, Bob, why didn't you tell anyone? I mean, how could you live for six months without telling someone?

BOB *(No emotion)*: Oh, I don't know. A little cunning. A little fortitude. A little perseverance. *(Pause)* I couldn't believe it. Not the last time anyway. They put her in this room. I don't know what you call it. They bring everybody there just before they kick the bucket. They just sort of lie there looking at each other, wondering what the hell they got in common to talk about. I couldn't believe that anyone could look like she looked and still be alive. *(Pause)* She knew. I'm sure of that. *(Pause)* Once, I remember, she tried to tell me something. I mean this noise came out of somewhere around her mouth, like somebody running a stick over a fence or something, and I thought she's trying to tell me something. So I leaned over to hear better and I caught a whiff of that breath. Like fried puke. And I was sick all over her. *(Pause. Brighter)* But you want to know something funny, and I mean this really is funny, so you can laugh if you like. There was this lady dying next to my mother and she kept talking about her daughter Susan. Well, Susan came to visit the day I puked on Mom. And you know what? It was only Susan Weinfeld, which doesn't mean anything to you, but she happens to have been the girl I spent a good many of my best months as a sophomore in high school trying to lay. In fact, her virginity almost cost me a B plus in history and here we were, six years later, staring at each other across two dying mothers. I want to tell you something, Kathy. She looked fantastic. And I could tell she was thinking the same thing about me. I mean

that kind of scene doesn't happen every day. It was like . . .
(thinks) . . . it was like how we were the first time. Maybe,
just possibly, a little better. So we went out and had a coffee in Mr. Doughnut and started groping each other like
crazy under the counter, and I mean we just couldn't keep
our hands off each other, so I suggested we get a cab
down to my mother's place since, you know, there happened to be no one there at the moment. But the funniest thing was when we get down to Mom's place and you
know all those stairs you have to go up and there's Susan
all over me practically screaming for it and I start fum-
bling around with the keys in the lock and none of them
would fit. I must've tried every key about fifty fucking
times and none of them would fit. Boy, what a drag.
(Pause) Oh, we got in all right. Finally. I had to go downstairs, through the Salvatores' apartment, out the window, up the fire escape, and through Mom's place, but
when I opened the front door, guess what? There's poor
old Susan asleep on the landing. She really looked cute.
I hated to wake her up. Anyway, by the time we'd made
coffee and talked and smoked about a million cigarettes
each we didn't feel like it anymore. Not really. We did it
anyway but, you know, just to be polite, just to make
some sense out of the evening. It was, taken all in all, a
pretty ordinary fuck. The next morning we made plans
to meet again that night. We even joked about it, you
know, about what a super-fucking good time we'd have,
and if you ask me, we could've probably really gotten
into something incredible if we'd tried again, but when I
went to the hospital I found out good old Mom had
croaked sometime during the night, and somehow I still
don't know why to this day . . . I never got in touch with
Susan again. And vice versa. It's a funny thing, you know.
At the funeral there were all these people. Friends of
Mom's—I didn't know any of them. They were all crying like crazy and I . . . well . . . *(Pause)* I never even got
to the burial. The car I was in broke down on the Merritt
Parkway. Just as well. I didn't feel like seeing all those
people. I'd sure love to have fucked Susan again, though.

KATHY: Bob . . . I . . .

BOB *(Abstract)*: Anyway . . . I just didn't feel like telling anyone. I mean, I wasn't all that upset. I was a little upset,
mostly because I thought I ought to be more upset, but
as for your actual grief, well. Anything interesting happen to you this semester . . . Kathy? *(Kathy has risen)*
Going? *(Kathy is going out the door)* Give my regards to
that guy you're rescuing at the moment; what's-his-
name? *(Kathy is gone. Bob shrugs. The cat wanders in
from the hallway)* Hey, cat, what are you doing hanging
around here? All the humans gone west. *(Puts the cat
outside and shuts the door. He nudges the tiles with his
toe and looks around at the empty room)* Hey, guys,
guess what happened to me? I want to tell you about this
really incredible thing that happened to me . . . *(He is fal-
tering now, choking slightly, but he doesn't know he's
about to crack. His body is doing something strange,
unfamiliar)* Hey, what's happening . . . *(He's crying now)*
Oh, fuck, come on, come on. Shit, no, no . . .

(Fade.)

End of Play

FISHING

Fishing was first presented by the New York Shakespeare Festival (Joseph Papp, Producer) on February 8, 1975. Peter Gill directed the following cast:

ROBBIE	Guy Boyd
BILL	Tommy Lee Jones
SHELLY	Lindsay Crouse
RORY	Ray Barry
MARY-ELLEN	Kathryn Grody
DANE	John Heard
REILLY	Ed Seamon

The play was revived in a slightly rewritten version by Second Stage Theatre, New York (Robyn Goodman, Carole Rothman, Artistic Directors) on April 17, 1981. Amy Saltz directed the following cast:

ROBBIE	Richard Cox
BILL	Daniel Hugh-Kelly
SHELLY	Penelope Milford
RORY	John Spencer
MARY-ELLEN	Robyn Goodman
DANE	Timothy Phillips
REILLY	Ralph Roberts

Characters

ROBBIE
BILL
SHELLY
RORY
MARY-ELLEN
DANE
REILLY

Place

The play takes place in one day
somewhere on the coast
of the Pacific Northwest
in 1974.

Act One

Scene 1

A living room in a rented shack on the Pacific Coast. Bare feeling, a transient place being made permanent. Couch, a few tattered easy chairs, eating table, bookcase with mildewed books and a few new ones, mostly paperbacks. Franklin stove. Indian rug. Against wall a .22 rifle, a cavalry sword, three fishing rods. Portable Sony TV. And like that. It's morning. It's drizzling. The Northwest. Robbie sleeps on the couch with a powder-blue sleeping bag pulled over him and an open book on the floor.

Lights up. Enter Bill, holding an egg. He sees Robbie asleep. Checks him out. Makes a loud rooster noise. Robbie stirs. Bill walks around the room, strutting and crowing like a rooster. He stops.

ROBBIE: Oh shit. Is it Tuesday?

BILL: Wednesday, m'boy. No, wait. It's July, definitely.

ROBBIE: Let's skip today. I want to have tomorrow, O.K.

BILL: O.K., it's tomorrow. Look what I got.

ROBBIE *(Looking)*: Small . . . whitish object. Spheroid. I give up.

BILL: An egg. I found it underneath the chicken out in the coop.

ROBBIE: Coincidence. Eggs come from Safeways. I hate waking up.

BILL: Our chicken has laid a egg. A white egg. And just wait'll you taste it. Country chicken eggs are amazing, young Rob. They are tasty and they are funky and they are real.

ROBBIE: You know what I think?

BILL: You just don't want to admit country living is far out. Well, you're wrong 'cause country living happens to be far out and if you don't believe me read your *Whole Earth Catalogue* and your crazy Euell Gibbons and you'll see it written in plain undeniable black and white.

ROBBIE: Shelly put that egg under the chicken.

BILL: Now why would a nice girl like Shelly go and do a deceitful thing like that?

ROBBIE: 'Cause you said you'd chop off its head and serve it for dinner if it didn't crank out an egg by today.

BILL *(Pause)*: How come you're sleeping in here?

ROBBIE: My room's haunted. I was having a nightmare.

BILL: Want to shoot some gophers?

ROBBIE: No.

BILL: Want to go fishing? High tide's 10:27. I got bait.

ROBBIE: I was down at Angel Point, night, you know, pitch black and the tide was way, way out and I was stepping along these rocks. Except they were all wet and covered with seaweed and I kept losing my balance. Then I was lying down. Yeah. My face was right up close against the rocks and I was looking down at them like I was in a helicopter over a city. Hovering, sort of. And I couldn't believe it how every single inch of those rocks had some kind of living thing on it, every chink, every crevice. Mussels. Gooseneck barnacles. Anemones. Stuff I don't even know what it's called, all of it clinging for dear life and I wanted to reach down and . . . and . . . Then I felt myself moving, like gliding real slowly just above the rocks and I realized I was heading straight for the ocean faster and faster and I got real panicky and started reaching out toward the rocks trying to find a place to grab on to but there was no room, everything was covered with all this slippery, living stuff and I tried to scream but the surf was too loud . . . *(Pause)* I want to sleep.

BILL: Me too.

ROBBIE: What?

BILL: I had the same dream.

ROBBIE: Leave me alone.

BILL: Remember when you used to dream about flying and cowboys and chicks with wet sissies.

ROBBIE: Yeah. Sheeet. *(Spits)*

BILL: Sheeet. *(Spits)* Shelly dreamed she had a job. She's really upset. It was sort of a nightmare.

ROBBIE: Well, we've had dreams now. Time for emptying of the bowels and cleansing of the skin. Another day, another trip. Where's Shelly? *(Robbie begins dressing)*

BILL: Safeways. Morning milk run. And by the way, in case you forgot, last night Reilly said he was gonna come today.

ROBBIE: Oh, shit, Reilly. That's real life, isn't it?

BILL: Yep. Time for a joint.

ROBBIE: That's going to be a problem because I smoked the last of our stash last night. I couldn't sleep.

BILL: Things are really getting desperate. Like twenty-one fifty-seven in the bank desperate. And no dope.

ROBBIE: And not a whole lot of food either.

BILL: Fuck food. I'm talking basics.

ROBBIE: At least we got eggs. One a week at the present rate. That is, if Shelly isn't behind this sudden mysterious egg phenomenon.

BILL: I figure we can get Reilly down from fifteen hundred. I don't think the boat's worth that. If we go really heavy on the condition the boat's in I bet we can jew him down to a thousand.

ROBBIE: Twenty-one fifty-seven in the bank. You're the Jew, you do the talking.

BILL: Maybe nine hundred.

ROBBIE: That's nine with two zeros after it.

BILL: We're a nice bunch of kids.

ROBBIE: Straight from the shoulder, I have reservations.

BILL: We can dig up a thousand. There's gotta be a way. I mean between you and me and Shelly, and maybe someone else'd come in for a share like maybe crazy Rory the undertaker.

ROBBIE: I'm talking more about Reilly's boat. I mean, I'm not exactly an old salt or anything, but if we're gonna do commercial salmon fishing we have to have a boat with certain basic things, right, like a tendency to stay on top of the water. I heard Reilly's boat sunk three times last winter.

BILL: Yeah, but that was at the dock, that wasn't out on the ocean.

ROBBIE: Is that supposed to make me feel better?

BILL: Boats leak. You gotta be around them so you can bail them out. If you're not there, of course they'll sink.

ROBBIE: I'd only like a boat that didn't sink. Even when you weren't there.

BILL: All boats leak.

ROBBIE: How do you know so much about boats all of a sudden? Listen, pal o' mine, it just so happens I've read all kinds of seafaring books, and the one distinguishing factor about all the major historical oceangoing hot shits is they all had boats that floated, dock or no.

BILL: You always sit around figuring out the bad news, don't you? Ever since you got here.

ROBBIE: I just know your dreams, Billy-boy. I can see your fleet of five hundred fully automated vacuum-cleaner-type fishing tankers with radar-equipped salmon detectors and canning plants in the hold and stereophonic P.A. blasting out Pink Floyd on the quarter deck or whatever the fuck you call it; William-Acid-Rock-Where-Did-The-Sixties-Go-Barenberg Pacific Salmon Outta Sight Enterprises, Inc.

BILL: Some of us don't have lots of bread in the family, fuckhead. Some of us have to make a living.

ROBBIE: My old man's bread is not *my* bread. Leave me alone.

BILL: Come on, bummer, don't tell me you haven't heard that old ocean calling. You're the one that sat out there on Angel's Point all day, and all night, and all the next day staring at it when you first got here. Ah, silence. High tide, calm sea, beer and dope and some funky sounds on the cassette, sea trout crawling up your line begging to be fried in bread crumbs with a little garlic and sage. I'm telling you, man, that old ocean is just one great big mamma with a smile on her face and food in her belly. All we need is a boat and a few smarts and she'll lay great abundance upon us at seventy-nine cents a pound and that adds up.

ROBBIE: Ho-hum, another day, another trip.

(Shelly enters with brown paper bag.)

SHELLY: Guess what?

ROBBIE *(Pause)*: What?

SHELLY: Ed Nolan's taking all my pots. Every one of 'em.

BILL: Did he pay you?

SHELLY: No, on consignment. It's cool. The tourist season's almost starting, and he's gonna put the fruit bowl and the yellow mugs right in the big display window.

BILL: When do you get some money?

SHELLY: When he sells one of my things, stupid.

ROBBIE: Congratulations.

SHELLY: Thanks. *(Pause)* So, what's happening?

BILL: Shelly-pie.

SHELLY: What?

BILL: Shelly-pie.

SHELLY: What's on your mind?

BILL: Have you been out to the chicken coop this morning?

SHELLY: Why should I go out there?

BILL: Think carefully, Shelly-pie. Have you had any social interaction with Guinevere in the past twelve hours?

ROBBIE: Look out, it's a trap.

BILL: Did you put an egg under Guinevere's body this morning?

SHELLY: She laid an egg?!! Guinevere laid an egg?! Oh, Guinevere, you little sweetie-pie. I knew she'd figure it out. Didn't I say she'd come through in the end? Where is it? Let's see.

ROBBIE: Stand back with awe.

(Bill raises the egg slowly. He and Robbie do the "Also Sprach Zarathustra" theme from 2001.)

SHELLY: Guinevere is a genius. She definitely gets an extra cup of scratch today and I'm going to knit her some booties.

BILL: Shelly-pie?

SHELLY: I mean two years of art school and I could never do an egg like that. It'll have to be scrambled for three ways . . . I'll make some bread for toast.

BILL: You're avoiding me, Shelly-pie.

SHELLY: Why am I avoiding you?

BILL: Did you slip this egg under Guinevere so I wouldn't chop off her head today? Did you?

SHELLY: I bet she lays an egg tomorrow. Another one.

BILL: That's not what I asked.

SHELLY: How come you always think I'm doing something sneaky?

BILL: Shelly-pie, honey, sweet baby cake. *(Bill advances on Shelly. An old game)*

SHELLY: Oh dear! Help! No, no please don't Oh! Oh! Oh! *(Bill tickles her. She shrieks, but you know)* Leave my body alone. I have a surprise.

BILL: You were a very naughty Shelly-pie, weren't you?

SHELLY: No. Yes. Yes.

BILL: Yes, what?

SHELLY: Yes I was.

BILL: Yes I was what?

SHELLY: Yes I was a very naughty Shelly-pie, wasn't I? Now stop it and I'll tell you what I got.

BILL: Repeat ten times I was a very naughty Shelly-pie.

SHELLY: I was a very naughty Shelly-pie. I was a very naughty Shelly-pie. I was a very naughty Shelly-pie. I was a very naughty Shelly-pie. I was a very naughty Shelly-pie. I was a very naughty Shelly-pie. I was a very naughty Shelly-pie. I was a very naughty Shelly-pie. I was a very naughty Shelly-pie.

BILL: That was only nine.

SHELLY: I have my pride. Yikes, stop.

ROBBIE: Who wants a third of a scrambled egg. *(Bill and Shelly stop)*

SHELLY: Oh. Hi, Rob.

BILL: Rob isn't feeling all kinds of positive today. He wants it to be a bummer, so we have to do everything in our power to help him out.

SHELLY *(To Robbie)*: For real?

ROBBIE: I don't know. The weather's sort of shitty and Reilly's coming and we don't have a thousand dollars for a boat that keeps sinking anyway and on top of that this house is haunted by evil spirits.

SHELLY: Are these the reasons you're not feeling positive?

ROBBIE: I'm horny.

BILL: Ah, that's the reason you're not feeling positive.

ROBBIE: We're out of smokables.

BILL: Anything else?

ROBBIE: And we're a lost generation in search of meaning but unable to grasp a sense of values in a shipwrecked century.

SHELLY: That's true, but then again, fuck it. Let's have an egg.

ROBBIE: Can I use your room?

SHELLY: Sure.

ROBBIE: If the weather clears up, and a girl comes by who wants to get laid and we get our hands on some dope and Reilly decides to sell for twenty-one fifty-seven, then wake me up. *(Robbie exits)*

BILL: Bummerville, oh, bummerville. *(Hummed, that is)*

SHELLY: I can never tell when he's being serious.

BILL: The thing about Rob is he's full of shit. You know that, you know Rob.

SHELLY: Why? I mean you're probably right . . . or wrong, but why? You're the man, hon, so what you say goes, but like why is he full of shit as opposed to you or me?

BILL: He wouldn't give a damn if this whole fishing thing fell through.

SHELLY: I bet he would.

BILL: I bet he wouldn't.

SHELLY: I bet he would.

BILL: I bet he wouldn't.

SHELLY: I bet . . . *(Bill dives for her, more tickles)* Hey, don't. *(Pause)* You asked him to come out here. I mean, he is your best friend and everything.

BILL: I don't know. I mean, our fathers were best friends maybe. They really were. That was a long time ago, and you know, once his old man started doing well he just like cut himself off. Never kept in touch with the old gang. Like he was embarrassed or something. I remember this time, my old man needed some bread and he had to ask me to ask Robbie to ask his dad . . . absurd. He just thinks it's all some kind of joke, this boat. Not a joke exactly. If he had to work, you know, if he couldn't just drive around having a groovy time spending his old man's money maybe I could feel, like, more trust, that's all I mean. He's a good guy. I dig him.

SHELLY: What if it doesn't work out with the boat?

BILL: It'll work out.

SHELLY: I know, baby, but what if it doesn't?

BILL: Like crazy Rory says, "Wow, man, you want to get into something you like, put your energy right there and the whole thing just happens, right." *(Pause)* It just has to work. It feels right. What can I say? Just being out there on the ocean with no one to hassle you. No assholes trying to get rich and coming down on you 'cause you don't want their fucking crazy trip. Just me and Rob and the fish. Us and them. And the boat.

SHELLY: As the sun sinks slowly in the west.

BILL: So it's romantic. Nothing wrong with that. Nothing at all. I'll wear a cowboy hat, so what?

SHELLY: The farm was sort of romantic.

BILL: That was different.

SHELLY: Why?

BILL: It just was. A farm is just a bunch of dirt and cows shitting in the fields. I'm not a land person. I'm a water person. Pisces. Why the fuck is everyone closing in on me today, I'm a nice guy.

SHELLY: Hey, I wasn't closing in, baby. I think it's a fine idea. And I think it's going to work out really good. The old Ching said, "After Initial Setbacks, Great Abundance."

BILL: You throw it?

SHELLY: Yeah, last night.

BILL: Well, all right, all right. That's better. In fact, that's kind of far out. That definitely calls for an egg, and a little smokeroo. Oh, shit.

SHELLY: Just sometimes I don't know I think about it. About how things don't work out sometimes or not work out exactly more like not work out the way you want them to. Or even work out but not be what you thought they'd be. And how you adjust. I know you have to fight. I know that. But you oughta be able to get your head into a place where whatever's happening around you . . . outside of you . . . it's O.K. It's just O.K. no matter which way things go. Anyway, I know what I mean. It's like, some people always go around looking for a beautiful place to be in and other people make whatever place they're in beautiful. *(Bill laughs)* It's not funny.

BILL: In case you forget, Shelly-pie, I read that book, too, and it's not like I don't dig Swami whatever his name is. A lot of my favorite gurus are fat little Indians but all that stuff is bullshit.

SHELLY: It is not.

BILL: It is too.

SHELLY: You don't know what you're talking about.

BILL *(Pause)*: I hope we get some sun today. *(Pause. Truce)*

SHELLY: I got peyote.

BILL: Did you say something?

SHELLY: Yup.

BILL: As in the psychedelic-parts-of-certain-cactuses-native-to-the-American-Southwest peyote?

SHELLY: Cacti. Yup.

BILL: What how when where why?

SHELLY: That chick that's always at the marina, the hippie chick with that weird lizard. She was in Safeways over by frozen foods. I was just getting milk and she came up and said, "Hey, man, I've seen you around, you want some dynamite peyote, man, hey, man," you know, and she handed me a bag, a hundred buttons. They picked 'em last week in Arizona "or Chicago, or something, like they grow, right." Boy, was she out of it. And the manager guy that always tails you when you're shopping—

BILL: Shit-Shoes.

SHELLY: Yeah, Shit-Shoes, he's standing right at the end of the aisle and he knew what was going down and he was shitting in his shoes because if he hassled her there'd be a big hippie-drug scandal in Safeways and you can't have a big hippie-drug scandal in Safeways. So I gave her ten bucks. That's fair.

BILL: A hundred buttons for ten bucks. That's disbelievable. Let me see.

(Shelly takes them out of the bag and shows them.)

SHELLY: Did I do good, huh-huh?

BILL: They're fresh! They're not even dried. They're juicy and green and sunkist and, Shelly, you're a genius. I knew there was a reason I kept you around.

SHELLY: Aw gee.

BILL: God in his infinite wisdom and mercy has seen fit this day to lay upon us the means to get very stoned for many hours, and if I can jew Reilly down to a thousand today, I say we celebrate with a trip of unforgettable magnitude and duration.

SHELLY: Sounds like a good plan.

BILL: *Far out!* O.K. Time for the cooking and the eating of the breakfast. What's for food?

SHELLY: Ah. That's the hitch. See, after I gave the lizard chick the money I realized an embarrassing thing.

BILL: You silly girl.

SHELLY: I got milk. We can have coffee. And an egg. And milk.

(Rory enters. He's 30-ish. Red and black lumberman's shirt and jeans. Soaking wet from the rain. Bottle of beer in hand. He's drunk.)

RORY: First thing is I gotta pee and how are you and where's the party?

SHELLY: Hi, Rory, how's tricks?

RORY: Tricks is tricks and kicks is kicks and always the twain shall meet as the chipmunk said to the tractor. What? Whew. All *right*. Yeah. Water. There seems to be a little water around here and most of it's on me. Must be raining, know what I mean. The big boy is taking a pee. On you and me. And that makes three. Yessiree. How 'bout some tea? Whew, nine o'clock A.M. in the morning and I'm already drunk as a skunk in a bunk.

BILL: Sit down, Rory. Or kneel or something so you don't have far to fall.

RORY: Right, right. *(Sits)* So how's your ass and pass the grass.

BILL: We're all out.

RORY: Whew, tragedy-tragedy-tragedy. Famine in the lamine.

BILL: Don't you have any?

RORY *(German)*: Do I heff der grass geschmoken? Nein, mein hippeez. It's juice all the way till the end of the day, and I definitely have to do something about the u*ri*no in my blad*dero*.

SHELLY: Why don't you go to the toilet.

RORY: I like that girl, yes I do. You oughta be in the toilet business. Hey, I want you to remember something. Six-thirty. Remember that. Six-thirty. Very important time of the day. Big changes at six-thirty.

SHELLY: O.K. What about six-thirty, Rory?

RORY: You want to know and here we go. Party-arty-o at the big house on the cemetery.

SHELLY: Again?

RORY: Dass rhat, Missy Shelly. Gotta play de fiddle while de ciddy burns. Lotta foods gonna happen. Big salad, apple crumble, and Delores is doing this whole number with a twenty-five-pound Ling cod all wrapped up in pastry and baked for two hours.

BILL: Twenty-five pound Ling cod? Where the hell did you catch that?

RORY: We haven't caught it yet. That happens this afternoon. Dope? Dope? I'll have some grass for you a little later. I got these friends coming by from movieland said they'd be bringing some dynamite marihootee from the land of Mehico. Mucho bene.

BILL *(Pause)*: You got any spare bread, Rory?

RORY: For Reilly's boat? No way.

BILL: How'd you know about that?

RORY: Reilly ain't so wiley. Word's out you guys want to go fishing. How the fuck you think you're gonna keep anything from the undertaker in a town this size? Leave the fish alone. That's what the fish are saying. "No, no, no, you groovy dudes, don't catch me don't sell me." What do you want to fish for? I mean—I mean—I mean, go fishing. That's all. Just go down to Angel Point and catch a few, eat a few. It's fun. But, go commercial? Leave the ocean alone. It's having a good time.

BILL: Thanks for the help.

RORY: Come on, amigo, I bum you not out. O.K., here's the deal. Why is Reilly selling? That's uno. Why's he selling so cheap? That's dos. And why's he in such a hurry? That's trey and you're out.

BILL: You know about something we don't know about?

RORY: Reilly's a corpse. He can still do the boogaloo, but he's dancing his last dance. Where does I work? I works in the graveyard. What do I do? I plants folks. Reilly's wife has a little deal going and I'll tell you about it but you never heard it, you dig?

BILL: Are you sure about Reilly?

RORY: His brain got all full of little cloteroos and one day they're just not gonna stay put and then "pop!," 'bye-bye Reilly. And since my graves is all the rave Missus Reilly comes to me and pays me to dig a grave pre-advanso of the big day. It's all dug. Last week. Whew. Got a piece of canvas over it keep the rain out. All he gotta do is crawl in and I dump the turf on him. And see, I don't have a whole lotta mind to invest in a boat when I just dug a hole for the man that owned it. I ain't superstitious, you understand, but I am superstitious.

BILL: Fuck.

RORY: Heaviness.

SHELLY: Well, yeah, sort of, but it's not our fault that he's dying. We can't do anything about that and we could probably get him to come down a couple hundred since he has to sell.

RORY: You just care too much, lady, that's your hang-up.

SHELLY: Someone's gonna get the boat. And anyway, he's just dying, it's not all that big a deal. People die all the time. Forget it. Bill.

RORY: Six-thirty. Party at the graveyard. I gotta pee, yessiree.

(Mary-Ellen and Dane stand awkwardly in the kitchen doorway.)

MARY-ELLEN: Excuse me, is Rob here?

RORY: Hey, you guys were driving around in a red Volvo.

DANE: That's right.

RORY: I saw you on the way over and I thought wow, they're lost, whew! How the hell are you?

DANE: Fine. The door was open so we just let ourselves in.

RORY: What's the word on Volvos? I been thinking of getting one.

DANE: We're pretty happy with it.

RORY: That's good to know. What time is it?

SHELLY: It's nine-thirty.

RORY: Nine-thirty and I is smashed out of my grapefruit. Gotta get this day together. Pee first, pay later. Arriverderci. Ciao. Guten Tag and kung fu. Scusi. *(He brushes past Mary-Ellen and Dane. Stops. All cramped in doorway)* About twenty-five a gallon.

DANE: What? Oh, yeah, we've been doing about that. A little more on long trips.

RORY: Beautiful beautiful. *(He exits)*

MARY-ELLEN: I hope we didn't interrupt anything. I mean I hope this is the right place.

SHELLY: You're friends of Rob?

MARY-ELLEN: He stayed with us before he came here. We just decided to drive up. You didn't have a phone or anything.

BILL: He's asleep.

MARY-ELLEN: Oh.

DANE: We could come back later.

MARY-ELLEN: Maybe we could wake him up. Could you tell him that Melon and Dane are here to see him?

BILL: Do you guys have any dope?

SHELLY: I'll wake him up.

BILL: I don't think you should. The sun's not out yet.

MARY-ELLEN: Is he all right?

SHELLY: What do you mean?

MARY-ELLEN: Rob.

SHELLY: You mean like is he sick or something?

DANE: I guess we ought to come back later.

SHELLY: Did you say Melon?

MARY-ELLEN: It's Mary-Ellen, but no one's called Mary-Ellen, right, so it's Melon. Cute, huh?

BILL: The thing about Rob is he's sort of hiding for the day 'cause he's horny and depressed and we're out of smokes and he's pretty sure the house is haunted.

MARY-ELLEN: Same old Rob.

DANE: Maybe I ought to bring the car around. *(Enter Robbie)*

ROBBIE *(Casual)*: Hi. Listen, Rory's peeing on the side of the house—and it stopped raining. *(Pause)* Have a nice trip up?

MARY-ELLEN: Yes, thank you, shithead.

(Mary-Ellen and Robbie bust up laughing and screaming. Dane smiles. They all hug each other. Shelly and Bill look at each other. Fade.)

Scene 2

Front of the house, porch and yard. Lots of farm-type junk on the porch. Maybe a makeshift birdhouse on a post.

Bright sunlight. Mary-Ellen is sunning herself, eyes closed, face up. Shelly is shooting at an offstage target with the .22.

SHELLY *(Fires)*: Bull's-eye. Guess we're about ready for the bank job. Hey, Bill, I hit three out of ten.

BILL *(Inside)*: Don't waste bullets.

SHELLY: Mah man.

MARY-ELLEN *(Continue)*: I guess it's just my imagination. Eight years, though, that's a long time. And the way he's been going around visiting all his old friends. I mean it's great that he feels like doing that but sometimes . . . like when he stayed with us, you couldn't tell if it was more of a hello visit or a good-bye visit.

SHELLY: Well, if I was gonna pick someone to worry about . . . and I never would unless I really had to . . . it wouldn't be Robbie.

MARY-ELLEN: We're not really worried.

SHELLY: Want to try a few shots?

MARY-ELLEN: No, thanks, I don't like guns.

SHELLY: I didn't used to, but now I love 'em. Not really, but I feel it becomes a young woman of today to be handy with a rifle. I cook and sew too. I'm sort of Renaissance-y. *(Fires)* Shit.

MARY-ELLEN: Do you feel anything?

SHELLY: I haven't exactly seen God or anything but I had a few rushes.

MARY-ELLEN: I feel like I'd sort of like to puke, but I don't really want to do that. If I'd already puked I'd probably feel better than I do.

SHELLY: How many buttons did you take?

MARY-ELLEN: Five. I've never done peyote before. I'm not sure what's supposed to happen.

SHELLY: I had eight. I feel pretty good.

MARY-ELLEN: I feel pretty nauseous.

SHELLY: Let's not talk about it.

MARY-ELLEN: I'm sorry.

SHELLY: Hey, I don't mean to be like heavy about it. I mean. Shit. *(Controlled)* I don't like to know when people are feeling sick because that's something they have to deal with and there's nothing you can do about it. *(Pause)* Wow. That was great. That was exactly what I wanted to say. That doesn't happen a lot. *(Guinevere clucks offstage)*

MARY-ELLEN: What's that?

SHELLY *(Going around house)*: I'm coming, baby, I'm coming.

ROBBIE *(He enters)*: Any reports from the land beyond the shadows?

MARY-ELLEN: I don't know about this peyote. How do you feel?

ROBBIE: Fan-fuckin'—tastic. Look at that sun. It's weird the way the weather keeps changing around here. God, that mountain. I'm sure it wasn't that close to us yesterday.

MARY-ELLEN: Rob . . .

(Enter Shelly, with Guinevere in her arms.)

ROBBIE: Any more eggs yet?

SHELLY: She's doing O.K. Don't hassle her. She's no good under pressure. *(To Mary-Ellen)* Have you met Guinevere? You can hold her if you want to.

MARY-ELLEN *(Backing off)*: Please take her away. I'm sorry. I just have a thing about chickens. *(Shelly goes off. Bill enters)*

BILL: How ya feeling?

ROBBIE: Like shit in a swamp. I'll tell you something. Peyote may turn out not to be my gateway to the beyond.

BILL: I feel like another shit in a swamp.

ROBBIE: Hi there. What's a nice shit like you doing in a swamp like this?

MARY-ELLEN: Where's Dane?

ROBBIE: Dane? Dane? Where'd you go, Dane? Dane, baby, come to papa. *(Robbie looks in his shirt pocket, his pants pocket, takes off his shoe, looks there. Bill and Shelly join in. This is hysterical)*

BILL: Hey, Shelly, what'd ya do with Dane?

SHELLY: I didn't mean to eat him. I'm sorry, I'm sorry. There was only one egg.

ROBBIE: Ah, come to the scenic Northwest and groove.

MARY-ELLEN: Has anyone seen Dane? Sometimes he wanders.

SHELLY: Dane's here.

(Dane stands in the front door holding a cutting board with buttons on it, like a serving tray.)

DANE: O.K. I think I've figured it out. We're feeling sick because of the strychnine in these buttons. Strychnine is a convulsant and its chemical action is to make the stomach tense up. Now the other thing that happens is the actual hallucinogenic effect of the drug that's in this stuff, and I'm not sure what that is, but there's a point where the curve traced by the poison and the curve traced by the high cross each other and from that point on the high is predominant. And this depends on the dose. Now there's less strychnine than there is drug, so it stands to reason that the more you take, the less chance there is of getting sick.

ROBBIE: Good thinking.

DANE: Yes. So what I've done is I've brought out more buttons.

SHELLY: Those are our buttons.

BILL: Cool it, Shelly.

SHELLY: But that's our peyote.

DANE: Oh. I'm sorry, Shelly, that didn't occur to me. Is it all right? I thought as long as we're committed to the trip we ought to try to make it as good as possible.

MARY-ELLEN: You want us to pay you for the extra dose?

ROBBIE: Hey, what's the matter with everyone? Dane has had a very excellent good idea which I think we all oughta throw our support behind. O.K.?

SHELLY: If I was their guest I'd at least ask . . .

BILL: Shut up, baby.

ROBBIE: It's great how we're all getting off on each other. If there were a few more guns in the house we could shoot it out.

SHELLY: Forget it. I'm just weirded out by everyone being sick when I'm feeling O.K.

BILL: If there were some way we could share our sickness with you we'd do everything in our power. Don't, baby. That's enough.

DANE: I also got ice cream, that's the other thing. I figured part of our sickness was because of the taste of the buttons, so the ice cream might help to mask it. You know.

ROBBIE: Yeeeech, ice cream.

DANE: Peppermint chip. Peppermint's very strong.

SHELLY: Why don't all you guys just have one big communal puke and get it over with?

MARY-ELLEN: I hope the trip at the end of this is worth the getting there.

SHELLY: The trip is in your head.

MARY-ELLEN: Shelly, can we do something later?

SHELLY: What do you mean?

MARY-ELLEN: I feel there's some kind of negative energy between us. I don't know exactly what it is but I feel it very strongly and it's gonna get in the way of a good event today if we don't do something about it, and just generally, you know, bad vibes ought to be avoided because they're an outside force and you don't want to be controlled by an outside force. What I want to suggest is that when we're more into the high maybe we could concentrate on finding some good energy inside of us and we could work at directing that good energy toward each other, and then later we'll be able to refer back to that energy whenever we feel bad vibes developing between us.

DANE: Mary-Ellen's doing a lot of confrontation work.

SHELLY: I haven't got a single negative feeling about you. Not one. I feel completely, positively wonderful about you.

MARY-ELLEN: I don't feel that's true. *(Shelly looks helplessly at the others)*

DANE: Why don't you two work that out later?

MARY-ELLEN *(Emphatically to Shelly)*: All right?

SHELLY: Sure. Fine.

BILL: The ice cream's melting.

(All are glad for a chance to break and get into something physical, like eating more of the stuff that created the situation from which they were glad to break and get into something physical, like eating more of the stuff . . . eat in relative silence. Some faces. Dane talks as he eats.)

DANE: Five months ago. Less. On this mountain. Me and Mary-Ellen hiked to the top and took acid. What a strange trip that was. The sounds you can hear on acid, just lying there naked on our backs. We were naked, you see. We took all our clothes off. Except our socks. Leaves. Breezes. You could hear the sun moving through the sky. Whhsssh. And roots moving through the ground under your head. Insects. Ants all over our bodies. Thousands of ants, thousands of tiny legs running all over us. I sort of freaked out. I was terrified. Mary-Ellen couldn't feel them. Well, there weren't any, you see, I was just imagining it and, anyway, Mary-Ellen was dancing. But this friend of mine had told me about a time when she'd been stoned on top of a mountain, a different mountain, and she'd woken up with ants in her hair and her eyes and in her ears and crawling around her crotch and I just flipped out and everything in my body came out. I was urinating and defecating and crying and my nose was running and I was sweating and I felt so Christ-awful alone way on top of that mountain with nothing above us except sky and just a mountain underneath us, which isn't very much. Trapped in between. Mary-Ellen didn't seem to notice. She was rubbing against trees. It got better.

MARY-ELLEN: I remember. I was being a grizzly bear.

ROBBIE: Oh, God, this ice cream, this ice cream, it's so green and so runny and it tastes so weird. It's like they didn't even bother to mix the chemicals together. I swear I can taste every single chemical separately. Green. Oh, I love it. It's so Twentieth Century. I would defend this ice cream against attack.

(Shelly begins to move in a kind of rhythm, dancing to music she hears in her head, very funky.)

SHELLY: Come on, baby, let's dance.

BILL: Stop it, Shelly.

SHELLY: Please dance with me.

BILL: Cut it out. *(Shelly moves off and dances on her own)*

DANE: I'll dance with you, Shelly.

BILL: Cut the shit, Shelly.

ROBBIE: What's the matter with you, Billy-boy?

SHELLY *(To herself)*: Ohhh, it's soooo good, it's sooo good. *(Bill gets up, takes the rifle. Dane grabs it from him)*

DANE: Hey, man, take it easy. What are you doing?*(Bill looks at him blankly)*

BILL: I'm going inside. How does that strike you? *(Bill takes the rifle back and exits indoors. Immediately, Shelly goes in after him. Pause)*

ROBBIE: Nice to see you guys. Nice of you to drop by.

DANE: You have some weird friends.

ROBBIE: Oh, Bill's just . . . he's like that sometimes. Life is a freak show, right?

DANE *(Seriously)*: That depends really on how you look at it. *(Robbie bursts out laughing)*

ROBBIE: You're the fucking limit. Hey, thanks for coming. *(He hugs Dane warmly. Dane returns the gesture but awkwardly)*

MARY-ELLEN: We missed you.

ROBBIE: So, what do we all feel about life at this point in time?

MARY-ELLEN: Honey, why don't you take the ice cream back before it melts?

DANE: O.K. You could say leave me and Rob alone, you know.

MARY-ELLEN: Leave me and Robbie alone.

DANE: Yes. All right. I'll be inside. *(He exits inside with the cutting board)*

ROBBIE: How'd you find out where I was? Did I leave clues?

MARY-ELLEN: Where are you going after this?

ROBBIE: I haven't thought about it. Maybe I'll stay, settle down, who knows? Countryside, ocean, and there's this check-out girl in Safeways. I mean, why not? What more could a man ask for? A wife, a life, a little bit of strife. Look, I enjoy moving around right now. O.K.?

MARY-ELLEN: I don't know. Is it?

ROBBIE: Sure, the call of the highway, new horizons, adventure, old friends, laughing, good times, saying hi.

MARY-ELLEN: I worry about you.

ROBBIE: Well, don't. I'm fine.

MARY-ELLEN: Are you?

ROBBIE: Lay off, Mary.

MARY-ELLEN: I realized after you left . . . we'd never really talked. A whole month with us and I never learned anything about you. My husband's best friend.

ROBBIE: What? Is that what he said? I mean, sure, we went to school together but I always thought . . . well, it was more you and me. Sort of. You know.

MARY-ELLEN: I know. Why did you leave so suddenly? I was really upset.

ROBBIE: Oh, I don't know. I thought it was time to go. *(Pause)* What do you want, Mary?

MARY-ELLEN: I want to know what's going on with you. How you're feeling.

ROBBIE: You came all the way up here today to find out how I was feeling?

MARY-ELLEN: Just talk to me, that's all. I've been thinking about you.

ROBBIE: What if I don't want to talk? What if I don't really want you to know me? What if I want to guard the big secret? Stay mysterious, elusive. What would you say to that?

MARY-ELLEN: I just want to be able to think about you in a certain way. I want to feel good about you. You remember the day you and me and Dane went to that park and . . .

ROBBIE: No. *(Deliberate)* I don't. Look, Mary, whatever it is we could say to each other, the thing is, afterwards you'd go back to Dane and have dinner and talk and live your life . . . and that's very nice for you . . . and Dane . . . and I'm very happy for both of you. And I would just move on to some place else. Which is very nice for me. But it's different. Things are just a certain way, and the way they are is that we can't do anything about what both of us think it might be nice to do something about. And anyway, it wouldn't be very nice.

MARY-ELLEN: Hold my hand. It's all right.

ROBBIE: Oh, God, you get things so mixed up sometimes.

MARY-ELLEN: No I don't. Tell me what you're really thinking.

ROBBIE: I just fucking did. Tit.

MARY-ELLEN: What?

ROBBIE: Tit. Teat. Bosom. Breast. That's what I was really thinking, O.K.? Being suckled at your breast. May I do that?

MARY-ELLEN: Of course not.

ROBBIE *(Laughing)*: And you want me to trust you?

MARY-ELLEN: Stop being like this, Rob.

ROBBIE: Like what? I just told you exactly what was going on in my mind. I had this very simple, straightforward urge to be suckled at the breast of my best friend's wife, in that way that friends do. End of conversation. Next question.

MARY-ELLEN: All right. Go ahead.

ROBBIE: Let's talk about something else, Mary.

MARY-ELLEN: God, you're the loneliest person I've ever met.

ROBBIE: Fuck off, Mary, just fuck off. Leave me alone. I haven't done anything to you. *(Calmer)* Golly. Nice sun. For a while there I didn't think it was going to come out today. *(Pause)* See, there's no point. *(Enter Reilly from the corner. He's about forty-five or so. He clears his throat)* Ah, Reilly, you old son of a gun, just in the nick of time. How the hell are you?

REILLY: Can't complain, can't complain.

ROBBIE: This is Mary-Ellen. Mary-Ellen, Reilly.

MARY-ELLEN: Hi.

REILLY: You found yourself a friend, eh?

ROBBIE: Yes, yes indeed. How is the missus?

REILLY: She's well, she's well.

ROBBIE: Good. I'm glad to hear it.

REILLY: Yes, she's doing fine.

ROBBIE: Great. Everyone's sort of . . . ah . . . inside. I'll tell them you're here.

REILLY: Could I trouble you for a glass of water? Just a glass of water, if you could manage, that is, if it's no trouble.

ROBBIE: Sure. Come on inside.

REILLY: I'll stay out here if it's all right with you. Just a glass of water. *(Enter Dane)*

DANE: Whew, boy, I think that last batch must've done the trick. I'm getting incredible rushes.

ROBBIE: Dane, this is Reilly. He's, ah. We're just now in the process of. Jesus, this is pretty complicated. Inside my head, I mean. Reilly, fix on Reilly. We're buying a boat from Reilly. Well, we're considering. It's a fishing boat. We're going to fish. Commercially. Me and Bill. I didn't tell you that. This is, oh, Reilly, this is Dane.

DANE: You look exactly like a picture of my grandfather.

REILLY: That a fact? Well, I could do with a glass of water. I could use that.

ROBBIE: Sure. Whew. Some shit! *(He exits into house)*

REILLY: Little something to wash down the pills. Got those little red ones here for the headache.

DANE: You get migraines?

REILLY: Couldn't get far without the red ones. The green ones I don't know. They're supposed to make you sleep better. I just about forgotten what the hell sleep is, you know? Oh, I take 'em, but. Total bitch this pain business. Never mind, hell, don't you pay any attention to me. Shit, I'm all right. I'll be fine. Don't believe I caught your name.

DANE: Dane.

REILLY: Dane, that's it! I remember now. Sure, Dane. I forgot the first time, that's what happened. Goes in here, comes out there. *(Ear to ear)* Concentration's shot. It's a humiliating thing what pain does to you. When it keeps going on, I mean. Dane, that's it, got it now. Like a Great Dane. That's the way to remember it. Great Dane. Great Dane.

MARY-ELLEN: Look at how the trees keep shifting colors. It's incredible. Did you bring the camera?

DANE *(He mimes a camera)*: Click, got it.

MARY-ELLEN: Wow, pictures. Get one with me and Reilly over by the trees.

REILLY: Beg your pardon?

DANE: Whoops.

MARY-ELLEN *(Explaining)*: We just . . . ah . . .

DANE: Oh, have you met my wife Mary-Ellen?

REILLY: How do you do? Your wife. I thought you were friends with whatsit. Paul.

MARY-ELLEN: Rob.

REILLY: Oh, Christ, my head, my head. *(He presses his hands over his eyes)*

MARY-ELLEN: Dane, do something. He's in pain, Dane. *(Dane giggles)* Dane?

DANE *(Laughing)*: I'm sorry, honey, I can't help it. It was just how you said that. I can't stop, I'm sorry. *(Reilly recovers)*

MARY-ELLEN: Hey, are you all right?

REILLY: I think it's over. Yeah, better, better. It comes in spurts like that. Comes and goes, Jesus, I wish to hell I was dead and that's the truth. Much better now, thank you. Just waiting for the water.

MARY-ELLEN *(To Dane)*: You make me sick, Dane.

DANE: Hey-hey. I'm sorry. I couldn't control it. *(He hugs her. Mary-Ellen exits into house)*

REILLY: I guess we're in for a spell of good weather. Fellow at the Coast Guard said a few weeks of sun. Warm up the water. That's good for the silver. Yep, silvers are on top, you see, right near the surface. Fifty degrees and they bite. Funny thing about that. See, your Chinook stay right close to the bottom and your silvers stay on top. Both of 'em salmon, but I don't suppose they ever even see each other. Figure that. You ever done any fishing there, Dane?

DANE: Fish talk to each other. Each species is supposed to have its own separate language and it can't be understood by any fish that isn't the same species. There's even supposed to be dialects. Complete sublanguages. Like up in Manitoba there's these bass that talk more like trout than . . . wait, it's not bass . . . it's pickerel . . . bass or pickerel . . . ?

REILLY: Oh, hell, yeah, there's all kinds of fish, that's true enough. Now, fish don't feel anything, there's an interesting fact while we're on information. Think of that. No such thing as a migraine in a fish. *(Enter Robbie)*

ROBBIE: Hey, I can't find them anywhere.

(Enter Bill and Shelly, in a hurry.)

BILL: Hey, Reilly, we just saw your truck coming off the highway.

SHELLY: I'll make some hibiscus tea. Would you like some tea, Reilly?

REILLY: I'll just have some water, if it's no trouble.

ROBBIE: Water! That was it. Sorry, Reilly. *(Shelly exits inside)*

REILLY: Just for the red pills, you see. What do you say, boys? Gonna catch yourself some fish?

BILL: Sure, why not?

REILLY: That's what I like to hear. Just got a new coat of paint on her. Looks real sweet. Don't know as I ought to sell her even.

BILL: Well, we're definitely interested.

ROBBIE: We're sort of wondering why she sank three times last winter.

REILLY: What's that?

ROBBIE: And why you never mentioned it.

BILL *(To Robbie)*: You fuck.

REILLY: Now let me tell you boys a thing or two about last winter. That boat . . . the third time I didn't have nothing to do with it. And them first two times neither. Goddamn son of a bitch fool kid I hired to look after it. Shit, he didn't know a boat from a shoe full of snot. Hippie jackass is what he was. Up from California. Shit. I told him a thing or two. *(Reilly has another attack in his head)* Damnit to holy fuck.

(Robbie makes a move toward Reilly but Bill restrains him, watching in fascination. Reilly blacks out.)

ROBBIE: He's dead.

BILL *(He goes over to him)*: Hey, Reilly. *(He shakes him. Reilly stirs. Sits bolt upright)*

REILLY: Where the hell am I? Oh. Jeeesus. How you boys doing? Could you get me a glass of water, could you? *(Enter Mary-Ellen with a glass of water. Shelly behind her)*

MARY-ELLEN: Here you are, Reilly.

REILLY: Ah, you're a darling . . . ah . . .

MARY-ELLEN: Mary-Ellen.

REILLY: I appreciate it. *(Mary-Ellen exits inside with Shelly. Reilly takes his pills)* Ah, that's better. That'll do it. Yes, sir, it's a good little boat. I started up that engine this morning and she purred like a kitten. All new valves. All new exhaust. Yeah, she's a good boat. You boys have a good think on it and I'll be around first thing tomorrow morning. First thing. *(Rises)* You can't go wrong. Lick of paint. I'll tell you. I'm not feeling too hot. No. Take it easy. *(He exits around the house)*

ROBBIE: You drive a hard bargain, sonny.

DANE *(He has been watching from the side)*: He's in bad shape.

ROBBIE: He's gonna be stone dead a long time before we ever lay our hands on a thousand dollars.

REILLY *(He reenters)*: Say, ah . . . oh, it's in the pickup. Can't keep track of paper. Take it easy. *(He reexits. Bill follows. Stops)*

BILL: He's dying. Rory's right. The guy's dying. He's standing here talking to us and he's dying. How can he do that?

ROBBIE: So, what's wrong with dying?

BILL: No, I mean how can the guy just be walking around like that when he's dying? It's fucking evil.

(Car engine starts offstage. Car leaving.)

ROBBIE: What do you want to play now?

DANE: I have a frisbee in the Volvo. Should I get it?

ROBBIE: Yeah, get the frisbee.

DANE: It's in the Volvo. I'll get it. *(Pause)* I'll be right back. *(He exits)*
ROBBIE: Hey.
BILL: What?
ROBBIE: Where's Dane?

(They laugh. Enter Shelly and Mary-Ellen. Mary-Ellen is laughing hysterically. She has a pot on her head like a helmet.)

MARY-ELLEN: Hey, look at me. What do I have on my head?
BILL: A pot.
MARY-ELLEN: I'm a pothead. *(All laugh hysterically. They stop. Mary-Ellen takes the pot off)* Where's Dane? *(Bill and Robbie bust up)*
ROBBIE: He's getting the frisbee from the Volvo.
MARY-ELLEN: The frisbee? Why?
ROBBIE: He wanted to.
BILL: We told him it was all right. *(This is giggly. Enter Dane with the frisbee)*
DANE: What's going on? *(They laugh. Can't explain)*
SHELLY: Hey, is this really as funny as I think it is?
BILL: I'm not feeling nauseous anymore.
ROBBIE: Do you . . . realize what this means . . . doctor?
ALL: WE'RE STONED . . .
ROBBIE: Again! *(They all cheer. Light changes to somber, dark, to suggest a cloud passing over the sun. All stop)*
MARY-ELLEN: What was that?
DANE: Look. *(They all look toward the mountains)*
MARY-ELLEN: Holy Jesus. Look at it.
ROBBIE: An Indian fog. Incredible.
DANE: What's an Indian fog?
ROBBIE: When it comes in like that without any warning. It's supposed to be when the gods screwed up something on earth. They roll a fog in over the mountain, then they can creep around straightening things up without anyone seeing them. That's what the Indians said. Spooky.
SHELLY: That's gotta be a miracle. Can we go to the lookout?
BILL: Sure.

DANE: What's the lookout?

SHELLY: It's this place over the ocean. It's incredible in the fog.

MARY-ELLEN: Oh, wow, yes, let's go there. *(General assent)*

DANE: We'll take the Volvo.

SHELLY: Far out.

ROBBIE *(To Bill)*: You got the keys to the cycle?

BILL: Sure.

SHELLY: Don't be a party-pooper. Come in the nifty red Volvo.

ROBBIE: I'll take the cycle.

BILL: Shelly, baby, it's cool on the cycle.

MARY-ELLEN: Are you sure it's safe? I mean, the fog. Why don't you come in the car?

ROBBIE: Jesus, would you please stop making a fuss. Give me the keys.

DANE: You should make up your mind if you want us to be worried about you or not.

MARY-ELLEN: Dane!

ROBBIE *(He does a mock baby cry)*: You're not supposed to notice that, Dane, and if you do notice it, you're not supposed to say anything, and if you do say anything, it's supposed to be a joke. *(He exits with keys)*

BILL: Hey, follow our lights.

DANE: Let's go. *(He and Mary-Ellen exit)*

SHELLY: Hey, what happened to Reilly?

BILL: He went home.

SHELLY: Well? Are we fisherfolk?

BILL: It's weird.

SHELLY: Is everything cool?

BILL: You mean like all around.

SHELLY: Yeah. You know.

BILL: Isn't it always?

DANE *(He calls from offstage)*: Hey, let's go.

SHELLY *(Imitating)*: Hey, let's go. *(They exit arm in arm)*

Act Two

Scene 1

"The lookout." A ledge of rock bordered by a wire fence with a run of barbed wire on top. A lighthouse just visible at the side. Its rotating light illuminates the stage every forty-five seconds. There's a set of binoculars on a rotating stand that you pay a dime to look through. It's fogged in. The actors can't see each other more than five feet away. No special effects, just acting. Everything has a slow quality about it. They are all in a private mood, the way you get on peyote in the fog. The Volvo is parked onstage. So is the cycle, a Norton Atlas, 1969.

At the start, this: Bill is looking through the binoculars. Shelly sits huddled against the fence. Mary-Ellen looks out at the ocean. Slow, distant waves, below. Robbie and Dane are conducting an experiment in visibility. Dane stands still while Robbie backs slowly away.

DANE: Further. Further. Further. There.

ROBBIE: No, I can still see you.

DANE *(Peering)*: Oh yes. O.K. A little more.

ROBBIE *(He goes back further)*: There! I can't see you now. Stand still and I'll pace it off.

DANE: No, you stay there. I know my shoe size exactly.

ROBBIE: So do I. Nine D.

DANE: You have to know the inches. Mine are exactly ten and three-eighths from toe to heel.

ROBBIE: I hope I'm having a good time.

DANE: I'm coming. *(Robbie feints back and circles around the vehicles to Shelly while Dane paces his way offstage. Exiting)* Boy, distances are really deceptive in the fog. *(Robbie settles down by Shelly)*

SHELLY: Wouldn't it be far out if you were a bird and you could just fly through the fog, nothing on any side of you, just fog?

ROBBIE: With my luck I'd crash into the lighthouse. *(The light pulses. They look up)*

SHELLY: It's so incredibly beautiful.

ROBBIE: I don't know. I can't see anything.

DANE *(Offstage)*: Hey, Rob!

ROBBIE: Over here.

DANE *(Offstage)*: You shithead!

ROBBIE: Dane? Dane? Come in, Dane. I've lost radio contact. Commander . . . there's something sinister about this planet. I don't know what it is but . . . yes, yes, I understand what it is that's making the hair stand up straight on the back of my head, Commander . . . the spatial relations are all wrong. Straight lines are . . . curved. All facts are untrue here. There's nothing to grab hold of. Dane. Come in, Dane, come in. *(Mary-Ellen turns from the fence and begins acting like an alien life form with antennae. She makes weird noises)* Do you hear something weird, Varga? Something sinister in the fog.

SHELLY: I'm just into being . . . still.

ROBBIE: It's got you in its power, Shelly. It's dulling your mind. I feel like I've been drugged.

MARY-ELLEN *(She finds her way to them)*: Beep-beep-beep. Hello . . . earthling . . . beep-beep. What . . . brings . . . you . . . to . . . our . . . pranet . . . beep . . . planet?

ROBBIE: I am looking for my colleague, Commander Dane . . . can you help me?

MARY-ELLEN: Do . . . you . . . really . . . want . . . my . . . hep . . . beep . . . help . . . beep . . . beep . . . I . . . mean . . . really?

ROBBIE: Yes, O strange little alien life form. Give me a message I can bring back to earth.

MARY-ELLEN: Listen . . . carefully . . . earthling.

ROBBIE: Yes? Yes? What?

MARY-ELLEN: I . . . love . . . you . . . beep. *(She turns abruptly and goes away, still being a spaceman. Robbie makes a slight involuntary gesture toward her. Dane appears at the edge of the stage)*

DANE: Rob? Mary-Ellen? *(Mary-Ellen goes to the Volvo, gets in and honks the horn, a long, loud honk. Dane runs to the window and knocks. Tries the door. It's locked)* Mary-Ellen. MARY-ELLEN, OPEN THE DOOR. SHE'S LOCKED HERSELF IN.

MARY-ELLEN *(She opens the door and comes out as a spaceman)*: Herro . . . Hello . . . earthling. Do . . . you . . . like . . . my . . . Volvo?

DANE: You're wearing the battery down, Mary-Ellen. Let's play frisbee.

MARY-ELLEN: I . . . love . . . you . . . earthling . . . *(She turns and exits, still as spaceman)*

SHELLY: Boy, does she get on my tits.

ROBBIE: She's a friend of mine. A really good friend.

SHELLY: I'm trying, Rob, I really am. But she's just one of those people that gets on my tits. There aren't many, but when they do, they really do. My uncle was like that.

DANE *(He gets the frisbee out of the car)*: I think it might be a lot of fun to play frisbee in the fog. Would anybody like to play frisbee?

ROBBIE: No, Dane.

SHELLY: No.

BILL: No.

(Dane tosses it up and catches it. Starts to put it back in the car, changes his mind. He finds his way to Bill.)

DANE: Can you see anything?

BILL: Yeah. *(Dane watches him, looks at the fog)*

DANE: The lighthouse flashes exactly once every forty-five seconds. *(Bill continues to look through the binoculars)*

SHELLY: What does the fog make you think of?

ROBBIE: Death.

SHELLY: Really?

ROBBIE: Yes. Or life. In that area.

SHELLY: I had a flash that we were on this giant movie set. The fog was just a veil, or something, and if it lifted suddenly we'd see these banks of lights on us and movie cameras and God would be sitting in one of those chairs with his name on it, Director, Mr. God, and he'd be yelling cut, cut, do the whole thing again.

ROBBIE: Oh, I hope so . . .

SHELLY: What?

ROBBIE: . . . that we can do the whole thing . . . *(Stopping)* Never mind.

SHELLY: You know, I have regular contact with the dead.

BILL: You want to have a look?

DANE: I don't understand how you can see anything in the fog.

BILL: You have to put a dime in. *(Bill does. Dane looks)*

ROBBIE: No, I didn't know that.

SHELLY: I've been talking to King Solomon for two years.

ROBBIE: How's he doing?

SHELLY: I know this sounds weird. That's why I never tell anyone.

ROBBIE: Shelly? Shelly-friend? Shelly-Bill's-Old-Lady? Hello?

SHELLY: He's been explaining why you shouldn't be afraid of death, because it doesn't stop there. You keep going on to higher forms of energy, until . . . I don't know. I can't understand him when he starts that rap. But you're not supposed to take life. It makes it harder for you to move up to the next state of energy after you die. That's where "Thou shalt not kill" comes from.

ROBBIE: Oh, that's where.

SHELLY: According to him. *(Back to Dane and Bill)*

DANE: I can't see anything.

BILL: You don't see the fog?

DANE: Of course I can see the fog.

BILL: Just look at it and let the images come to you. It's like a screen. If you don't want to do it . . .

DANE: Oh, I see. Let me try that. *(Rob and Shelly)*

SHELLY: This is between us, O.K.?

ROBBIE: Bill doesn't know?

SHELLY: I get so worried about the way he gets violent. If he'd killed Guinevere.

ROBBIE: Ah. You *did* put the egg there.

SHELLY: Don't tell him.

ROBBIE: He wouldn't kill Guinevere.

SHELLY: Last year, when we had the farm, he killed our cow. Shot it in the face.

ROBBIE: Bill did?

SHELLY: He said it wasn't giving enough milk.

ROBBIE: Oh, no wonder.

SHELLY: Why, what kind of a person did you think I was?

ROBBIE: What?

SHELLY: Didn't you just say . . . oh. I'm so stoned. I love this stuff.

ROBBIE: The other day I went in the bathroom right after you'd been, there was the most amazing turd I've ever seen lurking at the bottom of the toilet. I was just completely overcome with awe at the sight of this perfectly formed solitary turd and all I could think was, that's Shelly for ya. Down to earth. Calm. Complete. I'm just . . . you asked what kind of person I thought you were. You don't mind my talking to you like this, turd to turd.

SHELLY: You want to know something amazing? I remember that. Last week.

ROBBIE: Yeah.

SHELLY: Well. That wasn't mine. It was Bill's, and I had exactly the same thought except just the opposite. I couldn't figure out how he could be so violent and have such a calm turd. I'm not calm at all, you know.

ROBBIE: I really like you, Shelly.

SHELLY *(She lays her head on his shoulder)*: I feel sad.

ROBBIE: Why?

SHELLY: I don't think I'm going to be staying with Bill.

ROBBIE: Shelly?

SHELLY: I don't know yet. Don't say anything, please.

ROBBIE: But why?

SHELLY: I can't help him. He won't let me. He's just never gonna do anything with his life.

ROBBIE: I thought you guys were happy.

SHELLY: I love him, you see. That's the problem. Yeah, I think that's the trouble. *(She hears Mary-Ellen)* Shit.

MARY-ELLEN *(She enters as a spaceman)*: Where . . . is . . . everyone . . . beep . . . beep. *(She finds Dane)*

DANE: This is incredible. You should try this, Mary-Ellen.

MARY-ELLEN: What . . . do . . . you . . . see . . . out . . . there . . . beep . . . beep.

DANE: You can project perfect visual images onto the fog. There's some chemical in this peyote that activates the optical centers or something. It's like watching your own movie.

MARY-ELLEN: Beep . . . beep . . . far . . . out . . . good-bye . . . *(Mary-Ellen goes to Shelly and Rob)* Hello . . . Rob . . . beep . . . hello . . . Shelly . . . beep . . . beep . . . do . . . I . . . get . . . on . . . your . . . tits . . . Shelly? *(Pause)* Beep.

SHELLY *(She gets up suddenly)*: Would you please leave me alone.

MARY-ELLEN: Beep . . . beep . . . I . . . do . . . not . . . understand . . . your . . . request. Beep. Please . . . go . . . deeper. Beeper.

SHELLY: Because I'm not into it, O.K.? Do it, but leave me out.

MARY-ELLEN: Still . . . not . . . connecting. Beep. Please . . . go deeper . . . beeper. *(Shelly screams. This turns to a kind of hysterical laugh)*

SHELLY: You're crazy, you know that. You're completely goddamned crazy.

MARY-ELLEN: I . . . know . . . beep beep . . . I've . . . had . . . analysis. *(Straight)* I can't understand why you don't like me, Shelly. Please like me.

ROBBIE: Will you please like her. She's my friend, Shelly.

SHELLY *(She goes to Bill)*: I want to go for a walk.

BILL: Have a nice time.

SHELLY: Will you come with me?

BILL: No.

SHELLY: Please.

BILL: No.

SHELLY: Why not?

BILL: I don't feel like it.

DANE: I'll go for a walk with you.

SHELLY: I don't want to go with you. I mean . . . thanks, but I want to go with Bill.

BILL: And I don't want to go.

SHELLY: Bill!!! Who wants to go for a walk?

MARY-ELLEN: Me me me me me me . . . *(Mary-Ellen and Robbie exchange smiles)*

SHELLY: Oh, fuck it. Come on, let's go. Where are you? *(Mary Ellen and Shelly go for a walk)*

ROBBIE *(Apart)*: The fog's getting thinner. I can see you guys' outline. *(Bill watches Dane looking through the binoculars. A pause)*

BILL: What's architecture like?

DANE: Huh?

BILL: You're an architect, right?

DANE: Yeah, I'm an architect.

BILL: What's it like? You like it? I mean, I bet it's a good job, being an architect. You seem pretty . . . like someone with a good job.

DANE: It's O.K. In fact, I like the actual work very much, and I like the people I work with. And a lot of jobs get created as a result of the work we do, which isn't the most important thing, but it's good to know. I guess some people don't care so much but I really like having a good income, you know, being able to think about the future, plan things, give my kids a good education, take care of my folks when they're older . . . Mary-Ellen's folks. Oh, I remember now, the really incredible thing about architecture, and I just realized this the other day, it's something about the structures you work with, I mean the way you have to train yourself to think about your materials from the point of view of an underlying structure, it means that you're always looking for the order behind things, and when you apply that kind of thinking to the whole world, you find that everything becomes clearer and clearer all the time, everything makes more and more sense, you know, falls into certain patterns, like a sort of design that you can keep filling in as you learn things. I mean I didn't know that I'd think about things that way when I was studying architecture. It just happened, and then the other day I realized that I'd had a kind of perfect accident happen to me . . . I had this work that would always illuminate things about the world for me. I don't know, maybe a lot of people feel that way about their work. Oh, that's not what you asked, is it? I guess I got carried away. What did you ask?

BILL: Let me see your frisbee. *(Dane gives it over abstractly)* Don't you want to play, Dane?

DANE: I just want to look through here a little more. I'll be with you in a little while.

BILL *(He goes near Robbie)*: Hey, Cisco. Looks like you and me.

ROBBIE *(Turns)*: Yeah, right, sheet! *(Spits)*

BILL: Sheet! *(Spits)*

ROBBIE *(He backs up toward the fence and holds up his pinkie)*: On the pinkie . . . *(Bill throws. The frisbee sails over the fence into the ocean)* Whoops.

BILL: Whoops? Oh. Um. I wonder if Dane's got another frisbee?

(Bill and Robbie lean up against the fence looking out onto the ocean, fingers clutching the wire.)

ROBBIE: Bill, Bill, we've lost the frisbee.

BILL: Frisbee gone to Great Waters to join Father Frisbee.

DANE: This is just absolutely amazing. I mean, I just wouldn't have believed this is possible. *(Dane doesn't seem to be speaking to anyone, but he's intense)*

BILL: You got some weird friends.

ROBBIE: Yeah, they kill cows and stuff.

BILL: What's amazing, Dane?

DANE: Out there. No, wait a minute. I guess I mean "in here."

BILL: It must be really quiet, down there.

ROBBIE: Do you really want to go through with this boat thing?

BILL: No, asshole. I just moved out here for my fucking health. Look, if you want out, just say and I'll get Larry or Ed Nolin to come in with me. There's hundreds of guys that want to have a boat.

ROBBIE: I just asked.

BILL: Well, I just answered. *(Robbie takes an envelope out of his pocket and hands it to Bill. Bill opens it. It's money)* What the fuck is this?

ROBBIE: It's fifteen hundred dollars in denominations of one hundred.

BILL: Where's this from?

ROBBIE: My rich daddy.

BILL: When did this happen?

ROBBIE: I've had it for a while. I just wanted to be sure you were for real about the boat.

BILL: Me? What about you?

ROBBIE: Well. Strictly speaking . . . to keep the record accurate it isn't a sort of life-or-death affair for me, salmon fishing. I'm very used to living off Pa. In fact, I've reached a point where I honestly get deep pleasure spending his money. Not in a bitter, spiteful, hate-filled, self-destructive way. I feel generous and wise and even helpful as I spread it around. He doesn't really know how to enjoy it, and I do. And in the long run, which is the only run that counts, he's going to die and you're going to die and the earth is going to crumble into dust when the sun burns out, at least that's what I've been told, so what the fuck. And, of course, I adore the sea.

BILL: Hang on. I appreciate this, man. I really do. But why didn't you let me know you had the bread? I mean I've been busting my ass trying to figure out a way to get a hold of that boat and you've been holding on to all this bread, am I for real, what kind of bullshit game is that?

ROBBIE: You haven't been busting your ass, Bill. You've been thinking about it, sure, sort of, maybe even a whole lot, sure, kind of. Listen, I like you, man, I really like you a lot, but I see you. I can't help it. I see the game, what you're doing. The farm. The trucking business. The pot plantation in Brazil. What else? A million beautiful trips, Billy. But someone or something always fucked you over. The shits out there always beat you back. Well, what happens if the great salmon enterprise fails; some other great shit comes along and dumps on you only this time, this time you don't get away with blaming it on everything around you. What happens if you realize the fucking up is built right into you like an extra liver, and you're gonna have to take it with you wherever you go? For the rest of your life? I don't want to finance a move that's gonna break you. You're thirty, man. It's starting to be really important.

BILL: Well, just who the holy fuck do you think you are, all of a sudden.

ROBBIE: Forget about me. I'm a rich son of a bitch with nothing to do. I drift around. I live off the friends I have. Oh, I pay, but it's not even my money. Look, I've seen it, Billy. I know what I am and it's O.K., I'm indestructible. I live off your happiness. O.K. Your energy. I dig on the fact that things really matter to you, that you have lives. They do things. All my friends. See, I want you to do this thing, I want you to have a fleet of five hundred boats if that's what you want and I want your life to be good and I want you to be happy with your life and your Shelly and your chicken and . . .

BILL: You're spooky.

ROBBIE: Shit, I didn't mean to say any of that. It's not even true. I find most of my friends pathetic, including you. Take the fucking money. I conned it out of some weird old guy. He buys stocks in dog shit.

BILL: Rob. What's up?

ROBBIE: Take the money. I'm just talking. That's what I do.

BILL *(Cheering)*: We're gonna get that fleet of five hundred boats, fuckhead, you and me. You wait and see. And one day just for the pure dumb hell of it I'm gonna line 'em up end to end and sail around the whole fucking planet with a stereo playing rock-and-roll and I'll be laughing so hard they'll hear it on Mars. Put that money in your pocket. We're going fishing.

ROBBIE: I don't trust myself with that much cash. You hold on to it.

BILL *(Taking it)*: Hey, man.

ROBBIE: What, man?

BILL: You got an ugly soul.

ROBBIE *(Laughing)*: Right, right.

(They shake. Bill whoops for joy, yells, laughs, whatever.)

BILL: We're going fishing, goddamn. We are going fishing. *All right.* Hey, Dane, you beautiful motherfucker, stoke up the Volvo, we're buying a boat. A BOAT. A fishing boat, man. And I'm gonna buy you two hundred and fifty new frisbees and a tank of gas and we'll have a Chinese meal and take more buttons and holy shit, man, it's all coming to-fucking-gether.

DANE: You want to go into town. *(Bill busts up at Dane's low-key reaction)*

BILL: Oh, Dane, Dane, Dane, you're so together.

DANE: You want to go right away is what I meant.

BILL *(He gets mock calm-serious)*: See, the thing is, there's this fisherman Reilly . . . Oh, you met him. Well, he has a boat, and we're gonna buy it. O.K. You drive us into town and you get to watch us sign the papers. I got the cash right here. Fifteen hundred buckeroos.

DANE: Well. We ought to get the girls.

BILL: Shelly! Shelly-baby! We're buying a boat, wanna come?

DANE: Mary-Ellen!

BILL: Shelly. Mary-Ellen and Shelly.

MARY-ELLEN: Yoo-hoo. We're coming, don't go without us. *(They enter)*

SHELLY: They're over here. *(During all this Robbie is climbing over the fence on the other side of the lookout)* What's going on? What's this about a boat?

BILL: Shelly-baby-pie, we're getting us a boat. We got the money. Rob just put up fifteen hundred. He had it all along. Look.

SHELLY: Ahaaaa? Cripes. That's just . . . oh, my God . . .

BILL: Yeah . . . ain't it just . . . *(They laugh hysterically)*

MARY-ELLEN: Is this for the fishing thing? I thought both of you guys were doing it together.

BILL: Yeah, me and Rob.

MARY-ELLEN: Why did he give you the money?

BILL: Why did he give me the money? What difference does it make? You want to hold it?

MARY-ELLEN *(Worried)*: Where's Rob?

BILL: He's here. What's the matter with you?

MARY-ELLEN: ROB? ROBBIE!! *(Silence)*

DANE: Mary-Ellen, is something the matter?

MARY-ELLEN: ROB? ROBBIE??!!! *(She wanders toward the fence)* ROBBIE!!! *(She sees him outside the fence on the cliff, leaning out over the edge, staring down. The others follow her)* Rob. What are you doing? Robbie?

ROBBIE *(Distant)*: What?

MARY-ELLEN: Come on, we're going to town.

ROBBIE: The frisbee's down there. We ought to get it.

BILL: That's sort of a shitty idea, Rob, 'cause that's an eighty-foot drop.

ROBBIE: I can throw it up. Fuck it, we'll get a new frisbee. *(He starts climbing back over the fence)*

MARY-ELLEN: Careful, Rob.

DANE *(Helping)*: Put your hand on my shoulder.

(Robbie jumps down to safety. Awkward pause.)

ROBBIE: Come on, let's buy a boat.

MARY-ELLEN: Can't you wait till tomorrow with the boat?

ROBBIE: Strike while the iron's hot, that's what I say. I always say that. Always.

BILL: I'll follow you guys on the cycle.

ROBBIE: I'll take the cycle.

MARY-ELLEN: Rob.

SHELLY: You take the cycle, Rob. We'll meet you in town.

MARY-ELLEN: NO! I mean, for Christ sakes, everyone.

ROBBIE: What's the matter? Come on, let's go to town.

BILL *(Hands over keys)*: Meet us at Reilly's.

ROBBIE: Have a nice drive. *(He exits with cycle)*

MARY-ELLEN: This is wrong.

(Cycle engine starting, roaring off.)

BILL: Who was that masked man?

SHELLY: Let's buy a boat.

MARY-ELLEN: We shouldn't let him go. *(Shelly gets in the car. Bill too)* Dane, you know him. He was going to jump.

DANE: Get in the Volvo, Mary-Ellen.

MARY-ELLEN: Why are you ignoring me?

DANE: Because there's only two things he can do. He can either kill himself or not kill himself, and either way, I don't care. *(Pause)* I'm sorry. I just went to school with him. I don't care. *(Dane gets in the car. Mary-Ellen alone. Car starts. Fade)*

Scene 2

Back to square one. The living room. Dane is asleep on the couch, his head on Mary Ellen's lap. Shelly is curled up on the easy chair. Rory is on a chair. Long pause.

RORY: Whew. The end. I've seen a lot of dead dudes in my day but I want to tell you that dude was dead. I'll tell you the good news, though. When it's funeral time, they got a cosmetic guy in town that'll make that bod look like Saturday night at the Roxy. It's a fucking miracle what they can do with cosmetics. Whew. Really. It's an art.

SHELLY: I've never been . . . seen anyone dead up close like that. I mean that I knew. It's such a waste. *(Shelly cries)*

MARY-ELLEN: Do you believe in God?

RORY: I do, man. I believe in everything.

SHELLY: It's just not the same as what you think. God, he was such a mess on the road. It didn't even look like a body.

RORY: Really. Death is the ultimate trip, right? Right!

SHELLY: Shut up, Rory.

RORY: Hey, babe, don't back into me, like my head is there, my mouth is there. Zip zip. That's how I am. I care. I'm feeling all kinds of stuff. I dug him. He was a truly far-out dude.

ROBBIE *(He enters with a tray of coffee)*: Come and get it. What did Dane want? *(He sets the tray down. They help themselves)*

MARY-ELLEN: He's out.

ROBBIE: Where'd Bill go?

SHELLY: He's taking a walk. You should see the stars out there. It's gonna be a really nice day.

ROBBIE: Do you think he's really cut up about Reilly?

SHELLY: I guess. He really dug that Reilly was a fisherman. You know.

ROBBIE: Yeah.

RORY: It's better this way. Fffft. Out like a fuse, nothing to lose. Blood clots are a bummer. My dad cashed in on a hemorrhage. One day. Twenty-two hours. Blubbering and pissing in the sheets. Messy scene. Didn't even recognize the kid till the last minute. Weird. Weird. You know what the old fucker said to me on the way out. Big exit line. Kid, he says, how come you're such a jerkoff? Man, what do you say to that? Know what I did? Springfield General Hospital. Into the men's room and jerk off. Really. Very heavy day. Oh, things can get so fucking beee-zarre.

MARY-ELLEN: I don't think I like peyote.

RORY: Any of that shit left? Lay some on the kid for partytime?

SHELLY: In the icebox. I'm sorry we can't make it.

RORY: I'm hip, I'm hip. Be cool. Be mellow. Remember me in your dreams. Listen. We're putting Reilly in the turf in a few days. Don't know when yet but like he didn't have a whole lot of friends, you know? Just Mrs. Reilly.

SHELLY: We'll be there.

RORY: Beautiful. Beautiful. *(Pause)* It's such a fucking shame, ain't it? *(Nods and exits)*

ROBBIE: They found his head a hundred feet away from the body.

MARY-ELLEN: Even the last couple of acid trips haven't been all that great. I used to get off a lot more on tripping.

SHELLY: Do you have any children?

MARY-ELLEN: Not yet. We're not into . . . no.

SHELLY: My body's falling apart. Just in little ways, but enough so you notice it. In the thighs. Around here. It has to happen sooner or later, I guess. I'm sorry I don't like you more, Mary-Ellen. It's stupid.

MARY-ELLEN: That's life.

ROBBIE: Hey, come on, come on, let's play a game or something. Put on some music. Play a game. Yuk it up.

SHELLY: No.

ROBBIE: Is Dane asleep?

MARY-ELLEN: Looks like it.

ROBBIE: Would you make sure? I want to tell you something.

MARY-ELLEN: Danie. Arf-arf. Woof-woof. Frank Lloyd Wright! *(To Robbie)* Well?

ROBBIE *(Pause)*: Hey, let's go off some place together, us three. Canada. Start a commune.

MARY-ELLEN: Rob.

ROBBIE: Up on the lookout before. When I went off on the cycle, I really did intend to . . . as much as I ever intend anything . . . no, more, much more . . . I was going to . . .

MARY-ELLEN AND SHELLY: I know *(They exchange glances)*

ROBBIE: Yes, I guess I knew you knew. I mean, I know you knew what I wanted you to think, but I have this way of not being serious about things and I was *very* serious about . . . Was it really that obvious?

SHELLY: You know it was.

ROBBIE: It felt so amazing in the fog. Like flying. A hundred miles an hour. One-ten. I was sort of scared for a minute but the scared went into just perfect control, perfect peace. And I thought, O.K., do it. Just like that. Next set of headlights. I got to that uphill curve around Angel Crest, leaned into the left lane and closed my eyes. Waited. Nothing. Then this image came into my head . . . these rocks in front of my face, right in front, and all this life clinging to them and I'm talking to these rocks, I'm saying, Why? What are you doing there? What's the point? What's so important you're holding on to it? And I'm really asking, I really want to know, but all I can hear is the motorcycle. All this slimy stuff is silent, it's just there. And I suddenly realized that that silence was an answer in a way. I mean, all that stuff is holding on just to be alive, that's all, nothing more. And that's a reason. It's something to know. And it's up to me. No one's listening. No one's moving aside to make room, and it's O.K. because it's up to me. Then I felt my hands hurting and I opened my eyes and my hands were white from holding the handlebars so tight . . . and . . . and I felt great. I was holding on and it felt great. I wanted to shout I was so happy, I wanted to wrap my arms around the whole fucking world and kiss it. I couldn't wait to see you guys again. I couldn't wait to buy that boat. I couldn't wait to see what happened next and then, oh, man, this was the really weird part. I saw all those cop cars up ahead in the fog, all the lights flashing. I knew there'd been an accident and for a minute I thought, I really thought, Oh, shit, it's me. I must've already crashed and now I'm a ghost on this motorcycle and I'm seeing my own accident, that's how it must work . . . The second you die you realize how much you wanted to live and then it's too late. Then I saw the truck all smashed up, and all I could think was, Thank fucking Christ they chose Reilly. You know, the Indian fog . . . I must've been really stoned . . . but just, thank Christ it's him and I'm still alive. *(Pause)* Anyway, I'm sort of glad I saw that. If you'll pardon my being heavy for a moment.

MARY-ELLEN: I guess we ought to be starting back. We have a long drive. Dane. Dane, baby . . . *(She shakes him. He sits bolt upright)*

DANE: Birds. Damn, it was birds. That's why I couldn't think of the kind of fish. It was birds. Bird calls. They have dialects, you see. Never mind.

MARY-ELLEN: We have to get going.

DANE: I'm getting so inaccurate. That's unforgivable. Birds.

(Bill enters with Guinevere, dead and plucked.)

SHELLY: You didn't! Bill, Bill, Billy, why?

BILL: Cook it up. There'll be enough for all of us.

SHELLY: You're a bastard. And you're a failure. And you're pathetic. *(Shelly goes off through the kitchen door)*

BILL: Who's hungry?

DANE: What was that?

BILL: Nothing. This used to be Guinevere. She was a game we were playing.

MARY-ELLEN: We have to go. Thanks. Dane has to work tomorrow. Monday.

ROBBIE: It's Sunday. It's Sunday. That's what today is. It happens to be a very important fact.

BILL: Right. Sunday.

DANE *(He rises)*: Well, thank you very much.

MARY-ELLEN *(She and Rob hug)*: Take care of yourself. Come have a suck one day.

ROBBIE *(He goes to Dane)*: Thanks for dropping by. Happy building.

DANE: Good luck. That was excellent peyote. I enjoyed that. Say good-bye to Shelly. *(He exits with Mary-Ellen)*

ROBBIE *(Spits)*: Well.

BILL: Sheet. *(Spits)* Back to square one.

ROBBIE: What do you mean?

BILL: Looking for another boat.

ROBBIE: Isn't Reilly's still for sale?

BILL: You gotta be kidding. That's all I need. Ride around the high seas in a dead man's boat. That'd be real cute.

ROBBIE: I didn't know you were superstitious.

BILL: The guy's a jinx. Look at the way he went out. His boat goes down three times at the dock and he gets splattered all over the highway. Stinking blood clots. One little wodge of red snot in his brain and . . . it's so stupid.

ROBBIE: Dying's dying.

BILL: The cop told me they found Reilly's head . . .

ROBBIE: I know.

BILL: He must've really been traveling.

ROBBIE: I guess.

BILL: It's weird. You'd think he'd've slowed down if he blacked out. Don't your muscles relax and you go limp.

ROBBIE: If Dane were here we could find out for sure.

BILL: Holy shit. That beautiful old fart. You know what that means?

ROBBIE: It means he's dead.

BILL: It means he killed himself. He went out on the highway and deliberately offed himself. He couldn't take the idea of walking around looking like such a mess, so he did it himself.

ROBBIE: What difference does it make?

BILL: Oh, asshole, can't you see anything? You think lying around in a hospital full of pills and rubber tubes and stink everywhere . . . you think that's the same as gracing out on a highway. This puts it right, what he did. We gotta have that boat, man. We gotta.

ROBBIE: Bill . . .

BILL: Don't sit there all calm on me, Robbie-boy. I can't spell this out in black and white but I know what I'm saying and I know it's right just the way I know everything is full of shit most of the time and I don't know why it's full of shit and I can't write a book about it for you but it's all gray . . . everything in the middle . . . everyone's under shadows, under rocks like a bunch of moles and all this totally ridiculous stuff keeps happening to them and they just take it and take it and take it and never raise a stink, never fight back and Reilly did it. He saw what was coming and he said, No, man, fuck this, I don't have to swallow this last piece of shit, don't say anything *(Bill in a rage kicks the couch that Robbie is on, kicks other things, tears Guinevere apart. Robbie rises calmly, goes to him and starts fighting mechanically. It's a long, awful ritual. Robbie finally pins him. Bill lies panting)*

ROBBIE: Another day, another trip.

BILL: Oh, man, what the fuck is wrong with me? How come you're always so calm?

ROBBIE: Good toilet training and a happy youth.

BILL: A lot of the time I feel like busting your head open.

ROBBIE: I still wouldn't lay any eggs.

BILL: What? Oh. You ever had chicken stew?

ROBBIE: Dane's building a city. My buddy. Dane. A whole new city someplace. Bolivia. Peru. One of those places. If his idea is accepted there'll be this whole new city someplace with people living their lives in it and he designed it. Dane. The frisbee champion of my high school.

BILL: Dane's an asshole.

ROBBIE: Yeah.

BILL: He's O.K.

ROBBIE: Yeah.

BILL: Fishing is a pretty dumb idea, isn't it?

ROBBIE: Yeah.

BILL: I mean, I've never even been on a boat before. What if we get seasick? What if we sink? What if we can't make a living? I mean, *I* can't. What if you decide to take your money back.

ROBBIE: I won't.

BILL: You gonna stay out here?

ROBBIE: Yeah.

BILL: And fish.

ROBBIE: Sure.

BILL: Why?

ROBBIE: 'Cause it's something to do. Oh, you're right, it's a dumb idea, no doubt about it. You and me. Two of the finest minds of our generation. But it's something to do. And, you know, if we approach it just the right way, after a while, if we manage to stick to it, and we don't get seasick and we do catch fish we might find there's a good reason for doing it.

BILL: You're serious, right?

ROBBIE: I just want to keep an eye on my investment.

BILL: Yeah, and fuck you, too, man. I can do it on my own, you know. I don't need your help.

ROBBIE: I know.

(Shelly enters.)

SHELLY: Give me Guinevere. I'll cook her.

BILL: Shelly-baby.

SHELLY: Don't talk to me. I'm tired and I'm upset.

BILL: I'm sorry.

SHELLY: I don't care. *(Shelly exits with pieces of Guinevere. Bill starts after her, stops, caught between her and Robbie)*

BILL *(To Robbie)*: Ugh-oh. *(He exits)*

(Robbie looks around for a moment, takes the .22 rifle, opens front door, aims at target outside, and fires. Brief pause. Bill rushes in, alarmed.)

BILL: What the fuck are you doing, man?

ROBBIE: Bull's-eye.

BILL *(Covering)*: Don't waste bullets, they're expensive.

ROBBIE: Whatever you say, Billy-boy.

BILL *(He smiles suddenly)*: Hey, Reilly's boat, first thing in the morning.

ROBBIE: I think maybe after the funeral.

BILL: Right. Right. *(Pause)* Sheeeeit. *(Fake spit)*

ROBBIE: Sheeeit. *(Fake spit)*

(Bill exits back into kitchen. Robbie sets down rifle, takes up fishing rod and exits. We watch the room for a moment. Blackout.)

End of Play

At Home

Split, Part 1

At Home was first performed at Second Stage Theatre, New York (Robyn Goodman, Carole Rothman, Artistic Directors) on April 4, 1980, as the first half of a double bill. The title of the evening was *Split*. Carole Rothman directed the following cast:

PAUL	John Heard
CAROL	Brooke Adams

Characters

PAUL
CAROL

Table set nicely for four, dinner. Tasteful but not-quite-matched dinnerware. Of the chairs, three are of a set, the other not. Three elegant wine glasses, one tumbler.

Paul is seated at the table with a glassful of wine. Two bottles of wine on the table, one opened and partly drunk. Paul stares straight ahead. Pause. He drinks. Enter Carol from the kitchen. She wears an apron. She stands watching Paul for a moment.

PAUL: I'm sorry.

CAROL: It's not your fault.

PAUL: It's partly my fault. I'm sorry for the part that's my fault.

CAROL: Me too. It was just an argument. It didn't happen, O.K.

PAUL: O.K.

CAROL: Will you make the salad?

PAUL: What are we doing this for? I mean, I don't want company tonight. Not now. I don't want to see anyone.

CAROL: Me neither. I didn't in the first place, but it's too late, they're coming, we invited them, whoopee.

PAUL: I could maybe call. Maybe she hasn't left yet. *(Carol exits)* Should I call? *(Pause. He goes to the phone, dials)* I'm calling.

CAROL *(Off)*: What are you going to tell her?

PAUL: I don't know. I'll think of something. *(He listens into phone)* Shit. *(Imitating)* . . . speakaslongas . . . recordtillyouhangup.

CAROL *(Off)*: What?

PAUL: Nothing. *(Into phone)* Hi, Jean? Anyone there? Jean, are you listening? If you're there please pick up, it's some-one you're dying to talk to. It's Paul. Of Paul and Carol. You're not there are you. No. Well, I was just calling 'cause . . . I was . . . well, we'll see you in a little while. No, that's not true, is it? No, by the time you listen to this we'll have already seen you. And we'll have all had a great time and you'll be back home listening to this . . . so what? Well, we really enjoyed it. It was great to see you, and your new guy, we really like him. He's great. You really know how to pick 'em. And if we seemed a lit-tle weird tonight, I'm sorry, it's just . . . or maybe we didn't seem weird, in which case . . . *(Takes phone away from mouth)* What am I talking about? *(Into phone)* 'Bye Jean.

(He hangs up, goes to table, pours more wine. Carol comes into doorway.)

CAROL: Well?

PAUL: She's on her way. She's not there.

CAROL: Who were you talking to?

PAUL: Her machine.

CAROL: Oh. How is it?

PAUL: Fine. Her machine is fine.

CAROL: Are you going to give me a hand?

PAUL: What happened to the other wine glass?

CAROL: It broke.

PAUL: It broke? It just sat there and broke?

CAROL: I broke it.

PAUL: When?

CAROL: A few weeks ago. You put it at the edge of the shelf. I opened the door and it fell out.

PAUL: I did not put the wine glasses near the edge of the shelf. I never put the wine glasses near the edge of the shelf. I always put them in back.

CAROL: Some people broke in. Four men. They moved the wine glasses to the edge of the shelf, closed the cabinet door and got away undetected. I didn't call the police because I didn't want to upset you, I know how important those wine glasses are to you . . .

PAUL: They're a wedding present, Carol. It's not funny.

CAROL: All right, it was only two men . . .

PAUL: Why does everything get broken around here? Why don't we have a single complete set of anything anymore.

CAROL: We'll get married again and cash in. We'll get divorced and then get married again.

PAUL: You say the most incredibly stupid things sometimes.

CAROL: So do you. This is still the argument, isn't it? We're still arguing.

PAUL: No. I mean, I don't know.

CAROL: Come on, give me a hand with the salad and show me what I'm supposed to do with the potato-thing you started.

PAUL: I thought I fuck everything up in the kitchen.

CAROL: Sweetie, I was angry. You're not supposed to listen to what I say when I'm angry. You're just supposed to listen to the noise. It's just noise, it's not words. It didn't happen. I didn't say anything. I take it all back.

PAUL: But why did you get angry, that's what I don't understand. What did I say? What did I do?

CAROL: Nothing. There was no reason. I just got angry, that's all.

PAUL: I thought you liked her. I thought you two were friends.

CAROL: Who? Jean? I do. I like her. I think she's super-duper.

PAUL: She's a friend.

CAROL: That's right, she's a friend. That's why I think she's super-duper. That's why I'm dying to meet her new boopsie, that's why I'm dying to know all about him, and it's going to be a great evening and then they're going to go home and leave us alone and we can talk about them behind their backs. Now please, sweetie, give me a hand.

PAUL: You're jealous of her, aren't you?

CAROL: Oh, you know us married women, we're always jealous of the single gals.

PAUL: That's right, make a joke out of it.

CAROL: All right, yes, I'm jealous of Jean. No, I'm not jealous of Jean per se. I'm just . . . I'm pissed off, that's all . . . I'm tired of her . . .

PAUL: Of what?

CAROL: Of her goddamn fucking insinuations. I'm tired of her hovering around all the time . . . I'm tired of . . . I don't like the way she keeps making such an effort to be my friend when she doesn't like me all that much really and I barely like her at all and she knows it and I . . . why does she keep wanting me to go shopping with her and take yoga classes and have lunch?

PAUL: But she *does* like you.

CAROL: She likes you, Paul. She's your friend. She keeps wanting to hang around with me so we can all be friends so she can be your friend and it won't look so obvious what's going on.

PAUL: That's bullshit.

CAROL: You know what she talks about when we're together? You. What a great guy you are. How lucky I am. How she wishes she had someone like you. How much fun she has with us, meaning you, what a perfect couple we are. I mean, I get the point.

PAUL: Well, if you feel that way why do you keep hanging around with her?

CAROL: Because I'm not going to give her the satisfaction of not hanging around with her.

PAUL: You're being absurd, you know that? Jean is a friend. She happens to be a woman. What's wrong with that? What's wrong with the fact that I have a best friend that's a woman? I'm a freak, all right, I'm not normal, I don't like baseball, I don't like poker, I don't like talking about women I'd like to sleep with . . . I don't like beer. I like women, I like to be with them, I prefer it. It's not sexual. I just enjoy spending time with Jean.

CAROL: Well, that's terrific.

PAUL: You have men friends. It's not sexual.

CAROL: Who?

PAUL: Who? Well, Larry, for one.

CAROL: Larry's gay.

PAUL: Gay? He's living with Vickie.

CAROL: He needs time. He's a slow developer.

PAUL: I don't believe this conversation. This isn't us. I don't recognize us in this conversation.

CAROL: Paul. I'm sorry about . . . before. I was just in a good mood. I don't know why you took it the way you did. I mean, don't you think it's a little much for you to get so worked up over a carrot? It's not the end of the world, you know. We do have other carrots. Can I have some wine? *(Paul pours her a glass. She drinks. After a moment)*

PAUL: It wasn't the carrot.

CAROL: Then what was it?

PAUL: It was your poking the carrot with a pencil.

CAROL: This is a really grown-up conversation. I feel really adult.

PAUL: You asked.

CAROL: Paul, could we please have a talk-talk. This is stupid. This isn't getting us anywhere.

PAUL: We have to do the meal.

CAROL: I don't care about the meal right now. If we don't figure out what this was all about before they get here, I swear when she walks through that door with her Elrod or Ogden or Travis or whatever his name is I'm going to shove the roast down her blouse. I can't stand this, Paul, I can't stand it.

PAUL: All right, we'll talk-talk.

CAROL: Good.

PAUL: You first.

CAROL: Can I have a little more wine? *(He pours for both of them. She giggles)*

PAUL: What?

CAROL: You're just so cute. *(They drink)*

PAUL: Well? It's your turn.

CAROL: All right. Talk-talk. I want to tell you what I think happened. This is how I see it. You were making the salad. You were cutting the carrots. I was putting the roast in the oven. You were talking about Jean. Do you agree so far?

PAUL: Yes.

CAROL: O.K. Now . . . you were saying how much fun Jean is. How she really listens to what you're saying, how she really seems to understand you, how she's really interesting. *(Pause)* Well, isn't that what you were saying?

PAUL: What are you getting at?

CAROL: Well, I am too, goddamnit, I'm all those things.

PAUL: I never said you weren't.

CAROL: It's still my turn, let me finish.

PAUL: May I just say one thing?

CAROL: What?

PAUL: I think you're all those things, too. It's just that I happened to be talking about Jean.

CAROL: O.K., you can tell me when it's your turn.

PAUL: I love you, Carol.

CAROL: O.K., don't forget anything you're going to say, but let me finish.

PAUL: You're beautiful . . .

CAROL: You were making the salad . . .

PAUL: You're sexy . . .

CAROL: Thank you . . . so I looked at the salad . . .

PAUL: I want to make love . . .

CAROL: Babe, please, let me finish. Let's just clear this up and don't keep trying to change the subject.

PAUL: All right, but I just want you to know while you're talking, I want you to keep in mind the fact that I have an erection.

CAROL: Paul, why do you always do this!

PAUL: Get an erection . . . ?

CAROL: Forget it . . . *(Carol rises angrily and starts out)*

PAUL: All right, I'm sorry, I'm sorry, I'm sorry. I'm an asshole. Come back.

CAROL: Will you listen to me?

PAUL: Yes, I will listen to you. Come on, sit down. *(Carol sits back down)*

CAROL: You were cutting the carrots and talking about Jean and you didn't see me but I was looking at you. And I was wondering why you always think everyone is so great and interesting and wonderful all the time. And then I wondered what it would be like if I was the same way . . . if I felt the same way about everything . . . maybe that would be better, maybe I'd be a better person . . . I'm just telling you what I was thinking about, and then suddenly I thought you're the most beautiful man I ever saw and that surprised me because we've been married six years and sometimes I look at you and you seem like someone I just met and I want to have a date with you and make you fall in love with me and then I realize you're my husband and it seems amazing to me. So, anyway, I saw you cutting the carrots and I thought wouldn't it be nice if we were bunny rabbits.

PAUL. Bunny rabbits?

CAROL: Yeah. We could be furry brown bunny rabbits and dig a hole in the ground and cuddle up together and . . . and never ever see anybody . . . and that'd be all I want. It was just a thought. But I also thought this isn't the kind of thing I can say to you because . . . well, because that kind of thing makes you uncomfortable so . . . so instead I . . .

PAUL: You poked my carrot with a pencil.

CAROL: Sweetie, I was just joking around. It's a carrot, for Christ sake. I thought it was funny. I was having a good time, like wives can have with their husbands, just like their husbands can have with their best nonsexual female friends.

PAUL: I asked you to stop. I didn't get angry at first. I asked nicely. The carrot is for the salad. You don't poke a pencil into a carrot that is going into a salad. It's unsanitary, you could get lead poisoning.

CAROL: Graphite poisoning, they don't use lead in pencils. Look, Jean's weird, she's very weird, but she's not so weird that she's going to go rooting through the salad looking for carrots with puncture holes. We're not suspected of being carrot puncturers.

PAUL: Why did you do it, that's all I want to know.

CAROL: I told you, I wanted to be a bunny rabbit.

PAUL: Bunny rabbits eat carrots. They don't poke pencils into them.

CAROL: I was being a bunny rabbit with penis envy. *(They laugh briefly)*

PAUL: This still feels like an argument. *(Suddenly Carol cries openly, no warning. Paul holds her)*

CAROL: What we said before . . . we didn't mean it, did we?

PAUL: God, I hope not.

CAROL: You don't want to split up, do you?

PAUL: Of course not . . . we were just . . . I don't know.

CAROL: Why did we say it?

PAUL: It doesn't matter. We didn't mean it.

CAROL: We're the best couple I know. You're not tired of being together, are you?

PAUL: Carol, we were just angry. That's all. Let's forget about it.

CAROL: Jean told me people think we're the perfect couple.

PAUL: Well, then we can't split up, can we? We have too much to live up to. We can't disappoint all our friends.

CAROL: Splitting up was not mentioned tonight. I declare it to have never been mentioned.

PAUL: I second the motion.

CAROL: Let's get drunk before they get here. Let's be really disgusting hosts. See if we can gross-out Jean's new guy. Damn, the beans. Pour me a little more wine. *(Carol exits into the kitchen. Paul pours more wine)*

PAUL: I never thought you were jealous, that's all. You never have been. That's why I was surprised when . . . we have all these friends, we see them all the time, we talk about them behind their backs, they talk about us behind our backs, we all wonder who has the best life, the best relationship, the best sex, the best apartment, the most happiness. I mean, that's what friends are for. *(Carol reenters)*

CAROL: Beans are on. What?

PAUL: I said that's what friends are for, to make you feel your life isn't as good as theirs, or that it's better, or that it even makes any difference. What are you looking at?

CAROL: It scared me, the things we said.

PAUL: It scared me, too.

CAROL: Was it moving out of the city? Have you changed your mind?

PAUL: No, I want to get out of here.

CAROL: Was it having a baby?

PAUL: No, I want that. I want everything we've been planning. I want it. I'm happy.

CAROL: Then what was it?

PAUL: Do you really think Jean's trying to get something going with me?

CAROL: If she isn't, she's stupid. I would if I were her.

PAUL: Come here. *(Carol sits on his lap)* I don't know why we talked about splitting up. I don't want to. And I know you don't want to. So, therefore, we never said it. All right.

CAROL: I've had a terrible daydream . . . I've had it a bunch of times.

PAUL: What is it?

CAROL: You remember the first week? The vegetables?

PAUL: I remember.

CAROL: Did we ever get out of bed?

PAUL: No. Except for the vegetables.

CAROL: Remember that note they sent up, the people downstairs?

PAUL: "We appreciate the fact that you are in love but some of us have to go to work in the morning and we'd appreciate it if you could express your moments of pleasure without jungle noises. Regards, 4B." The Millers.

CAROL: Yeah.

PAUL: Is that the daydream?

CAROL: No, but it's like that a little . . . we're lying in bed watching TV . . . but the bed isn't really there and the TV and the room and the apartment aren't really there . . . it's more like a hologram, you can just put your hand through it, but we're there. We're the only things that are solid, and we're sort of suspended. That's how it feels. And on the TV there's no programs, just commercials, all commercials and we keep waiting for a story to begin but it never does. And all the actors in the commercials are friends of ours. Bob and Marge are selling Toyotas. Jean's selling fur coats and then the ads get weird and they start plugging new identities and countries you can have sent to you in the mail for a one-week trial period, and all our friends on TV look so happy, kind of like they're in a trance. And then we look at each other and realize that all we want to do is make love suspended in the middle of all this, so we roll over and start sliding around and just then . . . just right when we're about to disappear into each other, the doorbell rings. That's all.

Ding-dong. It's terrifying. We're both scared out of our minds but we don't know why.

PAUL: That's it? That's the daydream.

CAROL: Marge thinks I should see a shrink.

PAUL: Marge thinks everyone should see a shrink. *(The phone rings)*

CAROL: Don't answer it.

PAUL *(To phone)*: We're not here, sorry. We went out. We don't live here anymore. We went to Canada. We don't have a phone up there. Carol's having a baby and I'm writing a book and we're happier than you are, so fuck you. Maybe it's Jean? *(The phone rings once more, then stops)* Whew, that was close. What's that smell? Shit, the potatoes. Hang on. Pour me some wine. *(He gets up, stumbles a little)* Heeey, I'm getting drunk. *(He exits. The phone rings. On the second ring . . .)*

CAROL: I'll get it. *(Answers the phone)* Hello? Oh, hi, Jean . . . no, no everything's, we . . . yeah, we've been in. Oh, well, it must have been a wrong number. Listen, Jean . . . it's O.K., we have plenty of wine . . . Well, it's up to you, if you want to . . . no, we have dessert. We don't need anything, Jean, we're fine, don't bring anything, don't even come. *(Pause)* I was just joking . . . it's from a TV show we were just watching. O.K., about ten minutes. See you. *(Carol hangs up. Paul enters with a tray of potatoes burnt to a crisp)*

PAUL: This didn't work.

CAROL: What happened?

PAUL: They're a little overdone. You're right, I fuck up everything in the kitchen.

CAROL: I'll make rice.

PAUL: I'll make the salad. Who was that?

CAROL: Jean.

PAUL: She's not coming?

CAROL: She's coming.

PAUL: Why didn't you tell her . . . ?

CAROL: We invited them.

PAUL: This is going to be one fucked-up dinner. Friends.

CAROL: Good old friends. *(They laugh)*

PAUL: When are they going to be here?

CAROL: About ten minutes.

PAUL: That means we have time.

CAROL: Now? Right now?

PAUL: Why not? Then when they come we'll know something they don't know. I wonder if it shows.

CAROL: I slept with someone.

PAUL: What?

CAROL: Else. Someone else. I slept with someone else.

PAUL: Oh. Why don't we sit down? *(They sit down)* You slept with someone else.

CAROL: Yes.

PAUL: I see. Um. Why?

CAROL: I don't know.

PAUL: All right, then, who?

CAROL: A friend of Eric's

PAUL: What's his name?

CAROL: I don't know. I don't know anything about him. I just slept with him. I met him on a bus with Eric. He bought me a coffee and then we went to his place and . . . it didn't mean anything. It really didn't.

PAUL: That's good to know. I feel better already.

CAROL: I bought a pound of apricots afterwards and I ate them all and got sick. And I felt better.

PAUL: So that's what's been going on here. That's what this was all about.

CAROL: I don't know what you mean.

PAUL: The argument. What happened in the kitchen. I wish I'd known the rules.

CAROL: No. There's no connection. I wanted to sleep with someone else, that's all. It didn't matter who. He just happened to be there. I thought about you when I was with him. I thought maybe now I'll be more interesting. Or at least maybe I'll feel more interesting.

PAUL: Is it my turn yet? Are we still having a talk-talk? I'm not sure where we are right now.

CAROL: Because I'm not very interesting, am I? We go out with friends and we have a great time and you get into a good mood and you joke around and then when we get home you're never like that. You get quiet. You don't joke around with me because I'm just not very interesting and I thought maybe if I did something I'd never do, then I'd be . . . instead of being the kind of person who'd never do certain things I'd become . . . I'd be different than you thought I was. And you'd joke around more. But it didn't change anything. I was still exactly the same as I was, and we were the same. Everything was the same. And then later . . . much later . . . I was happy that everything was the same. I was happy that it hadn't changed anything.

PAUL: What do you mean much later? When did this happen.

CAROL: About three years ago.

PAUL: Jesus, Carol, I mean, Jesus . . . and you're telling me now?

CAROL: Because it doesn't matter. I want you to understand that sleeping with someone doesn't necessarily mean . . . doesn't change anything. Between us.

PAUL: Your logic is really incredible, Carol.

CAROL: What I'm saying is that it doesn't matter that you've been sleeping with Jean. I'm jealous, but I don't care.

PAUL: What? Who says I've been sleeping with Jean?

CAROL: It doesn't matter.

PAUL: I'm not sleeping with Jean. I've never slept with Jean. I don't want to sleep with Jean!

CAROL: You've never slept with her?

PAUL: No. Who told you that?

CAROL: No one. It's just the way you keep talking about her . . . I thought you . . . Do you want to sleep with her?

PAUL: No. Not at all.

CAROL: I made a mistake.

PAUL: Yes you did. Oh, boy, did you ever! You're incredible, Carol . . . you know that . . . What are you trying to do here? You waited for three years to tell me this because you thought I was sleeping with Jean?

CAROL: I didn't wait. I never even thought about it. It just came up.

PAUL: I don't believe you.

CAROL (*Rage*): Why not? Why don't you believe everything about me? Why aren't I someone who could do anything and you'd believe it? Why can't I poke your carrot and it's

O.K.? Why do I have to be someone who doesn't poke carrots if I want to? Why do I always have to be me?

PAUL: Carol, calm down . . .

CAROL: No, tell me why I can't be someone else. Why can't I be you? Why can't I go out and teach history and have a roomful of kids who think I'm brilliant and funny and smart and who respect me . . . ?

PAUL: Stop it. Carol, stop it . . .

CAROL: Why don't you think I'm all those things? Why do you think I just cook and clean and go to bed with only you and take part-time jobs where people don't think I'm anything except someone doing a part-time job. It's not enough. Nothing is enough.

PAUL: I make you feel like you're not enough.

CAROL: Everything . . . everything. I'm not enough, you're not enough, nothing is enough. That's why you want to split up, isn't it?

PAUL: I don't want to split up.

CAROL: You said you did.

PAUL: I thought we decided we'd never said that.

CAROL: But we did. We said it. If we say something it's because we mean it. We may mean something else too, we may mean exactly the opposite, but we also mean what we say.

PAUL: You're the one that slept with someone. Why did you do that? Because I'm enough? You were so happy with me that you went out and fucked Eric's friend.

CAROL: I didn't. It just happened. I didn't do it. Nothing happened.

PAUL: Well, if that's the way you feel, then maybe . . . if this is what's really going on with us . . . maybe we . . . maybe we should think seriously about ending it.

CAROL: All right.

PAUL: All right.

CAROL: After dinner or before? *(Pause. They burst out laughing)*

PAUL: This is some argument.

CAROL: You don't have your period or anything, do you?

PAUL: Want some more wine?

CAROL: O.K. *(He pours more wine)* You've never slept with anyone else?

PAUL: So we'll be even?

CAROL: I'm not talking about Jean. I mean anyone.

PAUL: No.

CAROL: Look at me. Never? Not once?

PAUL: No. All right. Once. Twice, twice. Only twice.

CAROL: You did?

PAUL: Yes, once with . . .

CAROL: Don't tell me. I don't want to know who. I only want to know that it happened. And that it didn't make any difference.

PAUL: Actually it was twice with the same person.

CAROL: Twice? You mean you liked her?

PAUL: No. Not really. She wanted to. I wanted to. We thought it might be nice and we . . . I guess we wanted to know if what we thought was true.

CAROL: Was it?

PAUL: Yes.

CAROL: It was nice?

PAUL: Yes.

CAROL: Well then, that's that.

PAUL: What do you mean?

CAROL: We're even. We'll make your two equal one and it cancels out and that means we're . . . *(Carol cries and runs out. Paul pours the last of one wine bottle into his glass. Carol comes back into the doorway, calm)* Are you going to do the salad?

PAUL: Who'd get the apartment?

CAROL: What?

PAUL: It was mine before you moved in but you fixed up. We have to figure out who gets to stay here.

CAROL: This isn't an argument anymore. *(Paul slams a plate on the floor)*

PAUL *(Rage)*: I hate you, Carol. I hate the way you dress, I hate the way you do your hair, I hate the things you say, I hate your jealousy, I hate the way you've done the apartment, I hate the way you put everything emotional on your terms, I hate the fact that you don't like my friends, I hate the way you make love, I hate being in this apartment with you, I hate the way you look at me, I hate this city,

I hate teaching, I hate my life . . . *(Banging on the floor below. Paul looks down at the floor)* Fuck you, Mr. and Mrs. Miller, just fuck you, you don't like it when we screw, you don't like it when we fight, what do you want from us, this is our home, we live here, mind your own goddamned business. Man, I can't wait to get out of this city. *(Pause)* I'm sorry, Carol.

CAROL: Now we know what's happening to the dishes.

PAUL: I never did that before.

CAROL: You can break more if you feel like it. Then we'll get divorced and then we'll get married again and we'll get all new dishes.

PAUL: Carol, Carol . . . *(They embrace. They kiss)* What happened?

CAROL: I don't know.

PAUL: I even had a pretty good day.

CAROL: Let's forget it.

PAUL: It's so weird. We live here. We go out and work. We see . . . friends. We eat. We make love. We're married. This is our home. And that's all.

CAROL: I love you. We'll go to the country. You'll do your book. We'll have a baby. I love you *(They come out of their embrace)* I better put on the rice.

PAUL: Boy, do I ever not want company tonight.

CAROL: It's too late. They're hurtling toward us.

PAUL: You know what? Why don't we put a note on the door. An envelope with twenty dollars in it and a note . . . "Dear Jean, we changed our minds, sorry, here's some money, go out and have a good time. Love, Carol and Paul."

CAROL: Salad. Yummy yummy.

PAUL: I'll explain it to her tomorrow. We'll just turn off all the lights and pretend we're not here.

CAROL: We can't do that.

PAUL: Why not? What did they ever do for us?

CAROL: God, what would she tell Elrod.

PAUL: Emery.

CAROL: Paul . . . you're so beautiful. I love you so much. You know that's the first really bad argument we've had in . . . in a long time. I didn't like it.

PAUL: I didn't either. We really should fuck and make up.

CAROL: Really?

PAUL: We could even stand by the door when they knock. We could listen to what they say.

CAROL: Paul . . . tell me just one thing, O.K.

PAUL: What?

CAROL: Did it make any difference . . . being with whoever it was you were with?

PAUL: Not really.

CAROL: It's weird, isn't it? Something like that can happen and it's like nothing ever happened. Tell me about it.

PAUL: Let's just forget it.

CAROL: I told you about mine. We can make it a talk-talk. You never got a turn.

PAUL: You really want to know?

CAROL: Not who she was. I don't want to know her name. Is it anyone I know?

PAUL: No.

CAROL: Do friends of ours know her?

PAUL: Some.

CAROL: Tell me what happened. No, first open another bottle, and then tell me what happened.

PAUL: All right. *(Paul opens the new bottle, with a corkscrew. Carol watches him. He pours for himself. He pours for her. They smile at each other)* O.K., what do you want to know first?

CAROL: Let me see. What did she look like? Did she have nice breasts?

PAUL: Yes.

CAROL: Nicer than mine?

PAUL: No. Exactly the same. In quality. And quantity.

CAROL: Jean has nice breasts, doesn't she?

PAUL: So-so.

CAROL: She has a nice tush.

PAUL: Yes, that she has. But a nice tush does not a woman make.

CAROL: Then what happened. How did you meet her?

PAUL: At a party.

CAROL: What did you say to her?

PAUL: Hello, you have breasts just like my wife.

CAROL: You did not.

PAUL: No, I said hi, I'm Paul. Pretty clever, huh?

CAROL: What did she say?

PAUL: She said "Hello, Paul, if you make love to me, the world will go away and it won't matter that God is dead."

CAROL: Was she a student? She sounds like a student.

PAUL: I was kidding.

CAROL: I know. What did she say?

PAUL: Hello, I'm Carol.

CAROL: Come on, be serious.

PAUL: I am. That's what she said. Her name was Carol.

CAROL: I don't like that. You shouldn't sleep around with Carols.

PAUL: O.K.

CAROL: Then what happened?

PAUL: Then we were in bed . . .

CAROL: Wait a minute, what happened in between?

PAUL: Oh, well, first we went to a supermarket and bought a whole cartful of vegetables.

CAROL: That was us.

PAUL: I did the same thing with her. It's the only way I know how to seduce anyone. No, the real reason I bought vegetables was because the first week we were together was the nicest time in my life and I wanted to find out whether it was you or the vegetables.

CAROL: Which was it? No, just tell me what happened . . .

PAUL: We went to her place and chopped up all the vegetables and laughed because when we were all done there were so many vegetables we didn't have any place to put them.

CAROL: So you got a big plastic garbage liner . . .

PAUL: Yes, and dumped it all inside and took off all our clothes and put our arms in the bag and mixed it all up and we had enough salad for a week. And then we sat in bed for a week and ate salad from this big plastic bag whenever we were hungry, and the neighbors downstairs sent up this note . . .

CAROL: Paul, you're talking about us. I want to know about her.

PAUL: She doesn't exist. Nothing ever happened with her. I decree. Nothing ever happened except with us. It was the happiest time in my life. You, the way you smell, the way you touched me, and the sound of your voice . . . and the salad . . . and the bed . . . and there was nothing else in the world. Nothing else. And I thought this is the most perfect woman there ever was. She's all I need.

CAROL: Did you really think that?

PAUL: Yes.

CAROL: Do you still?

PAUL *(Faintest hesitation):* Yes.

CAROL: We'll pretend we're not here.

PAUL: And I won't teach tomorrow. We'll stay in bed all day and all night . . .

CAROL: . . . and eat salad and watch television. Bunny rabbits. See what I mean?

PAUL: You win.

CAROL: Paul, I love you, I love you, I love you.

(They embrace, starting to make love. The doorbell rings. They freeze. They look toward the sound. It rings again.)

(Blackout.)

End of Play

≡ABROAD≡

Split, Part 2

Abroad was written for and
is dedicated to Alan Schneider
and the drama students
of the Juilliard School.

Abroad was first presented at Ensemble Studio Theatre, New York (Curt Dempster, Artistic Director) on April 13, 1978, under the title *Split*. Carole Rothman directed the following cast:

MARGE	Mary Elaine Monti
PAUL	Mandy Patinkin
WAITER	Daniel Stern
CAROL	Elaine Bromka
JEAN	Kathryn Grody
JAY	Tom Noonan
BOB	Chip Zien

The play was revived at Second Stage Theatre, New York (Robyn Goodman, Carole Rothman, Artistic Directors) on April 4, 1980, as the second half of a double bill that began with the one-act play *At Home*. The title of the evening was *Split*. Carole Rothman directed the following cast:

MARGE	Pamela Blair
PAUL	John Heard
WAITER	Paul McCrane
CAROL	Brooke Adams
JEAN	Polly Draper
JAY	Rick Lieberman
BOB	Chip Zien

Characters

MARGE
PAUL
WAITER
CAROL
JEAN
JAY
BOB

Scene 1

Table—a café. Paul and Marge with coffee. Café noises.

MARGE: O.K. Stevie Wonder's blind. He's black and he's blind. That's a lot of things to have going against you, right, but instead of letting it mess him up he turns into this genius level songwriter-arranger-performer who's very fulfilled spiritually according to his songs anyway plus he's famous and rich and cool and he's able to write all these incredibly happy upbeat numbers . . . and here I am this white middle-class girl with two good eyes and a college education. That's what I was trying to explain to my shrink. Stevie Wonder makes me deeply deeply depressed. The fact that he exists is really depressing to me. And of course he said I was being adolescent, which he always says. I mean I don't need him to tell me I'm adolescent. I need him to tell me it's all right that I'm adolescent. *(Pause)* Do you want to stop talking and we'll just sit for a while?

PAUL: No, that's O.K. Talk. It's O.K.

MARGE: Why don't you tell me about what happened?

PAUL: There's nothing to tell.

MARGE: Well, for instance, was it more of a thing where you left her, or did she leave you or what?

PAUL: I don't want to keep boring my friends talking about it. People split up all the time.

MARGE: A lot of them haven't been married for six years.

PAUL: A lot of them have.

MARGE: A lot of them aren't my best friends.

PAUL: It's just over, that's all. It's over. There's nothing to say.

MARGE: You know what I think, Paul? I think it's temporary. You guys just belong together. *(Pause)* Look, you want me to move in with you?

PAUL: Move in? You?

MARGE: Just for a few days. While you're getting used to Carol not being there. I'd invite you to stay with me and Bob but Bob's learning how to play GO . . . it's this Japanese game and you'd probably end up having to let him teach you how to play, which might not be kind of what you want to be doing for the next few days.

PAUL: No it's not what I had in mind. Thanks anyway.

MARGE: I'm just trying to help. It's really lonely at the beginning. I remember when I left this guy once. He said he was a genuine Oglala Sioux Indian and I believed him for two years. Blond hair and blue eyes the guy had. He looked like Sven the Swede. Boy, was he full of shit. And I was really naive. Anyway, I really missed him at the beginning, even though I didn't like him. You don't look too good.

PAUL: There have been times in my life when I felt better, I must admit. It's crazy; last night I . . . I didn't feel like calling anyone. I didn't feel like doing anything. I was just sitting at home watching TV and getting a little drunk and I found I was thinking an awful lot about suicide.

MARGE: Well. It's something you should think a lot about before you take it up.

PAUL: I'm glad you called, Margie. And I have to start teaching again tomorrow.

MARGE: You want me to talk to Carol?

PAUL: What's the point? It's just over.

MARGE: I'll talk to her. First chance I get I'm going to talk to her. I like you guys. I hate to see this happening to you. Other people, I'm glad. You, I'm not glad. *(Pause)* Oh, that's the other thing I meant to tell you about Stevie Wonder. He has this manager, I forgot what the guy's name is, but he goes around killing people. Really. This guy I'm working with, the video guy I told you about before . . . Oh, I didn't tell you what he does, he takes movies, well, actually they're videotapes, he takes these tapes of himself dancing to all the hit tunes . . . all alone in his studio. That's one of the things he does, and the other thing . . . oh, and he doesn't wear any clothes. Well, he told me his sister works at a place where there's this guy who used to work for Stevie Wonder's manager and he saw the guy kill someone. He actually saw it. Isn't that amazing? Oh, and anyway, this video guy shows his tapes at parties. And all his friends dance to them, but they turn the sound off so they're only dancing to the way the guy moves and he's a terrible dancer. Don't tell him I said that if you meet him. I'll tell you next time he has a party. *(Pause)* Don't worry, Paul. I'll talk to her. It'll be all right. *(Enter Waiter with small tray)*

WAITER: Coffee and English?

MARGE: Me.

WAITER: And ice coffee.

PAUL: And some milk with that, please.

WAITER: Did you hear something about an assassination?

MARGE: What assassination?

WAITER: That's what I was wondering. I guess you didn't hear anything, huh? A guy just said. I think that's what he said. Maybe it was "examination." Gotta get my ears checked. Milk, right?

PAUL: Yes. *(The Waiter exits)*

MARGE: I know just what I'm going to say, too. Don't worry, Paul, really.

Scene 2

Carol alone. A street.

JEAN *(Off)*: Carol! Carol! *(Carol looks around. Jean enters)*

CAROL: Jeannie . . . hi . . .

JEAN: How's it going?

CAROL . . . Oh, pretty good . . .

JEAN: I thought you'd be at yoga on Tuesday but you weren't there.

CAROL: Oh, you know, stuff's been happening. Hey, you look great.

JEAN: Thanks. You look . . . you shouldn't skip yoga, you know.

CAROL: Which way are you walking?

JEAN: I'm waiting for someone. Oh, Carol, this guy is so funny you gotta meet him, he's a genuine totally crazy person. You doing anything. I mean, right now?

CAROL: Yeah. Well. Why?

JEAN: Jay's taking me to this friend of his's place, he's got a loft or something. We're gonna sit around, get stoned, eat organic peanut butter, pretend it's 1968, you know. Why don't you come with us?

CAROL: Well. I don't know. I'm supposed to meet someone.

JEAN: O.K., some other time. I almost forgot. I meant to call you and everything. I found a place.

CAROL: Great. Where is it?

JEAN: No, not for me, for you guys. For next year. I got these friends in Vermont, they're renting their farm and, Carol, I want to tell you this place . . . it's like you won't believe it . . . Trees all over the place and totally isolated . . . it's on the side of a hill looking over a valley with a lake . . . and . . . and and and . . . it's facing west. Well, you guys are into sunsets, right?

CAROL: Right, right. Sounds real nice.

JEAN: Real nice? Carol, this place is total nature city. And listen, all that money you guys've been saving . . . you won't have to spend half of it. These friends of mine aren't into heavy profit. I told them about Paul writing a book and you doing a baby thing and they got so into having that kind of year happen on their farm they'll probably let you have it for free. I got their number . . . *(Jean checks in handbag)* . . . well, it's somewhere in the garbage bag here . . . look, I'll never find it now. I'll call you. *(She has pulled out cigarettes and takes one out)*

CAROL: Can I have one?

JEAN: I never knew you smoked.

CAROL: I'm just learning. Jeannie, have you been out of town or something?

JEAN: No, but I would love to get out. Maybe we could take a trip up to the farm together. Are you free next weekend?

CAROL: Very.

JEAN: O.K., I'll tell you what. I'll call you . . . tonight. When'll you be home?

CAROL: Paul ought to be back after school.

JEAN: O.K., I'll call him at five. I'll call him at school. I have the number . . . somewhere.

CAROL: Jeannie . . .

JEAN: What?

CAROL: I'm not meeting anyone. I told you I was meeting someone. I'm not. I don't know why I said it. I can't believe you don't know . . . I thought everybody . . . it's all anyone seems to be able to talk about and now you don't know about it and I hate that too . . .

JEAN: What's going on? Hot news?

CAROL: Medium hot. Depends on how you look at it. Paul and I sort of parted company two days ago.

JEAN: What????!!!

CAROL: Yeah. End-of-marriage sort of thing.

JEAN: You and Paul.

CAROL: Me and Paul. Paul and Carol. Finito.

JEAN: I don't get it. Divorce and everything.

CAROL: Yeah. I guess so.

JEAN: This I don't believe.

CAROL: Why not? Everyone else is doing it. Don't want to be behind the times.

JEAN: Yeah, but you and Paul. I mean, you were married, you know . . . like *married* married.

CAROL: Yeah, well now we're like split split.

JEAN: Jesus Christ.

CAROL: That's exactly what I said this morning. I woke up and there was this funny moment when I didn't know where I was because the other side of the bed was unoccupied. After one thousand six hundred and thirty-eight mornings . . . And what I thought was Jesus Christ. So I went to church . . . first time in ten years.

JEAN: Carol . . . I don't know what to say.

CAROL: When I got there the place was cordoned off and there was this funny little bald priest running around telling everyone sorry, no one allowed in today . . . they're filming an episode of *Kojak*, sorry . . . and for some reason I found that really comforting. Bald priest. Bald Kojak. All these bald people.

JEAN: We should get together and talk, Carol.

CAROL: Yeah.

JEAN: Where you staying?

CAROL: The Gramercy Hotel.

JEAN: The Gramercy Hotel????

CAROL: I just want to be on my own for a while. I don't want people to know where I am. Everybody keeps inviting me out and I can't tell if it's because they really want to see me or they just feel sorry. I mean I don't need that . . .

JEAN: Oh, shit, here comes Jay . . . JAY!! JAY!! He is so funny. OVER HERE!!! I'll call you, Carol . . . *(Enter Jay very laid back and unfunny)*

JAY: There's a great accident around the corner. You want to go over and watch it?

JEAN: Jay, this is my friend Carol.

JAY: Hi. You want to come over and watch an accident with us? They're just clearing up. It's very interesting.

CAROL: I've got to go.

JAY: After that we're going over to this friend of mine's loft and get stoned and pretend it's 1968. You can come if you want.

CAROL: No thanks. *(To Jean)* He's not so funny.

JAY: What?

JEAN *(Hiding laugh)*: She has to meet a bunch of people. Jay. She wants to be on her own.

JAY: What's being said here? What did I miss?

CAROL: I'll see you at yoga.

JAY: You want to do some video, Carol?

JEAN: Not now, Jay. Let's go watch the accident. I'll call you, Carol.

JAY: With tape, you know. You show it on a TV screen. I'm ready to get into using a lot of new people and I get very strong vibes from you. That usually means good things for video. You have a very kinetic face. Have you ever thought about video?

CAROL: Well, I . . . no.

JAY: You should think about it. You'd be really beautiful on tape. Here's my card. Oh, yeah, that's the real-estate office. You can reach me there during the day. I don't have a phone in the loft. You know, like why give people a chance to invade your trip twenty-four hours a day? Right?

JEAN: The accident's going to be over soon, Jay.

CAROL: O.K. Maybe I'll call.

JAY: Ciao.

JEAN *(To Jay)*: Be with you in a moment. *(Jay walks off, not looking back)*

JEAN: He's not funny, is he?

CAROL: He's weird.

JEAN: Yeah, he is. Well, what do you do on Sundays, you know? Say hi to Paul when . . . Jesus. *(Jean goes. Carol takes a drag on the cigarette. Forces herself to like it)*

Scene 3

Rug—living room. Bob and Paul play GO on the floor.

BOB: No no no no no no no no no no. You remember what I told you that was called. That's Nichi no Tori. "Horse jumps pond, water goes away." That's what they call it in Japanese and it means I can take all your stones. You're not thinking conceptually. You can't play GO if you don't think conceptually.

PAUL: Bob. This looks like a good game, you know. It looks like a very interesting game, and some time I'd really like to learn how to play it. But not now, huh? Do you mind?

BOB: No. It's cool. You want to watch TV? There's the worst movie of the week on five.

PAUL: No.

BOB: Want to get drunk?

PAUL: No.

BOB: Leaving Carol hasn't made you a more interesting person to be with.

PAUL: I'm sorry. I wish someone would talk about something else.

BOB: Look. When something like this happens, two things happen. One thing is everyone wants to help out, right, because everyone knows what it feels like to break up, and the other thing that happens is nobody knows what to do because everybody realizes that the person they want to help feels terrible and wiped out and probably like they're not worth helping or even being with which makes it impossible for people who want to help to help.

PAUL: Marge is working pretty late.

BOB: She's working for this jerk who does videotape. I hardly ever see her. I mean, there's nothing going on. I think he's gay in the first place. He takes movies of himself . . .

PAUL: . . . Dancing naked, I know.

BOB: What a weird thing to do. I wonder if he'll still be at it when he's sixty. Can you just see it? Whole family comes over to his loft for Christmas and he shows tapes of himself as a young man dancing naked to "Voulez-Vous Coucher avec Moi Ce Soir." What did your daddy do for a living? Oh, he took off his clothes and danced naked in front of a camera in an empty studio.

PAUL: I heard he makes a lot of money in real estate.

BOB: Yeah. Boy. Everything's really weird.

PAUL: Anyway.

BOB: Yeah.

PAUL: What's this all about? You said you had something to talk to me about.

BOB: I did?

PAUL: What's the matter with you, Bob? You called me up and invited me over and you said you and Marge had been talking about me and Carol splitting up and you had this very important thing to tell me . . . isn't that exactly what happened?

BOB: We ought to wait for Marge to get home.

PAUL: Why? What's the big mystery?

BOB: There's no mystery.

PAUL: Then why are you acting so weird?

BOB: I'm not acting weird.

PAUL: You are too. You're acting very weird.

BOB: No I'm not. I am not acting weird, Paul. Your head's in a weird place, that's all. Everything looks weird to you.

PAUL: This is a dumb conversation. Let's change the subject.

BOB: Very good idea. What do you want to talk about?

PAUL: What I really want to talk about is what you and Marge invited me over here tonight to talk about.

BOB: You're right. This is a stupid conversation.

PAUL: I'm gonna go home. It's getting late.

BOB: No. Look. Just wait'll Marge gets home, O.K.? We wanted to talk to you together.

PAUL: Why?

BOB: O.K. Whew. I don't know. I guess I better tell you. Man, this feels strange. O.K. Well, it's kind of about. It's partly about me and Marge. And partly about. Has she told you much about what we've been into lately?

PAUL: Marge?

BOB: Yeah.

PAUL: No. I mean, maybe. I don't know. I mean what do you mean?

BOB: Well. We've been sort of exploring this area that we hadn't been aware of before. Well, we were aware of it. You know, marriage is . . . it can be very kind of very insular. You know. A man and a woman together all the time. Marriage can sort of cut you off from a lot of experience. And anyway, what me and Marge were thinking was that maybe you'd let that happen to you. You and Carol.

PAUL: That's what you thought.

BOB: Look, man, this isn't a criticism. Believe me. Believe me I know what it can be like. Me and Marge. It happened to us. I mean, we didn't even know we'd gotten into such a closed-in trip and then when we realized it . . . well, we knew we had to do something about it soon or else everything that was good between us . . . fffft!! You know?

PAUL: What the hell are you talking about, Bob?

BOB: Swinging.

PAUL: Swinging? You mean two couples together? Is that what you mean? You've been doing that? You and Marge? And two other people?

BOB: . . . or more . . .

PAUL: Together? Having sex? Together? All of you?

BOB: It surprises you.

PAUL: Yeah, I mean. Yeah. You and Marge. Whew.

BOB: Paul, I know what you're probably thinking, but believe me, it's a beautiful thing. It's brought an incredible amount of openness in our marriage and it's helped us not to be afraid of our . . . well, ourselves. And each other and other people. We're each totally free to explore other people, but we're also together, so we can enjoy each other's explorations and it's just amazing how you become aware of the fact that society has crippled you by defining sexuality in such a narrow and limited way. And we're all victims, Paul. You take Persia and India and some of those ancient civilizations . . .

PAUL: Horseshit, Bob, just horseshit. Horse shit. I mean, O.K., so you and Marge are getting tired of each other and you don't know what to do about it. What's that got to do with me?

BOB: We saved our marriage, Paul.

PAUL: Oh, man. Look. If you mean like you thought you'd try to help me and Carol get back together by inviting us over here for a little group sex, I mean, no, thank you. Is that what you had in mind? Is that what you wanted to talk about?

BOB: I guess I'm not explaining it right. I knew we should wait till Marge gets home. It's really more sort of her idea. I mean, I don't think it's a bad idea, don't get me wrong. I just sort of thought, I told her the timing's wrong. Anyway. It beats sitting at home alone.

PAUL: Anything beats sitting at home alone.

BOB: It's just we can't figure why you guys split up. You were such a great marriage.

PAUL: That's what everybody says.

BOB: No one expected it.

PAUL: Like that. *(Snaps finger)* Literally. We were joking around. We were making up after a fight, laughing and everything, and Carol said, "Well, if we're going to fight all the time maybe we ought to just split up." It was a joke. I mean, we never fight. Never. We laugh, we laugh all the time. And instead of laughing, suddenly we were talking very seriously about ending it and we were crying and stuff.

BOB: Jesus.

PAUL: Yeah. Just like that.

BOB: It was a mood. That's all. You've got to get together and talk.

PAUL: It was more than that. It must have been. I don't know what the hell it was.

BOB: You know what I think sometimes. Things just happen and you never know why. You figure out all these reasons to explain it, but it still doesn't make sense. Like a few days ago I started wondering why I was a carpenter. And I figured it out. I figured out a lot of reasons. I'm good at it. It pays a lot. I work my own hours. My uncle was a carpenter. All these reasons, but I still wonder why I'm a carpenter. I mean, I still wonder much more than I believe any of the reasons I came up with to explain why I'm a carpenter. *(Pause)* That was clear, wasn't it?

PAUL: So. You guys have been swinging, huh. *(Paul laughs. Bob laughs. They both laugh hysterically)*

Scene 4

Bare stage—video loft. Jay with video camera, running. Carol and the Waiter are being taped. Very awkward. Improvise.

WAITER: Well. Ah. What kind of stuff are we supposed to do, you know?

JAY *(Filming)*: That's fine. Anything that happens is valid.

WAITER: Oh. O.K. Well. Hmmm. Let's see. I'm Jeff. I'm a waiter.

CAROL: I'm Carol. I'm . . . I don't do anything at the moment.

WAITER: Hi, Carol.

CAROL: Hi, Jeff.

WAITER: Is that O.K.? Is that the kind of thing you want?

JAY: Great. Great. Keep going.

WAITER: What's your name again? Jay? That's it. This is a great loft, huh.

CAROL: Yeah. You're not a friend of his?

WAITER: I just met him. My favorite color is blue.

CAROL: What? Oh. My favorite color is . . . it used to be yellow but it's getting to be lime green. I feel really uncomfortable in front of the camera.

JAY: It's great. It's beautiful. You two are perfect together.

WAITER: You want to play a game?

CAROL: O.K.

WAITER: What do you want to play?

CAROL: I don't care. Whatever you want to play.

WAITER: Do you know that one where I start a story and then I stop and you take it up where I left off until you stop and then I keep on?

CAROL: I don't know. It's O.K. We'll play that. I mean if it's all right. Can we play a game in front of the camera?

JAY: Why do you keep asking for permission? Whatever happens let it.

CAROL: Well, I mean, it's your tape. I don't know what you want to do with it.

WAITER: Hey, I've got one.

CAROL: What?

WAITER: I've got the beginning of a story, O.K.?

CAROL: Go ahead. I don't know what I'm doing here, I really don't.

WAITER: Once upon a time there was a frog. *(Pause)* Go ahead.

CAROL: What?

WAITER: There was a frog. That's the beginning of the story.

CAROL: A frog?

WAITER: Yeah.

CAROL: What about him?

WAITER: You're supposed to say what happened to him next.

CAROL: I'm supposed to say what happened to a frog? I don't know. That's not what we're supposed to be doing, is it?

You didn't want us to come up here to tell a story about a frog, did you? I need a cigarette.

JAY: You both keep thinking there's something that I want. Please stop worrying about it. I want whatever happens.

CAROL: I just don't know what I'm doing here, O.K.? I'm sorry. I'm standing in front of a camera with a guy called Jeff because some guy who's a friend of Jean's said come up and make some tapes and I don't know what you want? It's not like I do this kind of thing all the time. I thought I'd be watching to start with.

WAITER: I have a different story. Two trucks . . .

CAROL: I don't even know Jean all that well. I have other things to do. That's all I'm saying. I mean I just find you really weird. Not you, Jeff, I mean him.

WAITER: That's O.K., that's O.K.

JAY: Beautiful, keep going, keep going . . .

CAROL: Look, I'm getting upset. I don't want this to be on film.

WAITER: Well. I have to get to work pretty soon. I mean, if we're going to do a story we ought to start pretty soon.

CAROL: Please turn the camera off. I don't know what's the matter with me. *(Jay stops)* Thank you. *(An awkward pause. Jay goes to Waiter)*

JAY: Jeff. That was beautiful. I want you to come by any time you're free and we'll do a tape.

WAITER: I don't have to go right away. Oh. O.K. Maybe tomorrow. This is really interesting. You got a great loft. You pay a lot of rent?

JAY: I own the building.

WAITER: Oh. O.K. *(Waiter goes. Jay sits down facing Carol on the floor)*

CAROL: Don't say anything. I just want to sit for a few minutes. Do you have a cigarette? *(Jay smiles. Offers her one)*

JAY: You're here in this loft. The loft is in a building. The building is in a city which is somewhere in the world which is somewhere in the universe and that makes you feel alone. But you're not alone. Do you know what that is?

CAROL: No.

JAY: Something I wrote. For you. So, tell me what's happening in your life. *(Carol laughs, louder and louder. Blackout)*

Scene 5

Table—a restaurant. Paul and Jean.

PAUL: Well?

JEAN: See, you're supposed to sit with your legs crossed and close your eyes and try to imagine this thing kind of just resting at the base of your spine. Like a little black pea or something. I thought of a thermometer.

PAUL: Well?

JEAN: And then a shoot grows out of the pea and up the inside of your spine and you have to be sure to not try to force it up. You think of it as something that has a life of its own. It just grows by itself when it's ready.

PAUL: Well?

JEAN: You're not listening.

PAUL: I'm listening.

JEAN: Then when it gets to your brain it grows out into this lotus-flower shape, that's the image he uses, and this little hole opens up in the top of your head and the Kundalini goes right out of your head and up into . . . oh, I don't know where exactly but somewhere, and when that happens you become sex. You *are* sex. You become the thing itself. Why don't you come along once, see if you like it. You've gotta get interested in something.

PAUL: I am interested in something. You know what I'm interested in.

JEAN: I don't know, Paul.

PAUL: Which way is it going, more yes or more no? Well?

JEAN: I feel like you're pushing me.

PAUL: That's because I am. I'm out of practice. And of course it doesn't help a lot to know that you think of me and Carol as a kind of . . . unit. You want to arrange a signal? When it's the right time for me to ask you if you'd like to come home with me tonight, please indicate by grabbing my leg under the table.

JEAN: I feel like I'd like to. It's not that simple, though. There's even stupid things. Being in the same bed . . . you know . . . that you and Carol . . .

PAUL: Oh, no problem there. We'll go to your place.

JEAN: No.

PAUL: I'll turn the mattress over. I'll buy a new one. Wait a minute. I just remembered. I don't have to. I bought a new mattress just this morning. Whew, that was lucky.

JEAN: I'm serious, Paul.

PAUL: I know. I know you are. I'm horny.

JEAN: And what if you and Carol get back together, like everybody thinks you will. Then I'll be someone who just came kind of in between for a while. That's not what I want.

PAUL: Why are you being so complicated all of a sudden? You want another drink?

JEAN: No.

PAUL: I mean, I thought I knew what'd be fun, call Jeannie, she's nice, she's a friend, we turn each other on I'm pretty sure, it'll be fun, go out, eat a nice friendly sexy dinner, see a nice friendly sexy film and go back to our place afterward . . . my place. And, you know. For the night. I don't understand it. Don't I turn you on?

JEAN: Of course you do, Paul. You know that.

PAUL: Are you seeing someone else?

JEAN: How come you can be so happy so soon afterwards. You were married five years.

PAUL: Because I'm smiling a lot and acting cute to get you into bed? Come on, Jeannie, you're too old to think that means anything. Please come back to my place.

JEAN: I don't think so. Not tonight.

PAUL: Why not tonight? What's wrong with tonight?

JEAN: I just don't want to. Not yet.

PAUL: When?

JEAN: I don't know. Soon. When I feel like I won't be being Carol.

PAUL: That was pretty low.

JEAN: It was just true.

PAUL: I really don't feel like being alone tonight.

JEAN: Neither do I, honey. That's the breaks. I have to work in the morning. You staying? Thanks for the dinner and the movie. And the drink. I like you, Paul. *(Jean kisses him on the head and starts to go)* I'll call.

PAUL: When?

JEAN: I'll call. I promise. *(Jean exits. Paul signals an offstage waiter. Lifts glass, pointing)*

PAUL *(Mouthing)*: Same again. Right. Make it a double. Double.

Scene 6

Couch—living room. Bob. Marge enters.

MARGE: I didn't have time to shop. All we have is a can of baby shrimp and some potato chips. I think there might be some beer.

BOB: That's O.K. I'll go out and get some chicken to go.

MARGE: I was seeing Carol.

BOB: That's O.K. Oh. Carol. How's Carol?

MARGE: O.K. She moved in with the video guy.

BOB: Yeah? What? The guy that dances?

MARGE: The guy I work for, Bob.

BOB: Jay.

MARGE: Yeah.

BOB: Why?

MARGE: I don't know. Why'd she and Paul split up in the first place? I don't know.

BOB: I could get a pizza instead of chicken. Or we could go out. You want to go out? I got paid for a job today.

MARGE: Either way. It doesn't matter.

BOB: You want to, though? You want to go out or eat in? If we eat in I could get a pizza or a chicken or something. Or we could just have the shrimp with some potato chips. That'd be O.K. with me.

MARGE: Well. What do you want to do?

BOB: Either way's fine with me. There's a pretty good movie on nine.

MARGE: Are we a good couple?

BOB: What?

MARGE: Are we a good couple? Should we stay together?

BOB: I don't understand. What did I say? Did I say something?

MARGE: Maybe we're just not a good couple. I don't think we're as good a couple as Paul and Carol were and they split up. Maybe we shouldn't be together. How do you feel about that?

BOB: I feel. I feel. Um. I don't agree. I feel that we should be together.

MARGE: Do you think we have a strong relationship?

BOB: I don't know. Yeah. I guess so.

MARGE: Do you think it's strong enough to stand on its own?

BOB: Yes. I do. Yes. Definitely. I think so. Definitely.

MARGE: Because I really don't want to play around with other couples anymore.

BOB: That's fine with me. Fine. Wait a minute. There was some chicken left over from last night.

MARGE: Chicken? I don't think so. Hang on, I'll look. *(Marge goes out)*

BOB *(Loud)*: I never liked swinging that much in the first place.

MARGE *(Off)*: Whaaa?

BOB: I said I never liked swinging that much in the first place.

MARGE *(Off)*: Just a minute, sweetie, I can't hear you.

BOB: Especially the men. *(Marge reenters)*

MARGE: We didn't have chicken last night. There's some cheddar. What were you just saying?

BOB: I said I never liked swinging all that much in the first place.

MARGE: You didn't?

BOB: No.

MARGE: Then why did you get us into it?

BOB: Me? Me? I didn't get us into it. You were the one that kept saying our relationship was limited sexually and you thought it would be an important step to expand it into new areas. That's what you said. Those are your exact words. Verbatim, almost.

MARGE: Come on, Bob. It wasn't me that started sending away for all those cheesy magazines with pictures of fat married couples and stuff . . .

BOB: You asked me to send for them. You said you were embarrassed.

MARGE: I asked you? Oh, bullshit, Bob, bullshit . . .

BOB: You asked me. I'm telling you, you asked me.

MARGE: I don't believe it. And it was me who asked you to go upstate to meet that bizarre couple with the leopardskin couch?

BOB: This is just what Paul said. One minute everything was O.K., the next minute . . . fffft.

MARGE: Do you want a separation, Bob? Is that what you're saying?

BOB: Is that what you want?

MARGE: I asked you first.

BOB: No. I do not want a separation.

MARGE: Neither do I.

BOB: I think it's ludicrous that we're yelling at each other when we both agree that we want to stop swinging.

MARGE: I just want to talk.

BOB: Well, that's what I want.

MARGE: Well then, let's talk.

BOB: O.K.

MARGE: So. You think it would be all right for us to not have sex with other couples anymore.

BOB: I do. I think it'd be all right.

MARGE: You think our relationship is strong enough to survive without it.

BOB: Yes. In my opinion.

MARGE: Good. I think I'd like to go out.

BOB: In fact, if you want to know the truth, I'm very glad we won't be with other couples anymore. I'm really glad.

MARGE: I'm going to have a beer before we go out. Want one?

BOB: Yeah. *(They look at each other. Smile)*

Scene 7

Paul with box and suitcase. Carol enters with plant.

CAROL: That's it.

PAUL: Yeah.

CAROL: Well.

PAUL: Can you stay for a while?

CAROL: I have to go to this video thing.

PAUL: Can I come? Sorry.

CAROL: Thanks for letting me have all the Stevie Wonder records.

PAUL: I never liked him much. Marge says he depresses her.

CAROL: Everything depresses Marge. That's why she's so happy.

PAUL: Do you have a number . . . in case I have to reach you for something.

CAROL: I left it on the bed.

PAUL: Would you mind if I called?

CAROL: Would you mind if I called?

PAUL: I asked first.

CAROL: Maybe we shouldn't. For a while.

PAUL: Yeah, I guess you're right.

CAROL: You seeing Jeannie?

PAUL: A little. How'd you know?

CAROL: Friends.

PAUL: Good old friends.

CAROL: Good old friends.

PAUL: Carol. What the hell happened? *(Phone rings)*

CAROL: Maybe it's for me.

PAUL: I'm expecting it. *(Carol picks up things. Paul puts plant in box)*

CAROL: You better get the phone. 'Bye, Paul. *(She goes)*

End of Play

≡LOOSE ENDS≡

This play is for Kathy.

Production Note

In its original production the scene changes of *Loose Ends* were accompanied by photographs. These showed scenes from Paul and/or Susan's life in the spans of time between the dates of each scene. Two things were accomplished by this. The audience's attention was taken off the stage where, in-the-round, there was nothing to hide from view the frantic scurrying of cast and crew while pieces of scenery were changed. And, more important, the pictures supplied information about the world of Paul and Susan and their friends. They were not intended to represent photographs taken by Susan. Their point of view, so to speak, was neutral.

Each scene ended with the actors freezing in position onstage as the lights dimmed and a slide of those actors in that position was projected on a screen. The photograph had been taken in a "real life" equivalent of the stage set. During the scene change there followed numbers of slides taken in various settings never seen in the play, then as a scene change was ending, we concluded with a slide of the next scene with actors in position. When stage lights came up we saw the theatrical equivalent of the last slide. There were no slides at the beginning and end of each act.

Loose Ends was first presented by Arena Stage, Washington, D.C. (Zelda Fichandler, Producing Director; Thomas C. Fichandler, Executive Director) on February 2, 1979. Alan Schneider directed the following cast:

PAUL	Kevin Kline
SUSAN	Roxanne Hart
JANICE	Robin Bartlett
BALINESE FISHERMAN	Ernest Abuba
DOUG	Jay O. Sanders
MARAYA	Celia Weston
BEN	Jordan Charney
SELINA	Jodi Long
RUSSELL	Stephen Mendillo
LAWRENCE	John Wylie
PHIL	James Jenner

The play then moved to New York, where it opened in June at Circle in the Square (Theodore Mann, Artistic Director; Paul Libin, Managing Director) with the following cast changes:

JANICE	Patricia Richardson
BEN	Steve Vinovich
RUSSELL	Michael Kell
LAWRENCE	Michael Lipton
PHIL	Jeff Brooks

Characters

PAUL

SUSAN

JANICE

BALINESE FISHERMAN

DOUG

MARAYA

BEN

SELINA

RUSSELL

LAWRENCE

PHIL

Scene 1

*Slide: 1970. A beach. Night. Full Moon. Waves. On bare stage,
Paul and Susan, early mid-20's, naked, clothes around. He sits
facing ocean (us) and she lies curled up.*

PAUL: It was great at the beginning. I could speak the language
almost fluently after a month and the people were fantastic. They'd come out and help us. Teach us songs.
Man, we thought it was all going so well. But we got all
the outhouses dug in six months and we had to stay there
two years, that was the deal. And that's when we began
to realize that none of the Nglele were using these outhouses. We'd ask them why and they'd just shrug. So we
started watching them very carefully and what we found
out was the Nglele use their feces for fertilizer. It's like
gold to them. They thought we were all fucking crazy
expecting them to waste their precious turds in our spiffy
new outhouses. Turns out they'd been helping us because
they misunderstood why we were there. They thought it
was some kind of punishment and we'd be allowed to go
home after we finished digging the latrines, that's why
they were helping us and then when we stayed on they
figured we must be permanent outcasts or something and
they just stopped talking to us altogether. Anyway, me

and Jeff, the guy I told you about, we figured maybe we could salvage something from the fuckup so we got a doctor to make a list of all the medicines we'd need to start a kind of skeleton health program in Ngleleland and we ordered the medicine, pooled both our salaries for the two years to pay for it. Paid for it. Waited. Never came. So we went to the capital to trace it and found out this very funny thing. The Minister of Health had confiscated it at the dock, same man who got our team assigned to the Nglele Tribal Territories in the first place. We were furious, man, we stormed into his office and started yelling at him. Turned out to be a real nice guy. Educated in England, British accent and everything. Had this office lined with sets of Dickens and Thackeray all in leather bindings. Unbelievable. Anyway, he said he couldn't help us about the medicine, he'd been acting on orders from higher up, which we knew was bullshit, then he said he really admired our enthusiasm and our desire to help his people but he wanted to know just out of curiosity, if we'd managed to start the medical program and save a thousand lives, let's say, he wanted to know if we were prepared to feed and clothe those thousand people for the next ten years, twenty years, however long they lived. He made us feel so goddamned naive, so totally helpless and unprepared, powerless. We went out of there, got drunk, paid the first women we could find and spent the rest of the week fucking our brains out. And then for the next year and two months we just sat around in Ngleleland stoned out of our minds counting off the days we had left before we could go home. Anyway, since you asked, that's what the Peace Corps was like.

SUSAN: Sounds pretty shitty.

PAUL: Well. At least now I speak fluent Nglele. You never know when that'll come in handy in Philadelphia.

SUSAN: You got another cigarette? *(Paul finds his shirt, gets out cigarettes, lights two of them)* I got this American newspaper yesterday, they sell 'em at that hotel by the marketplace, they're about a week old but I just wanted to read a newspaper . . . It was so weird. I took it back to the shack . . . Oh, we rented this shack just down the beach . . . me and Janice, the girl you saw me with . . . *(Paul hands cigarette to Susan)* Thanks . . . I should stop . . . anyway, I made a cup of coffee and sat on the beach and read this paper. And, you know, all the stories were out of date and I didn't know what most of 'em were about anyway because we've been traveling for over a month and I just started thinking, you know, all this news could be from another planet, you know what I mean, like is this stuff they're writing about happening on the planet earth because I live on earth, I'm sitting right here, right on the earth and none of this stuff is happening to me. I just thought of that while you were talking. I don't know why. Do you ever think about things like that? *(Paul starts chuckling)* What? What are you laughing at?

PAUL: Nothing.

SUSAN: You do that a lot, you know.

PAUL: Do what?

SUSAN: You start laughing when something isn't funny and when I ask you what you're laughing at you say "nothing."

PAUL: It's just . . . I don't know. I was just thinking I spent two years going through a lot of very weird stuff but when I try to talk about it it's just a story, just some stuff that happened and now it's over. It doesn't mean anything anymore.

SUSAN: That's not funny.

PAUL: No. No, it isn't.

SUSAN: You want me to tell you about something weird that happened to me? You know, that way we'll each have weird stories about each other.

PAUL: Sure. Go ahead.

SUSAN: O.K. When I was ten. No, eleven, I had my tonsils out and my dad was on a business trip, but I really wanted him to see my tonsils, so I made the doctor promise to put them in formaldehyde and I took them home. But they were real ugly and I decided I didn't want him to see them after all, so I made a little fire in the backyard and said a few prayers and had a tonsil cremation and then I put the ashes in this vase on the mantelpiece. That was my big secret. It was really great because wherever I went I knew something that no one else knew and that seemed like something very important. I don't know why exactly. Then the maid cleaned the vase one day and that was that. Except that a year later the maid choked to death and they found two grapes lodged in her trachea, so I knew my tonsils had had their revenge. I'm kidding. How long are you staying here?

PAUL: In Bali?

SUSAN: Yeah.

PAUL: I have a job that starts in two weeks.

SUSAN: Where?

PAUL: Philadelphia.

SUSAN: What kind of a job?

PAUL: Teaching English at this private school.

SUSAN: Is that what you're going to do? Teach English? I mean, you know, sort of forever?

PAUL: It's all I could get for now.

SUSAN: Do you know what you're going to do?

PAUL: When I grow up, you mean?

SUSAN: Yeah, you know.

PAUL: We'll see. What about you?

SUSAN: Oh, I don't know. I guess I'll travel with Janice for a while. Then I'll probably go home and do something or other that'll make me incredibly rich and respected and happy and fulfilled in every possible way and then, let's see, I'll move to the country and buy a little house with lots of stained glass and two cats, oh, and a solar heating panel and . . . and a servant called Lothar or something like that . . . I don't know.

PAUL: Sounds nice.

SUSAN: Want to go in again?

PAUL: Do you?

SUSAN: I asked first.

PAUL: Sure.

SUSAN: O.K. *(They stand)*

PAUL: Ready? One . . . two . . . three . . . GO! *(Paul runs forward. Susan doesn't. Paul stops, turns. Susan laughs. Paul chases her down the beach, offstage. Shrieks, happy yelling. Susan runs back on. Paul catches her. Tickle, kiss,*

passion. They roll on sand, kissing. Stop. Roll apart.
They are full) This is incredible. Fucking incredible.

SUSAN: Listen, what do you think if . . . me and Janice made a pact that if anything happened while we were on this trip it was O.K. to split up and go on alone. And I like her, you know, she's a good friend, but she's into this whole thing about a guru she heard about in India, that's kind of how this trip started in the first place, but I like it right here and I was thinking maybe . . . I mean, if I told her to go on alone, would you like to stay here for a while, see how things worked out and if it feels good maybe we could travel together, you know. Does that sound good? Paul?

PAUL: I have this job.

SUSAN: You didn't sound too enthusiastic about it.

PAUL: I'm not. That's not the point. I'm broke.

SUSAN: It doesn't cost anything to travel, you know. You can live for nothing if you do it right.

PAUL: Yeah, I guess so.

SUSAN: And I got a little saved up.

PAUL: I couldn't do that . . .

SUSAN: Why not? I mean, well, O.K. It's up to you.

PAUL: Is it? Yeah, I guess it is. I could just do it, couldn't I? I could just say fuck it. And I'd love to, Jesus God would I ever love to. *(Pause)* I don't believe this is happening. I really don't. *(They giggle. Paul suddenly alert)*

SUSAN: What's that?

PAUL: I heard something. *(They peer into darkness)* Over there, look, someone's coming. There's a flashlight. *(They start dressing quickly)* Hello! Hello! Who's there? *(Flashlight beam on them)* Americans. We're Americans. Tourists. Who is it?

JANICE *(Offstage)*: Susan, is that you?

SUSAN: Shit.

PAUL: What's the matter?

SUSAN: It's Janice. My friend.

JANICE: Are you all right? *(Enter Janice with flashlight)*

SUSAN: What are you doing?

JANICE: I just wondered what happened to you.

SUSAN: I went for a walk.

JANICE: I just got worried, that's all. You said you'd be back by five.

SUSAN: Things happened.

JANICE: Yeah, 'cause it's almost ten. I got worried.

SUSAN: This is Paul.

PAUL: Hi.

JANICE: Hi. So, are you coming back?

SUSAN: Janice, what's the matter with you?

JANICE: Someone was walking around outside the shack. I heard footsteps. I didn't want to stay back there. I mean a tourist did get killed here, you know.

PAUL: Wasn't that last year?

JANICE: The point is, it *can* happen.

PAUL: I thought I heard his wife killed him.

JANICE: Susan, I don't want to go back there alone. Those blue spiders are all over the place tonight. I tried to spray with a bug bomb, but it just makes the legs come off and they keep moving around. Please, Susan, I know it's a drag, I know we decided to be loose about the traveling, but I don't want to go back to that place by myself.

SUSAN: Can we talk about this later?

JANICE: Yes, I think we should do that, Susan.

SUSAN: Good night, Janice. *(Janice turns to go. Screams. Drops flashlight)*

JANICE: Oh, my God. *(They look. Nearby stands a Balinese holding a large fish)*

SUSAN: Who's that? *(Balinese advances with a smile, holds the fish out)*

BALINESE: *(Something in Balinese)*

JANICE: Oh, Jesus, it's him again.

SUSAN: Who?

JANICE: He's been following me around all day. He was in the marketplace. What do you want?

BALINESE: *(Something in Balinese)*

JANICE: I don't understand you. I don't speak your language. Please go away.

PAUL: Is that fish for us?

BALINESE: *(Something in Balinese)*

PAUL: Are you trying to sell the fish? You want money? Dollars. Dollars? *(Paul goes toward Balinese reaching into pocket for money. Balinese backs away and holds fish from him)*

BALINESE: *(Something in Balinese)*

PAUL: O.K., O.K., take it easy. *(Balinese kneels before Janice and proffers fish)*

BALINESE: *(Something in Balinese)*

JANICE *(Pause)*: Let's just buy the fish, O.K.?

SUSAN: What are we gonna do with a fish? We don't even have a place to cook it.

JANICE: We'll make a fire on the beach, I don't care. Let's just get rid of him.

PAUL: I think I read somewhere that the Balinese offer a fish when they're in love. Seriously, I think he's proposing marriage.

JANICE: O.K., mister, look, I've had enough of this. Get up, I'll buy your fish, O.K. Buy. Money. Then you go away and leave me alone. Do you understand me? Comprenez? Shit.

BALINESE: *(Something in Balinese)*

JANICE: You go away. Away. You go away.

BALINESE: Ooo gow weh.

JANICE: Here. *(Janice hands money to Balinese and takes fish)* . . . Now you go. Go. *(Balinese backs away, then stands watching)* No. Go all the way. Go completely away. All the way. *(Balinese backs away into the night)*

PAUL: He's gone.

JANICE: No he's not. He's just waiting out there. As soon as we start back he'll follow us.

SUSAN: Janice, I wish you'd cool it.

JANICE: I'm telling you, he's been after me all day.

SUSAN: All right, all right. He's gone now.

JANICE: Are you coming back?

SUSAN: Yes, I'm coming back. In a few minutes.

JANICE: It's really great to find out who your friends are. *(Exits)*

PAUL: Good night . . .

SUSAN: Oh, man, she is crazy. I mean I knew she could get a little weird sometimes, but this is ridiculous. This is a mistake. This trip is definitely a mistake.

PAUL: She seems O.K.

SUSAN: You don't have to travel with her. Do you have another
cigarette? *(Paul lights one for her)* I was feeling so good.
Was that really true about the fish?

PAUL: No.

SUSAN *(Laughs)*: I like you.

PAUL: You have a pen?

SUSAN: What for?

PAUL: Get your address. Maybe I'll see you back in the States.

SUSAN: But I thought . . . ?

PAUL: I can't. I mean, yeah sure, I could. I could. But I can't.
It's ridiculous. I mean, look at what I have after two years.
A bunch of stories and a ticket home. I have to do something now. You know, where I end up with something I
can . . . something that doesn't just go away, you know
what I mean?

SUSAN: Hey, that's O.K. You don't have to explain it. I had a
good time.

PAUL: Yeah.

SUSAN: You want to come back to the shack? I got a pen there.
You can stay tonight if you want, there's room.

PAUL: I have to confirm a flight back at the hotel.

SUSAN: You're staying at the hotel?

PAUL: After two years in Ngleleland, are you kidding?

SUSAN: Does it have a shower? I got sand everywhere.

PAUL: Want to come back?

SUSAN: If it's O.K.

PAUL: Sure. *(They start out. Susan stops)*

SUSAN: Shit.

PAUL: What's the matter?

SUSAN: I can't leave her alone. Janice, Jesus. Look, I'll tell you
what. Why don't I meet you at the hotel tomorrow. We could
rent a couple of bikes and go out to the mountains . . .

PAUL: I'm leaving in the morning.

SUSAN: Oh. You didn't say. O.K. Well, I'm in the Denver
phone book. Steen. That's two ees. We're the only Steens.
That's my family.

PAUL: O.K., Susan Steen. Two ees.

SUSAN: What's your last name?

PAUL: Baumer.

SUSAN: Paul Baumer.

PAUL: Right.

SUSAN: So. Maybe I'll see you.

PAUL: O.K. Take it easy. *(Paul and Susan stand for a moment. They exit in opposite directions. Fade)*

Scene 2

Slide: 1971. Doug and Maraya's yard. Noon. On one side of stage rear end of a shingle-covered trailer home on cinderblocks. Some shingles have fallen off and you can see painted metal beneath. There is a window in rear end. At other side of stage is nearly completed 2×4 frame for part of a house. Tools, etc. Doug and Paul, stripped to waist, working on frame.

DOUG: Listen, man, I've been there, you don't have to tell me about horny. Shit, when I found ole Maraya was pregnant with Baby-Jake I got a hard-on wouldn't go down for six months. Everything got me off and I mean everything. Even old Doofus the dog. Even looking at flowers.

PAUL: Well, what I was . . .

DOUG: Man, there was this one time it was raining and I was walking home from the swimming hole and I just started thinking wow, this rain reminds me of Maraya's big ole tummy. Don't ask me why. And before I knew what I was doing there I was standing in the rain, standing, man, holding my pecker in my hand, pumping away just like I was in the shower or something, I don't know. This dude came driving right by, I didn't give a shit, nothing was gonna stop me. He gets about fifty yards down the road and hits the brakes, tires screeching all over the place when he realizes he's just seen a sex maniac whacking off in the rain. I'm telling you, man, when the feeling hits you like that, fuck holding back, right.

PAUL: Yeah, but the thing is . . .

DOUG: I don't know. Maybe I'm just getting weird living up here. I'm not saying I'd ever go back to the city, ungh-uh, you can have that shit, but still . . . *(Paul hands him piece of 2×4)* What's this one for? Oh, yeah, damn, I interrupted you again. I *am* getting weird, I'm telling you. Cisco came up here a couple weeks ago, stayed for two days, I couldn't stop talking. Nobody up here talks. How do I seem?

PAUL: What do you mean?

DOUG: Since the last time you saw me. Do I seem any weirder?

PAUL: No.

DOUG: You do.

PAUL: What do you mean?

DOUG: I don't know. So you're walking on this beach in Bali and you see this chick, right?

PAUL: Well, you know, we started talking and it felt really good. I mean after two years in Africa it felt really good to be talking to someone again . . .

DOUG: So you whipped out the big boy and shagged her on the beach.

PAUL: Douglas, you have a mind like a sewer, you know that.

DOUG: You didn't fuck her? You mean I been listening to all this shit for nothing?

PAUL: You haven't been listening, you've been talking the whole time.

DOUG: O.K., you got five minutes to get to the fuck or I'm quitting for lunch.

PAUL: You want to hear this or not?

DOUG: Shit, man, she really got to you, huh?

PAUL: I guess you could say that.

DOUG: And I did. So it's real serious, huh?

PAUL: Well, you know, for now. What do you want me to say?

DOUG: You don't know if it's serious?

PAUL: We'll see.

DOUG: O.K., you go to bed at night sometimes and you lie there together but you don't feel like you *have* to fuck before you go to sleep, right?

PAUL: What are you talking about?

DOUG: Just answer me, does that ever happen?

PAUL: Sure, sometimes.

DOUG: Then it's serious. So you fucked her on the beach. Hey, O.K., I'm sorry, what happened?

PAUL: I've been trying to tell you.

DOUG: Well, I been waiting for it to get interesting. I can't help it if you don't know how to tell a story.

PAUL: O.K., look, the school closed . . .

DOUG: What school . . . ?

PAUL: Doug!

DOUG: What school? You didn't say anything about a school.

PAUL: Philadelphia. Where you wrote me that time?

DOUG: Oh, yeah. How come it closed?

PAUL: Oh, you know, it was one of those experimental places, develop the inner person, that kind of shit. Anyway, the parents must've got wise or something 'cause the school ran out of money halfway through the year and they had to close down. So there's me out of a job, nothing to do, so I got a bus up to Boston to check out a few possibilities and she was on the bus.

DOUG: You're shitting?

PAUL: I swear. I couldn't believe it.

DOUG: You didn't even know she was back in America? That's really far out. I mean that's definitely in the land of spooky events.

PAUL: Well, actually, I left out the part where I called her family in Denver and found out she was living in Boston.

DOUG: Why, you little devil . . .

PAUL: I mean I wasn't sure I was going to try to look her up or anything. In fact, I had a little thing going in Philadelphia and I wasn't sure I wanted to leave.

DOUG: Listen.

PAUL: What?

DOUG: She's real cute. I like her. Really. And I want to get back to the part where you fucked on the beach. And I want a sandwich. You want a sandwich?

PAUL: You're never gonna get this house built.

DOUG: Fuck the house, man, I'm hungry. *(Calls)* MARAYA! *(Maraya appears in rear window of trailer)*

MARAYA: What do you want?

DOUG: What's for food? We're getting hungry.

MARAYA: It's not ready yet.

DOUG: How 'bout a couple of beers?

MARAYA: Get 'em yourself. I'm not your waitress.

DOUG: I won't build your house. *(Maraya withdraws her head)* Want a beer?

PAUL: Sure.

(Doug goes toward the trailer, passes Susan, who is coming out. She has a camera over shoulder. She is eating an apple.)

DOUG: Beer, my dear?

SUSAN: Lunch is coming in a minute.

DOUG: There goes that darn Doug, ruining his appetite again. *(Doug goes into trailer. Susan comes to Paul)*

SUSAN: How's it going?

PAUL: Pretty slow.

SUSAN: Maraya told me about this waterfall where you can go swimming. It's only about a mile. You want to go after lunch?

PAUL: Come here.

SUSAN: What?

PAUL: I want to go right now.

SUSAN: You want to go after lunch?

PAUL: Sure.

SUSAN: It's nice here.

PAUL: Do you like them?

SUSAN: Yeah. Maraya's a little weird with that baby, but I like them.

PAUL: Are you O.K.?

SUSAN: Sure.

PAUL: You seem a little I don't know . . . something or other.

SUSAN: I always am a little something or other.

PAUL: Am I supposed to leave it alone? Am I supposed to not push it?

SUSAN: Babe, I'm fine, really.

PAUL: O.K. It's just, sometimes I'm not sure how you're feeling, that's all.

SUSAN: Don't worry about it.

PAUL: In other words, something's on your mind but you don't feel like talking about it right now?

SUSAN: It's nothing, really. I'm fine. Let's change the subject.

PAUL: O.K.
SUSAN: We'll talk about it later.
PAUL: O.K.

(Doug comes from trailer with three beers.)

DOUG: Maraya wants to know, lunch out here or in the west wing?
PAUL: Out here's fine.
DOUG. Did I interrupt something?
PAUL: No, no.
DOUG *(Yells)*: OUT HERE, AND HURRY UP, I GOTTA GO GET THAT BATTERY FOR THE TRUCK.
MARAYA *(Offstage. Yells)*: IT'LL BE THERE WHEN IT'S READY.
DOUG: I'm gonna haveta start whuppin' that woman if she don't behave herself better. *(Doug sits by Paul)* How come you didn't finish the house? *(Apple in mouth, Susan backs away and takes pictures of Paul and Doug together. Doug clowns)*
SUSAN: Hey, come on, just relax, I want to get you two together. Just act natural.
DOUG *(In a weird pose)*: I'm stuck, I can't move.
SUSAN: Doug. *(Doug relaxes)* O.K., now move a little closer.
DOUG *(Moves closer)*: Don't get fresh.

(Enter Maraya from trailer carrying Baby-Jake in one arm and balancing a plate of sandwiches with her free hand. She sees what's going on and stops, talks to Baby-Jake.)

MARAYA: Look, honey, they're taking pictures, see? That little thing she's holding goes click and that makes a picture and then you have something to look at so you can remember how it used to be. Done?
SUSAN: Yeah. *(Susan shoulders camera. Maraya sets plate down)*
MARAYA: O.K., troops, dig in.
BABY-JAKE: *(Cries)*

(Maraya takes out breast and feeds Baby-Jake.)

SUSAN: How much did you pay for this place?

DOUG: Fifteen. It's eleven acres. Goes right down to the bluestone quarry in back and then over to the woods that way. Be worth about sixty/seventy when the house is finished and you figure inflation. You guys looking for something?

SUSAN: I was just wondering. It's nice up here.

DOUG: Listen, there's a place coming on the market soon, no one knows about it yet, state land on three sides so no one can build. I'll check it out for you if you're interested. It'd be great if you guys moved up here. Want me to check it out?

MARAYA *(To Baby-Jake)*: Ouch, honey, you're biting really hard, you know. You shouldn't do that 'cause it just makes my nipples sore and I get all tense and that stops the milk from flowing and you'll just get angrier. It's a vicious circle.

DOUG: You want me to check out that land?

PAUL *(To Susan)*: What do you think?

SUSAN: I don't know. You want to?

PAUL: Do you?

SUSAN: I asked first.

PAUL *(To Doug)*: Sure. Why not?

DOUG: Hot damn, all right, you got it. This afternoon. Shit, I gotta get that battery. *(Stands)* Who's coming to town? *(No one moves)* Gee, I don't know if I'll have room for all of you.

PAUL: We're going to the waterfall.

DOUG: The waterfall, eh? We all know what happens at the waterfall, ho-ho. How 'bout you, Marsie, want to come to town?

MARAYA: I gotta do some stuff. Can you get me some smokes? Two packs. I'm trying to cut down, that's for all week. They say you can taste it in the milk, but I think that's bullshit. You can't taste it, can you, honey? No, of course not.

DOUG *(To Paul)*: Give me a push down the hill, wouldya? *(Paul and Doug exit)*

SUSAN: Do you mind if I take a few pictures?

MARAYA: No, that'd be great.

SUSAN: Just stay like that. Don't worry about anything. *(Susan takes pictures)*

MARAYA: Oww, shit, Jake, you're getting obnoxious, come on. Hold still. She's taking our picture.

SUSAN: Why don't you try the other one?

MARAYA: What other one? Oh. *(Maraya gives Baby-Jake the other teat)* Is that kind of a serious trip, the photography?

SUSAN: Oh, I don't know. I enjoy it.

MARAYA: You're taking a lot of pictures, is why I asked. Hey, this is a lot better, you know. He's not biting. I can't wait'll he can talk. It's weird 'cause you know he's got a lotta stuff on his mind, you can tell he's thinking about things all the time, but you can't ask him about it. It's really frustrating. Are you gonna have kids?

SUSAN: Probably. Someday. I don't know.

MARAYA: You should have 'em pretty soon, though. They come out healthier when you have 'em young and if you wait too long you might get a mutation. You'd probably be a good mother.

SUSAN: Why do you say that?

MARAYA: I don't know, just a feeling. Like how you knew about changing the breast. *(Pause)* You guys living together?

SUSAN: We're getting a place back in Boston this fall. Supposedly.

MARAYA: You sound sort of like you're not too sure.

SUSAN: Oh, you know. If we do, we do; if we don't, we don't.

MARAYA: I know what you mean. *(Susan is looking at Maraya)* What are you looking at?

SUSAN: Did you know a lot of guys before Doug?

MARAYA: Oh yeah, a lot. Well, a medium lot. I mean compared to some of my friends it wasn't hardly any, but compared to some of my other friends it was more than them.

SUSAN: Was it strange at first? Being with just one guy?

MARAYA: Well, I like Doug, you know. I mean he's not the easiest guy in the world, but then again he says I'm not all that great either. I guess it's how you look at it.

SUSAN: But did you . . . ? Like we decided we'd get this place together, right, but then when I thought about it . . . I don't know, you go through this whole number in your head, like are you really ready for this? Is this what you really want?

MARAYA: Try it out. What can you lose. You know, if it doesn't work, you split.

SUSAN: No, what I mean is . . . I thought this was supposed to happen a lot later . . . living with someone. You know how there's things you're gonna do now and things you're gonna do later, and living with someone was definitely supposed to be a later. But now I feel like really O.K. about it.

MARAYA: So tell him.

SUSAN: I already have. About five times. He always says, "yeah, great" and then he never does anything about it. I remember this one week I even left newspapers around his apartment, you know, open to the classified . . . apartments for rent. Really. You see yourself doing this stuff and you don't believe it's you. And like now, we're traveling around meeting all of his friends, right? And everyone wants to know where it's at with us and it's weird because I just don't know. I don't know. And I don't want to keep pushing him, either. I always hate it when people do that to me. I mean that's one of the things I really like about Paul. He always knows when to back off, but sometimes he's like so blasé you just want to strangle him. Shit. Listen to me. I'm making it sound like some kind of big deal. I don't even know why I brought it up.

MARAYA: That's O.K. Look, I'll tell you how I think about it. If you want something you ask for it. The worst thing that can happen is the guy says no and I'm used to that so it's O.K. and then sometimes he says yes and then you feel really good.

SUSAN: Don't say anything to Paul, O.K.?

MARAYA: My lips are sealed. Hey, Jakey-poo, you like that, don't you? That's nice, yes, nice. You can always tell when he's enjoying it from how he sucks. It's funny, it even turns me on sometimes. Really. I love sex. Sometimes when I'm real depressed I think, "How bad can it be if there's still sex?" *(Truck motor coughing to life offstage)* Yea, truck! They got the truck started, honey. Go "Yea, truck!" He could care less. Are you O.K.?

SUSAN: Sure. *(Goes back to loading camera)*

PAUL *(Returns, sweaty)*: O.K., who's for the waterfall? I gotta cool off.

MARAYA: Do you have a cigarette? *(Paul gets them out. Lights one for Maraya)* . . . Phew, Jake, you really stink. I swear, sometimes I think this kid borrows shit from somewhere. We don't feed him half of what comes out of him.

SUSAN: You want to come to the waterfall?

MARAYA: Can you just wait while I change the baby . . . maybe I better just put him to bed. Maybe I'll catch up with you later. *(Maraya starts offstage)*

PAUL: Hey, your cigarette.

MARAYA: Oh, thanks. I gotta stop, I really do. *(Maraya exits into trailer, puffing)*

PAUL: You ready?

SUSAN: Sure.

PAUL: O.K., let's go. *(Susan gets up, points camera somewhere)* Susan . . .

SUSAN: What?

PAUL: I want to talk.

SUSAN: Stay like that for a second. C'mon, don't look so serious. We'll talk at the waterfall. *(Susan takes a few shots)* O.K., let's go. *(Exits. Offstage)* You coming? *(Paul looks after her, follows. Fade)*

Scene 3

Slide: 1973. Back yard of Paul and Susan's apartment house. Children's swing and wrought-iron filigree table and chairs painted white but rusting. Low picket fence and gate. Susan organizes masses of small photos into rows on 4×8 panel which lies flat on the wrought-iron table. One complete board leans against frame of swing. Transistor cassette on ground plays Schubert's Trout Quintet, *3rd Movement, Scherzo. Hold on Susan at work for a moment. Then, through gate, enter Ben Baumer, 36, in seersucker suit, jacket over shoulder, tie undone, paper bag in one hand. He stops and watches for a moment.*

BEN: Susan?

SUSAN: Hi. You found us.

BEN: Oh yeah. You give a mean set of directions. Didn't get lost once. I'm parked right in front, is that O.K.?

SUSAN: Sure. Hang on a second. *(Susan turns off the cassette)* So. You're Ben.

BEN: Always was, always will be.

SUSAN: Well, it's nice to meet you at last.

BEN: Same to you. And everything you've heard about me is true.

SUSAN: I was expecting a mustache.

BEN: Oh, that. Shaved it off years ago. Paul told you about the mustache, eh?

SUSAN: No, in the picture.

BEN: No kidding. Funny, I don't remember any pictures with a mustache. I only had it a few months.

SUSAN: It's three couples on a beach.

BEN: Oh, God, no. Not the naked one.

SUSAN: It's a great picture. We put it on the bureau.

BEN: Well, goddarn! That little so and so! Wouldn't you know it. I have a hundred great pictures of myself and wouldn't you know he'd pick that one. What can you do? The whole family's crazy. Say, where is the little stinker anyway?

SUSAN: Who? Oh, you mean Paul. He's still at the editing room.

BEN: Editing room? What's that all about?

SUSAN: He's editing film. Well, he's learning.

BEN: I thought he was teaching.

SUSAN: He was. Now he's editing film.

BEN: You're trying to tell me he's editing film, right?

SUSAN: Right.

BEN: Well, you live and learn. He never said anything about it.

SUSAN: Can I get you anything . . . beer, Coke . . .

BEN: Leave the liquid refreshments to me. *(Ben takes champagne and paper cups from bag)*

SUSAN: What's that for?

BEN: Celebrazione.

SUSAN: Shouldn't we wait for Paul?

BEN: No, I got some cheap stuff for him. This is for us. The real thing, a little Dom Pergweenon. Chilled. Just got it in Cambridge.

SUSAN: What's the occasion?

BEN: Hahahaha. Just you wait, Mrs. Higgins, just you wait. *(Twists cork)* Hold your nose and wiggle your toes. *(Cork pops)* Ahhh, thank you. I needed that. O.K., one for you, one for me, quick, quick . . . waste not want not . . . a little more for you . . . a lot more for me . . . perfecto, O.K., here's glue in your shoe. *(They drink)* I'll tell you something. My little brother is a real so and so. He doesn't deserve a beautiful girl like you, and that's my humble opinion. I'll tell you what. Why don't you and me catch the next flight to London before he gets home?

SUSAN: Why London?

BEN: I thought you'd never ask. I got the job.

SUSAN: Oh.

BEN: The job. The London job. He told you about the job, didn't he?

SUSAN: I don't think so.

BEN: He didn't mention anything about . . . ?

SUSAN: He probably just forgot to tell me. We've had a lot of stuff going on.

BEN: Yeah. Well, I guess it's just not that important. Can't imagine how I got so excited about it in the first place.

SUSAN: What is it? Tell me.

BEN: It's only a little matter of opening a multimillion-dollar European operation which I'm in charge of. In fact, I created the idea. He did tell you I was in securities?

SUSAN: He said you were a salesman.

BEN: Near enough. Refill?

SUSAN: I'm fine.

BEN *(Pours for himself)*: No, you see Randle and Lane, that's my company, they've been kind of conservative on overseas markets, so I doped out a whole campaign, did a little presentation and they liked it. They liked it a lot. So now I'm in charge of setting the whole thing up. Europe.

SUSAN: That sounds fantastic.

BEN: Listen to this. Sixty thousand a year plus basic commissions. Free car. Six-week vacation a year. Five-room apartment overlooking jolly old Hyde Park. And the girls in London! I mean talk about yummy! All you want to do is tear the wrappers off and lick 'em to death, I swear.

SUSAN: Aren't you married?

BEN: Yep. Ten years. Great lady, the best. *(Drains cup)* Little more?

SUSAN: I'm O.K.

BEN *(Pours for himself. Looks at Susan's work)*: What's all this?

SUSAN: You like it?

BEN: Very nice. Very nice.

SUSAN: I'm serious. Do you really like it?

BEN: Absolutely. It's . . . different. You work for a photographer?

SUSAN: I *am* a photographer.

BEN: Oh, I'll be darned. So this is your stuff, huh? What do you sell it or is it a sort of a hobby or what?

SUSAN: I've sold a few. I might be having an exhibit next month. There's a guy that's interested. Just local but . . . gotta start somewhere.

PAUL *(Voice. Off, as from second-floor window)*: What's going on out there?

BEN: Hey, guy . . .

SUSAN: Hi, sweetie.

BEN: Get your rusty butt down here.

PAUL *(Off)*: Be right down.

SUSAN *(Pause)*: Listen, congratulations on the job.

BEN: Oh, thank you. Thank you very much. And, ah, fingers crossed for your exhibit. And you never know the way things catch on. There was that movie a couple years ago about surfing. A guy just went out and took a lot of film, just people surfing. Darn movie made him a fortune. You never know. *(Paul enters through gate)*

PAUL: Hi, Ben.

BEN: Hey, guy, look at you. *(They stand awkwardly)* You're just in time for a little warm champagne.

PAUL *(Kisses Susan hello)*: Hi, babe, how's it going?

SUSAN: O.K. The panel . . .

PAUL: Looks good.

SUSAN: It's coming. You're back early.

(Enter through gate Selina, very beautiful Chinese American. Totally American manner and accent.)

PAUL: Yeah, the lab fucked up the film again, so there's nothing to edit. They gave us the afternoon off. *(Ben is watching Selina)*

BEN: Can I help you?

SUSAN: Hi, Soolie . . .

PAUL: Oh, Selina, this is my brother Ben. This is Selina. She works in the editing room.

BEN: Ah, so that's why he stopped teaching.

SELINA: Excuse me?

PAUL: Soolie wanted to see some of the panels.

SELINA: I didn't know you had company. I'll stop by tomorrow.

SUSAN: Why don't you stay for dinner? Please. I want to show you one of the panels. It still doesn't feel right.

SELINA: How many panels are you going to have?

SUSAN: Twenty I think.

SELINA: Twenty, wow.

SUSAN: Well, I have like over a thousand pictures, right? I set the timer for once every fifteen seconds and the wedding was about nine hours. Figure it out.

BEN *(At panel)*: This is a wedding? I thought it was one of those you know, what do you call it . . . a happening . . .

SELINA: It was beautiful. That farm is perfect. If they ever want to sell it, let me know. I really love New Hampshire. Listen, I was thinking, you know, you could maybe try a series with the camera going around in a circle. You know. Time the shutter to the motor and you'd see the background changing a little in each picture.

SUSAN: I've thought about that, but I really like it to be one background—just one space and everything that happens in it so you have a reference point. You know, Space Portrait. That's what it is. A portrait of one space.

SELINA: You could call it Circular Space Portrait. I don't know. I was just thinking.

PAUL: Can I say something?

SUSAN: What?

PAUL: You're going up? With Soolie? To look at a panel?

SUSAN: Yeah.

PAUL: If you find yourself anywhere near the fridge . . .

SUSAN: Two beers?

BEN: What? Oh, sure. *(Susan and Selina start to go)*

SELINA *(To Ben)*: Nice to meet you.

BEN: Well, I hope there's more to come.

SELINA: Excuse me?

PAUL: Never mind. *(Susan and Selina exit, talking)*

SELINA: Avra's really sorry she missed the wedding. She has this great present for you guys. She wants to know when she can come over with it . . .

SUSAN: What is it?

SELINA: She made me promise not to tell. *(They are gone)*

PAUL: So, d'you drive up?

BEN: Wait a minute. Wait just a minute. I probably heard this wrong. Did that Oriental sweetie pie say something about a present for you? A wedding present?

PAUL: Oh, yeah, Avra. She wanted to watch Watergate so she missed the wedding. Avra's really strange.

BEN: Whose wedding?

PAUL: I was coming to that.

BEN: You're married?

PAUL: Yeah.

BEN: Well, surprise, surprise. When did this happen?

PAUL: Last weekend.

BEN: Gee, guy, excuse me for being a little surprised, here. I mean I talked to Mom on the phone yesterday and she didn't say anything about it. I suppose you didn't tell her, either.

PAUL: Not yet.

BEN: Jesus Christ, Paul, what is it with you?

PAUL: Is this going to be a lecture?

BEN: But your own mother.

PAUL: Did you tell Mom about you and Marlene splitting up? Did you tell her Marlene had enough of your drinking and fucking around and doesn't want to come to London with you if you get that job?

BEN: I got it.

PAUL: Congratulations. Did you tell Mom?

BEN: Of course I told her. I told her the moment I knew.

PAUL: But you didn't tell her about Marlene. Gee, Ben, are you trying to keep things from Mom?

BEN: Don't be a wise-ass.

PAUL: All right, then, don't start in about our duties to Mom. I'm not interested in this game you're trying to play about the two wonderboys living a great life, making their little fortunes, raising happy little families. What's the point? She's sitting there in Seattle bleeding Dad for all the alimony she can and dumping it into that ridiculous Ecole de Beauté she runs. I mean, come on, Ben. What's that got to do with my life?

BEN: I don't get it. Same family, same house, but I swear to God there's Chinamen I understand better than I understand you.

PAUL: I noticed. Look. Me and Susan . . . we've been together for like two years . . . more. It's working out real good, so . . . and if we pay joint taxes it'll be better for both of us and . . . Well, she needed to get a lot of people together for this Space Portrait she had in mind and we thought a wedding was a great idea. And we happen to love each other. So. And we didn't really dig the idea of a lot of relatives crying their ass off at the beauty of it all and shoving Waring blenders and matched dinnerware down our throat, that's all. O.K.?

BEN: No, it's not O.K. because that's not what I'm talking about and you know it.

PAUL (Exploding): How the fuck am I supposed to know what you're talking about? I haven't seen you for three years and I never understood you back then anyway. I just told you why I got married and why I didn't tell Mother. Now if that isn't what we're talking about, suppose you tell me just what the fuck we are talking about.

BEN: O.K., let's calm down.

PAUL: I'm calm. I'm calm. What? Tell me. What are we talking about?

BEN: Look. I know what you're going to say, but just listen to me and let me finish, O.K. I'm going to have a lot of contacts with this job, very important contacts . . .

PAUL: Forget it . . .

BEN: Just shut up a second. You've got fantastic qualifications . . . your background in the Peace Corps, your honors in college. They look at that résumé and it looks good. It looks real good and then they get to these years and what do they see? A little teaching here, a little what is it? Film editing . . . a little of that . . . And they want to know what was going on. Believe me, Paul, you can go anywhere you want from here, but you can't keep faffing around forever.

PAUL: Well, then I'd just better get my act together lickety-split or I'll miss my golden opportunity to sell securities, whatever they are.

BEN: I'm not talking about selling securities. I'm talking about diplomatic work, travel, foreign relations, all the stuff you were interested in in college.

PAUL: That was a long time ago.

BEN: O.K., look, Paul, I understand, you're going through something.

PAUL: Oh. What am I going through?

BEN: Well, don't ask me, for Christ sake, that's what I'd like to know. That's what we'd all like to know.

PAUL: All? Suddenly I'm so important. But what am I going through? You said you understood that I was going through something and I was just real curious to know what that was because I keep thinking of it as my life, but you seem to be anxious for me to get over it or through it or whatever.

BEN: I'm talking about . . .

PAUL: I know what you're talking about, but your arrogance just, I don't know, I just can't believe it sometimes. You come to me with your life in a shambles . . . oh, oh yeah, I know you got a great new job, but I'm not talking about your job. I'm talking about your life, Big Ben, your life. I have a little job. I like it. I know it doesn't take full advantage of my fluency in Nglele, I know it might raise questions about whatever happened to somebody or other everybody seems to have thought I was, but that's

. . . never mind. The point is, I'm happy. I have food in the icebox. When I'm hungry I go there and eat. I have a little money in the bank. Not too much, but enough; and it's more than many. There's someone in bed next to me. I'm not lonely. That's my life, Ben, that's all I want, just a home, Susan, some kids, just what I can see and touch. Do you understand what I'm saying? All the other stuff was and is and will be bullshit forever and evermore, amen. I'm happy. And this seems to worry you.

BEN: I'm not worried. I didn't say I was worried.

PAUL: Good for you.

BEN: Look, what are we fighting for? I haven't seen you for four years. Truce, huh? What do you say? Let me buy you guys dinner. We'll go out to the snazziest goddamn restaur . . .

PAUL: Susan's cooking.

BEN: Come on, give the little lady a break, huh? What do you say? My treat . . .

PAUL: We got food in. Some friends are coming over. We planned a big dinner for you. You don't have to impress us, Ben.

BEN *(Takes a swig of champagne)*: It's not final, you know. Me and Marlene. We're taking a year to think it over. There's the kids. *(Ben pours himself more champagne)*

PAUL: Why don't you hold off on that stuff 'til dinner. We got some nice wine.

BEN: What this? This is nothing. Carbonated French piss. So you're married.

PAUL: Yep.

BEN: Damn. *(Long pause)* Hey, how come there aren't ice cubes in Poland?

PAUL: Oh, Jesus, Ben not now.

BEN: No, this is a good one. You know why?

PAUL: Why?

BEN: I thought you'd never ask. The lady with the recipe died. *(Ben laughs. Paul laughs sadly at Ben. Ben thinks he's got Paul with him)* The lady died . . . dumb, huh? O.K., there's this convention of astronauts . . . this is a quickie . . . they're from all over the world . . . (Susan enters with two beers. Gives Ben one)* Thank you, little milkmaid.

SUSAN *(Walking away)*: It's beer.

BEN: What? Oh, oh, so it is, so it is. Well then, thank you, little beermaid . . . *(Susan hands Paul beer and starts out)*

PAUL: Hey.

SUSAN: What?

PAUL: Come here. *(Susan does)* What's going on up there?

SUSAN: Soolie's making a call. I'm just starting dinner.

PAUL: Want a hand?

SUSAN: It's all under control. She's just calling the gallery.

PAUL: O.K. *(Susan starts out)* Wait a minute. What do you mean she's calling the gallery?

SUSAN: She knows the guy. I mean, like real well. She's gonna get him to come over later. She thinks he'll give me my own show when he sees the new stuff.

PAUL: Serious?

SUSAN: Yeah.

PAUL: Well, I mean, how come you're so calm? Isn't this sort of whoopie-hooray-fucking incredible?

SUSAN: Yeah. I'm a genius. I gotta start the potatoes.

PAUL: Babe! *(They embrace, kiss. Ben stands awkwardly, wanders. Blackout)*

Scene 4

Slide: 1974. Paul and Susan's living room. Easy chair. Couch. Worn Indian rug. Bricks 'n' boards bookcase. On couch sit Janice and Russell. They wear loose-fitting Indian-mystic-style garments. Paul sits in easy chair, a pile of papers by his feet.

JANICE: Remember, this is a dream I'm talking about. Russell dreamed this. Anyway, then what was it? The girl climbed on the back of this huge white bird . . .

RUSSELL: . . . swan . . .

JANICE: What?

RUSSELL: Swan.

JANICE: Oh, yeah, right. The bird was a swan and he described this girl and it was a perfect description of

Susan, who he's never even seen a picture of, O.K.? But every detail. And that was on Sunday night, which was the same night you said Susan flew to New York. Now, I think that's more than a coincidence.

PAUL: She didn't fly. She took a Greyhound bus.

JANICE: Oh, I thought you said she flew.

RUSSELL: Swan. Greyhound. Animals. Travel. Animals carrying people to new places.

JANICE: And here's the amazing part. The swan put her down and she took out all these pictures out of a case she was carrying and started putting them up on these tall tall buildings and you say Susan's in New York putting up an exhibition of her photography. Russell dreamed this.

PAUL: You sure you don't want a beer or something?

RUSSELL: No alcohol.

PAUL: Oh yeah, I forgot.

RUSSELL: We'll take food later. Thank you.

JANICE: No, but you see what I mean?

PAUL: Well, I'm sorry she's not here.

RUSSELL: No problem. *(They sit for a moment)*

PAUL: If you say you might pass through New York I could give you her number there. You did say you might pass through New York, right?

RUSSELL: Yes.

PAUL: O.K. Well, I'll give you her number. I'll write it down. *(Starts writing)* So, you two met in India, huh?

RUSSELL: Yes.

PAUL: That must've been interesting.

RUSSELL: It was.

PAUL: Was it?

RUSSELL: Yes.

PAUL: How? In what way was it interesting?

RUSSELL *(Thinks)*: Have you been to India?

PAUL: No.

RUSSELL: You should go.

PAUL: Why?

RUSSELL: Different trip. Very different.

JANICE: We used to have these meetings in the ashram where Master would answer questions and . . . he's read a lot of

Western literature and he can explain things in a very clear way. He's very modern in a lot of ways . . .

RUSSELL: He's trained in a very ancient tradition.

JANICE: Yeah, the tradition is ancient. I'm not saying about the tradition. I mean, as far as that goes I'm not even sure they know how far back—I mean it's one of the oldest schools, right? But when he explains things you just feel he's talking to you, right now, today. Don't you think so, Russ?

RUSSELL: Yes.

JANICE: Yeah, you see, that's really what I mean, like even outside the meetings there was this incredible energy everywhere in the ashram—all kinds of different energy at different levels, spiritual, psychic, sexual . . . Oh, but let me give you example of the kind of stuff Master could get into. Like remember I told you that . . . oh, I didn't tell you this, O.K., they had this war, India and Pakistan, about something, and Master made the whole ashram, all the buildings and everything, he made it invisible from the air so the bombers couldn't see where . . .

RUSSELL: Jan. *(Janice stops immediately)* Certain times, certain ideas.

JANICE: I was only. I just meant . . . *(Russell smiles. Janice smiles back weakly. Russell takes her hand. She is reassured)*

PAUL: Here's the number.

(Enter Selina from the kitchen.)

SELINA: I can't find that pole thing for the middle of the coffeepot.

PAUL: I'll get it. *(Paul exits into kitchen. Selina sits. Pause)*

JANICE: So what's the film about? Paul said you and him were working on a script while Susan's in New York.

SELINA: We work on it while she's here too. Where do you know Susan from?

JANICE: We grew up together. We traveled around the world. We're like best friends.

SELINA: Oh, right, you're the one that bought the fish in Bali.

JANICE *(To Russell)*: We can stop in New York, can't we? All we need to do is change the tickets to New York/Tokyo.

RUSSELL: It could happen.

SELINA: You're going to Tokyo?

RUSSELL: Tokyo, Singapore, Agadir, Cologne, Paris, Leeds, New York again. Circles.

SELINA: You travel a lot, huh?

RUSSELL: Master can't be everywhere. The physical things. Someone has to check them.

SELINA: That's what you do? You check things for this guy Master?

RUSSELL: Master checks. I'm just there.

SELINA: What does he check?

RUSSELL: Everything. Anything.

SELINA: Covers a lot, huh?

RUSSELL: Really.

JANICE: What's the film about?

SELINA: The American Revolution.

RUSSELL: Heavy topic. Historical.

SELINA: It's mainly about this whorehouse in Concord where the British army used to get laid. The producers want to make kind of a porno-musical. We can't figure out if they're crazy or incredibly smart. They used to sell dope and write children's books. They keep their money in this old icebox. Big piles of it. Very weird. Anyway, I guess with the Bicentennial coming up they figure they can cash in if they get the film out in time.

(Enter Paul from kitchen carrying tray of cookies.)

PAUL: Who's that, Ira and Nick?

SELINA: Yeah. D'you find it?

PAUL: It's perking away.

RUSSELL *(Stands abruptly)*: Thank you.

PAUL: What?

JANICE: We're going? O.K. Well, I guess we'll see Susan in New York. Anything you want us to take her?

PAUL: No, that's O.K.

JANICE: Is everything all right?

PAUL: Fine. Fine.

JANICE: O.K. *(Janice and Russell exit. Paul picks up pages from floor)*

PAUL: So. Where were we?

SELINA: Do you feel like working?

PAUL: Sure. Why not?

SELINA: You seem distracted.

PAUL: I'm fine. I wasn't expecting company.

SELINA: You were out of it even before they came.

PAUL: No, it was just Janice. I knew what she was thinking . . . Susan in New York . . . you and me here. I mean, you can't say anything.

SELINA: O.K., let's work.

PAUL: You're right, I am out of it. She's only been in New York for five days and already I feel like a fucking basket case. You know, we haven't been apart for even a whole day since we started living together. Three years almost.

SELINA: Call her.

PAUL: She's probably still at the gallery.

SELINA: So call her there.

PAUL: She didn't leave the number.

SELINA: You know the name of the place. Call New York information.

PAUL: Soolie, she doesn't want me to call her there or she'd've given me the number. That's code for "this is my space, do not invade."

SELINA: You guys are so weird sometimes.

PAUL: Let's just work on the script.

SELINA: We'll get a lot done, I can tell.

PAUL *(Opens binder. Stops)*: She was out last night when I called. We usually talk at eleven. She wasn't there. She wasn't there all night. She never called.

SELINA: Look, if she was hurt or she got into some kind of trouble somebody'd've called you, don't worry.

PAUL: That's not what I was thinking exactly.

SELINA: You think she's fucking around?

PAUL: I don't know.

SELINA: What would you do if she was?

PAUL: How should I know?

SELINA: If I was in love with a guy and I found out he was doing something like that to me I know what I'd do.

PAUL: What would you do?

SELINA: I'd kill him.

PAUL: We've always had this kind of an understanding, not like a formal thing. Just we picked it up talking to each other, that it'd be all right if we . . . in theory, that is, in theory it was O.K. If we . . . we weren't like exclusively tied down to each other, you know. If we were attracted to someone . . . and we didn't have to necessarily tell each other if we ever . . . unless we were afraid it was getting out of hand . . . like it was getting too serious and we couldn't handle it. But the thing is, we've never been unfaithful. Unfaithful. Funny how it comes back to words like that. We haven't slept with other people. At least I haven't. And I don't think she has, except of course there's no way to know for sure since we said we didn't necessarily have to tell each other. But I really don't think she has. She's probably wanted to. I mean I've wanted to, so it stands to reason that she's probably wanted to and the fact that she hasn't, or probably hasn't, uncool though it is to admit it, the fact that there's probably this thing she's wanted to do but didn't do it because she knew how it'd make me feel . . . that always made me feel, like admire her. Not admire exactly. Maybe trust. Respect. Trust. Something like that. Some combination of those things.

SELINA: I know what you mean.

PAUL: Yeah, but now that I don't know where she was last night I've been feeling pretty ridiculous, you know. Kind of foolish. Stupid, I don't know what. I was awake all last night thinking about it. I mean, here I am all this time . . . I've known you for what, two years, and all that time I've found you like very very attractive, but so what? That's how it goes and now if she's just gone and slept with someone what was all this about? All this holding back for the sake of someone else's feelings . . . and the most ridiculous thing of all is maybe she was in New York thinking you and me were getting it on behind her back and that's what made her . . . if in fact she did do anything, maybe she did it to get even. Or maybe she hasn't done anything. In which case where was she? And why didn't she call?

SELINA: Do you want to sleep with me? Is that what you're saying?

PAUL: No, no, that's not what I'm saying. I mean, I have wanted to but that's not the point. Primarily. Although I did say it, didn't I? But I always assumed you sort of . . . it was just one of those things. Have you ever thought about it?

SELINA: Yes, of course.

PAUL: Well. How do you feel about that?

SELINA: About the fact that people are attracted to each other?

PAUL: Have you wanted to sleep with me?

SELINA: I've wanted to do a lot of things I wouldn't do.

PAUL: So you have wanted to. But you wouldn't.

SELINA: If Susan had been in last night, would you?

PAUL: I wish I hadn't brought this up.

SELINA: I think it was a good idea. Bringing it up, I mean. I smell coffee. *(Selina exits to kitchen)*

PAUL *(Calling)*: Selina?

SELINA *(Offstage)*: What?

PAUL: Thank you.

SELINA *(Offstage)*: You're welcome.

(Paul takes script, lies on couch, glances at a few pages. Pause. He lays script aside, can't concentrate. Enter Susan slowly. Carries small bag. She watches Paul for a moment.)

SUSAN: Paul?

PAUL *(Sits up)*: What happened? Why are you back?

SUSAN: Nothing happened. I took the day off. Are you working?

PAUL: Where were you last night?

SUSAN: I stayed with a friend. Are you glad to see me?

PAUL: Susan. *(Paul and Susan embrace. Selina appears with two cups of coffee. Stands for a moment)* You didn't call. I was worried.

SUSAN: I was going to. I'm sorry.

PAUL: Why didn't you? *(Selina withdraws into kitchen)*

SUSAN: I was here.

PAUL: Where? In Boston?

SUSAN: Yeah.

PAUL: Last night?

SUSAN: Paul, I have to tell you something.

PAUL: Oh, shit. What is it?

SUSAN: I stayed with Katie last night.

PAUL: Katie. Katie Moffatt? That's downstairs. You stayed downstairs? You came up from New York and you stayed downstairs?

SUSAN: Let me tell you what happened.

PAUL: Yeah, why don't you do that?

SUSAN: I came up. I flew up. I wanted to surprise you. And then at the airport just . . . I don't know. I just got angry that I'd come all this way because I missed you. I was gonna call. I was going to pretend I was still in New York, but then, I don't know . . . I didn't.

PAUL: I noticed.

SUSAN: Paul, I'm sorry, I'm trying to explain. I mean I don't feel wonderful about this. In fact, I feel pretty damn stupid. I know it was a dumb thing to do and I felt even worse when I realized why I'd . . . I wanted you to worry. I wanted that. I know it's shitty, but I wanted to get back at you for making me come all the way up to Boston when I should be working on the show . . . Yeah, I know. I just have to tell you that. What I'm trying to say is . . . I seem to have this little problem accepting the fact that I . . . I'm just so fucking in love with you, Paul. That's all it is, and I can't stand being away from you. (*Susan controlling herself. Paul comes to her. They embrace. Susan weepy*)

PAUL: Hey. Hey. (*They kiss. Passionately. Selina comes back. Stands. Fade*)

Scene 5

Slide: 1975. Central Park. Afternoon. Benches and garbage can. Paul, Susan and Maraya eat from "family size" bucket of Kentucky Fried Chicken. Paul holds Baby-Matty while Maraya prepares a bottle. Maraya is pregnant.

MARAYA: I don't know. I guess he was just pissed off about something. I don't even remember what it was anymore, but he picked up this big ole kitchen knife and slammed it into the table. Went in about an inch and that table's solid oak. I mean he was really mad. *(To Baby-Matty)* I'm just telling about Daddy, honey. Don't worry, everything's O.K. *(Maraya gives bottle to Paul, who feeds Baby-Matty)*

SUSAN: But how'd he hurt his hand?

MARAYA: Oh, he wasn't holding the handle tight enough. It slipped down over the blade.

SUSAN: Yech!

MARAYA: Really. Poor Doug. Twenty-three stitches. He's O.K. now, but he has to take these painkillers and that could be a drag in the interview 'cause these pills are like super zappo strong and they make you really high. And they don't kill the pain, either.

PAUL *(Looks at Susan's watch)*: It's ten past one.

MARAYA *(Yelling)*: DOUG!! *(To Baby-Matty)* Sorry, honey, I was just calling Daddy.

(Enter Doug looking back over his shoulder. He has a huge bandage-wrap and position brace on right hand. Dog barks offstage.)

DOUG: You heard what I said, Jake. Stay away from that doggie. Hey, man, I'm serious. I'll punch your fucking head in.

MARAYA: Doug, don't talk to him like that. He can play with the dog. It's not gonna hurt him.

DOUG: Yeah, and when it bites him and he gets rabies who's gonna pay the hospital bills?

PAUL: It's ten past, Doug. It'll take you a good half-hour to get down to Wall Street from here.

SUSAN: It takes fifteen minutes.

DOUG: I gotta have a joint. Where's your purse, Marsie?

MARAYA: You can't get stoned now, honey. You're going to see the president of a bank.

DOUG: Fuck him, man, my hand hurts. If he doesn't want to lend me the bread, I'll get it someplace else.

MARAYA: Doug, you're talking about five hundred thousand dollars. Another bank wouldn't let you in the door. *(To Susan)* The president is Cisco's uncle. .

DOUG: What do you know about it anyway? Man, if I can't get a few bucks from some sucker unless he's my buddy's uncle I don't even want it.

MARAYA: He's not just your buddy—he's your partner.

DOUG: Some fucking partner. If I didn't do all the work myself we'd finish about one house a century. Come on, where's the dope?

MARAYA: No, Doug, you can't have it.

DOUG: My hand's killing me. I can't think straight. *(Dog barks offstage)*

MARAYA: No.

DOUG *(Yelling)*: Jake, what'd I tell you about that doggie? Leave him alone or I'm gonna hurt you. If you want to stay over there . . . *(Barking stops)* O.K., that's better.

SUSAN: He's cute.

DOUG: I'll tell you one thing. If I get this bread I'm gonna buy Cisco out and run the business myself, unless you want to come in with me.

PAUL: Me?

DOUG: You never think I'm being serious. Man, I mean it. You don't know some of the shit I'm getting into. I'm gonna be a rich man. That guy I built the house for, you remember him. Mr. Conklin, the guy with the big lump on his neck? Well, he was real pleased with my work—real pleased. And he bought this big ole chunk of prime lake-front property and when he found out I was with the 23rd tactical in 'Nam . . . that was his outfit in the Second World War . . . that did it, man. Got the contract just like that. Fourteen houses. You know what that'll be worth?

MARAYA: Doug, you haven't even got the money yet.

DOUG: Listen, man, with this deal going any bank that ain't standing in line to lend me the bread is a bank with its head up its ass. One joint, Marsie, huh?

MARAYA: No.

DOUG: One toke. One fucking toke is all.

MARAYA: No, Doug, you can't.

PAUL *(Looks at Susan's watch)*: It's twenty past.

MARAYA: We better get moving.

DOUG: Yeah, O.K. *(Yells)* Hey, Jake, come on, kid, it's bank time. Man, I'll tell ya, I'm no good at this shit. I'm just not. I don't know why the fuck Cisco can't take care of it. It's his uncle.

SUSAN: Why doesn't he?

DOUG: He doesn't have a suit. Naa, I don't know. JAKE! He hates his uncle. In fact, I think it's mutual, but I'm supposed to promise this dude Cisco'll straighten out if he lends us the bread. The family's impressed that Cisco's a partner in a company. Shit-kicker Construction Unlimited. I'll tell you what I can't figure out is how anyone'd think it's worth half a million to get Cisco right. I like the dude. He's my partner and I'll carry him through a lot of shit for sure, but Cisco, man, you could get him straight as a ruler and I still wouldn't pay you more'n a dollar for the guy.

MARAYA: Are we going or not?

DOUG: Yeah, yeah, we're going. This is weird. This is definitely non-normal. I gotta go talk bullshit to a bank president. Doug Superfreak meets Mr. Straightmoney. You guys'll come up, right?

SUSAN: We'll see you soon. Good luck.

DOUG: I don't know how you can live in this city. Look at that squirrel. He's got hepatitis, no shit. Pathetic. Shooting up with a dirty needle. Give him an hour in the country and he'd forget there ever was a Central Park. You should move up. I'm serious. I dump Cisco, we go 50-50 on the business, you bring your camera, take pictures of trees and shit like that. It's so pretty up there.

MARAYA: Doug.

DOUG: O.K., O.K., take it easy. See you guys. Hey, Jakey-poo.
(Exits)

SUSAN: When are you expecting?

MARAYA: November, and that's absolutely the last one. It was a mistake, believe me. *(To Baby-Matty)* Not you, honey, the next one. All I can tell you is don't listen to doctors. They said I was safe for a couple months after Matty here . . . four weeks later, bang. Four weeks. On well, gotta

go. You guys take care, huh. *(For Baby-Matty)* 'Bye-bye.
Go 'bye-bye. 'Bye. *(Exits. Pause. Susan offers some chicken)*
SUSAN: Want some more?
PAUL: No. *(Pause)*
SUSAN: How've you been?
PAUL: Great. You?
SUSAN: O.K.
PAUL: So much for the good news.
SUSAN: Did you sell the script yet?
PAUL: No.
SUSAN: It'll happen, don't worry.
PAUL: No it won't. It's a piece of shit.
SUSAN: I read it. I thought it was good.
PAUL: Yet another point of agreement.
SUSAN: Paul, what's the matter?
PAUL: Why'd you have to go invite Doug and Maraya?
SUSAN: I thought you'd want to see them. They're your friends.
PAUL: But now?
SUSAN: They're only in town for the day. They have to go back
    this afternoon.
PAUL: Susan, for Christ sakes, we haven't seen each other for
    three months. We do have things to talk about.
SUSAN: I'm sorry. I thought you'd want to see them. We have
    all afternoon to talk.
PAUL: I thought you had to work.
SUSAN: I can take the afternoon off.
PAUL: Nice job.
SUSAN: Yes, as a matter of fact, it's a very nice job.
PAUL: Taking pictures of rich people's houses.
SUSAN: I knew that's how you'd see it.
PAUL: Sorry.
SUSAN: Paul, it does happen to be the best architectural jour-
    nal in the country. In fact, it's one of the best in the world.
    And I like working there. I like the people. I like their
    ideas. I like what they're trying to do with the magazine
    and I like the fact that I'm beginning to feel like I can take
    my work seriously for the first time.
PAUL: I said I'm sorry.
SUSAN: I heard you.

PAUL: Moving right along.

SUSAN: And another thing, Paul. I need to make my own living. I never realized it before, how much I hated taking money from you, from my family. Now I don't feel like I have to apologize for anything anymore and that's important, Paul. You're not the only one around here that's proud, you know.

PAUL: You're right. And I'm sorry. Really. That was stupid. I didn't mean to put you down.

SUSAN: I know you didn't. I just had to tell you. Oh, babe, it's so nice to see you.

PAUL: I miss you.

SUSAN: Well, I miss you too.

PAUL: A lot?

SUSAN: Yeah, pretty much a whole lot.

PAUL: Were you . . . have you been with anyone else?

SUSAN: As in guys? A few. How about you?

PAUL: Guys? Not many.

SUSAN: 'Cause I was with a woman. Once. Life's infinite variety.

PAUL: How interesting. Was it nice?

SUSAN: No. I mean yes, in a way, but no, not really. I miss making love to you.

PAUL: Yeah, that part was always pretty good.

SUSAN: Was? Why do you talk about it like it's over? *(Pause)* Is it?

PAUL: I don't know, is it?

SUSAN: Isn't that what we're supposed to be talking about? This wasn't supposed to be permanent. I thought we were just trying out a little time on our own. You want to end it?

PAUL: No.

SUSAN: So let's talk about it.

PAUL: That's what we're doing.

SUSAN: O.K. Things are going pretty well for me, you know.

PAUL: So I gathered.

SUSAN: What I mean is, I can't move back to Boston.

PAUL: Can't? You're being physically restrained?

SUSAN: I don't want to.

PAUL: Ah. So I'd have to move to New York, is that it?

SUSAN: You don't have to make it sound like the end of the world. You always talked about moving to New York.

PAUL: I'm just trying to clarify the situation.

SUSAN: You could do so well here, Paul.

PAUL: I'm doing just fine in Boston. All our friends are there. I've been made a full editor. I like it there.

SUSAN: But you said you wanted your own business one day. You can do it here. There's a lot more film happening here than there is in Boston. And I'm meeting a lot of people who might be able to help.

PAUL: You sound like my brother.

SUSAN: Well, what's wrong with getting a little help, for God sake? Soolie helped me. I've helped some people here. It's not just a favor, you know. You do it because you think someone's good. And you are, babe. You should be doing . . . just, something more like what I know you're capable of doing. Why do you keep fighting it?

PAUL: We should have a sex change before we think about getting back together.

SUSAN: Well, you're the one that always said it. "If you're white, middle-class and American you have to work twenty-four hours a day to not make it." So stop working so hard.

PAUL: O.K., let's say I move to New York. That's condition number one, right? So let's say I accept that . . .

SUSAN: Don't do me any favors.

PAUL: Well, for Christ sake, that's what you're saying, isn't it? If I want you, I have to have New York.

SUSAN: It isn't a condition.

PAUL: Everything is a condition, Susan. Everything.

SUSAN: What are you saying?

PAUL: I just want to know what I get in exchange.

SUSAN: What do you want?

PAUL: You know what I want.

SUSAN: Oh.

PAUL: Have you thought about it?

SUSAN: I don't think either of us is ready for that.

PAUL: That's bullshit . . .

SUSAN: I'm not.

PAUL: Well, when? We can't start when we're sixty.

SUSAN: I'm thirty-one.

PAUL: Great. Only twenty-nine years to go.

SUSAN: Would you want to be our child, Paul? I mean, honestly, at this point in time do you really think you'd want to have the two of us for parents?

PAUL: We're no worse than a few I grew up with.

SUSAN: That's what I mean. I want to have kids someday. I do. Just not now.

PAUL: So what's the score so far? Paul moves to New York. Susan remains childless. That's two to nothing. I need some points here.

SUSAN: We'll talk about it, O.K.?

PAUL: We'll talk about it? That sounds familiar.

SUSAN: Well, you can't just expect me to say yeah, great. "You want kids, we'll have kids." It is something we have to talk about.

PAUL: O.K. That's half a point, right?

SUSAN: Can you stay for the weekend? I think we should spend some time together. I'd like you to meet some of my friends. I've bored them to death talking about you. I don't think they believe you exist. There's a party tomorrow night. I have room at my place.

PAUL: Is that an offer?

SUSAN: Can you stay?

PAUL: Yeah.

SUSAN: Good. *(They kiss)* Let's clear up here.

PAUL: Are we going somewhere?

SUSAN: We can talk at my place.

PAUL: As opposed to here, where we can't talk?

SUSAN: You want to stay here?

PAUL: No, I want to go back to your place. And talk.

SUSAN: I'm expecting a call, that's all.

PAUL: Oh.

SUSAN: Come on. *(They rise)*

PAUL: Susan.

SUSAN: What?

PAUL: What is it? I feel like . . . I don't know.

SUSAN: It's been three months. We need time. Let's go. *(Exits. Offstage)* You coming, babe? *(Paul follows. Fried chicken on bench. Fade)*

Scene 6

Slide: 1977. Paul and Susan's living room, Central Park West. Evening. Painter's drop cloth on floor. Ladder, buckets of paint, paint tray, brushes. Pile of boxes covered with sheet. Armchair. Susan and Selina sit on floor finishing take-out Chinese meal. They are in work clothes.

SUSAN *(Looks into food container)*: Want some more?

SELINA: I'm stuffed.

SUSAN: All in all I'd call that a pretty shitty meal.

SELINA: It's better than I could do.

PAUL *(Offstage)*: What time is it?

SUSAN: Ten past.

SELINA: Is he really serious about the job?

SUSAN: Why would he joke about something like that?

SELINA: He's already got two editors working for him. I don't see why he needs me.

SUSAN: 'Cause Bert's a jerk. Paul ought to fire him but he won't so he's gonna need someone else around who really knows what they're doing. Look, it's a big deal. First feature film. He doesn't want to fuck it up.

SELINA: I thought he didn't have it yet. Isn't that why he's going to California?

SUSAN: That's just a formality. He already knows definitely they want him, but there's this whole ritual you have to do . . . meet the director . . . meet the producer . . . sit around for a few days snorting coke. That's how they do business.

SELINA: I've never worked on a feature.

PAUL *(Offstage)*: What time is it?

SUSAN: Quarter past. I wish he'd get a watch. Listen, I know you're worried. It's a big move. I mean I was terrified when I came to New York the first time. Remember my show . . . ?

SELINA: The Space Portraits?

SUSAN: Right. Jesus, the things I didn't know about photography. It feels like about a million years ago.

SELINA: I liked the Space Portraits.

SUSAN: Oh, sure, they were O.K., I mean for what I knew then, they were great, but until I met people who really knew what they were doing . . . 'cause if they see you've got something, they'll open right up . . . let you pick their brains, ask questions, tell you what you're doing wrong, show you all the stuff you have to know to get really good and, I mean, that's what it's all about finally. Just, when you can see yourself making real choices in the work and you know they're right, even though you don't know how you know anymore. Anyway. I'm rambling, aren't I? I keep doing that lately. What were we talking about? Oh, yeah, New York.

SELINA: I'll think about it.

SUSAN: Promise?

SELINA: Cross my heart and hope to die.

PAUL *(Offstage)*: What time is it?

SUSAN *(Ignores him)*: 'Cause Paul's really convinced you're one of the best editors he's ever worked with. You taught him, for God sake. But who's ever gonna know how good you are when you're stuck up in Boston?

(Paul rushes in with small suitcase. He wears a three-piece suit, has mustache, looks trendy.)

PAUL: Susie, what the hell did I do with my . . . oh, here they are. *(Pats his jacket)*

SUSAN: What?

PAUL: My joints. I forgot I had 'em. Man, do I hate flying. Let me have a little vino. What time is it?

SUSAN: Calm down, babe.

PAUL: I'm calm, I'm calm. *(Takes swig from bottle)* That's better. Well, I guess I'd better get moving.

SUSAN: Can't you wait a few more minutes? He's on his way.

PAUL: Who?

SUSAN: Lawrence.

PAUL: Oh yeah, right. What time is it?

SUSAN: Twenty-two past.

PAUL: I don't want to get caught in traffic. The plane's leaving in forty-five minutes.

SUSAN: There won't be any traffic.

PAUL: That's what you said the last time and it took an hour.

SUSAN: Last time wasn't the 4th of July weekend. Everyone's out of town. Calm down.

PAUL: Look, I saw Lawrence a few days ago. Just tell him I had to go. Tell him I'm sorry I missed him. I'm not trying to avoid him. I think he's a wonderful human being. I love the new beds. He has marvelous taste and we'll all have dinner when I get back, O.K.?

SUSAN: You know he's going to be hurt. He thinks you don't like him.

PAUL: He thinks everybody doesn't like him. Now come on. Wish me luck. I have to go.

SUSAN (Hugs him): Good luck. I'll miss you.

PAUL: I'll call as soon as I get to the hotel. You gonna watch the fireworks from the terrace?

SUSAN: I guess so.

PAUL: I'll tell the pilot to buzz Central Park West and waggle his wings.

SUSAN: O.K., we'll wave.

PAUL: 'Bye, Soolie. (They hug) You still be here Friday night?

SELINA: I don't know yet.

PAUL: If you're not, I'll call you.

SELINA: Good luck.

PAUL: It's in the bag. Shit, I hate flying. (Starts out)

SUSAN: Hey.

PAUL: What?

SUSAN: What about Bert?

PAUL: What about him?

SUSAN: You're not going to let him do that final cut on the Slumbermax commercial by himself? Come on, babe.

PAUL: I left instructions on the wall. He'll know what to do.

SUSAN: Like he did the last time?

PAUL: What can I do? Everyone else is tied up.

SUSAN: Everyone?

PAUL: Lindzee's busy, Stan's busy, Al's busy, Mike's busy, everyone's busy. (Pause. Susan is looking at Selina)

SELINA: Hey, come on, I can't . . .

PAUL: It's a piece of cake, Soolie . . .

SELINA: This is my vacation.

PAUL: You could do it in your sleep. It'll take a day. I've got it all laid out, even the frame counts.

SELINA: You guys are real subtle.

PAUL: Yes?

SELINA: O.K. One day.

PAUL *(To Susan)*: The logbook's on top of the filmrack. My work sheet's taped to the back of my office door. Warn Bert, by the way. Do you have his number in the country? Can you remember all that?

SUSAN: Logbook, filmrack, work sheet, back of door, warn Bert, country number, twenty-five past.

PAUL: What?

SUSAN: It's twenty-five past.

PAUL: Oh, O.K. Shit. 'Bye. *(Exits)*

SUSAN: Thanks.

SELINA: Yeah, good old Soolie. *(Susan sits, leans back)* You feeling O.K.?

SUSAN: Huh? Oh, yeah, I'm fine. I guess I had too much wine or something. Maybe it's the monosodium.

SELINA: Maybe you ought to lie down.

SUSAN: No, I'm O.K. Lawrence'll be here in a minute. I'll be all right.

SELINA: You don't look all right.

SUSAN: Excuse me. *(Rises, starts out. Stops. Breathes deep. Returns. Sits)* False alarm.

SELINA: Are you pregnant or something?

SUSAN: Yeah.

SELINA: Really?

SUSAN: Really.

SELINA: Paul didn't say anything.

SUSAN: I just found out, and don't say anything until I get a chance to tell him, O.K.?

SELINA: Man, I'd really like to be pregnant right now. I was thinking of just doing it, you know. Since it doesn't look like I'm having too much luck finding a guy I can put up with for more than a day or two. Just get someone to, you know, just contribute. Are you happy?

SUSAN: I had such an incredible feeling when I got the results of the test. Just . . . there you are, it finally happened. I was like totally serene, just sort of floated home and I had this whole fantasy, you know, all those pregnant women you see walking around with that funny little smile on their face, the big secret . . .

SELINA: . . . and huge tits . . .

SUSAN: God, Paul would love that. Oh, and I got this idea for a series of self-portraits all through the pregnancy, the different stages. You could do it with a permanent camera in the bedroom so everything would be the same in the picture except I'd be getting bigger and bigger. But the thing is, when I started thinking about it I realized I was really into the idea of the photographs, but I wasn't really all that into the idea of being pregnant.

SELINA: You don't really want to tell him, do you?

SUSAN: Of course I want to tell him. I mean, O.K., I guess maybe I just want to get comfortable with the idea first so I know how I feel about it. We're the ones who have to do all the work, right?

SELINA: Yeah, I guess.

SUSAN: I don't know. It's just so nice the way things are now and the thing is he hasn't said anything about a baby for like . . . well, ever since his business started doing well. Not one word. So I guess it really was some kind of competitive thing. You know, I get pregnant so I can't work as much and that makes me less of a threat. The old story. Does that make sense?

SELINA: Oh, yeah. It makes sense. Sure.

SUSAN: So what do you think?

SELINA: About what?

SUSAN *(Pause)*: Why do you always take his side?

SELINA: Whose side?

SUSAN: Whenever I try to talk to you about something you always . . . like, I really thought you'd understand about this . . . sisterhood and all that. I mean I have a right to my own thoughts, don't I? It's not so terrible that I don't want to say anything to him until I know for sure how I feel about what my body is going to have to be doing for the next however many months and then when I know for sure I'll tell him about it and that way it won't get all messy with me getting my feelings all tangled up in the way he feels about it until we don't know who feels what about anything anymore, which is what always seems to happen with us. But whenever I try to talk to you I feel like you think I'm being . . . I don't know . . . like you automatically think I'm doing the wrong thing. Well?

SELINA: What are you asking me?

SUSAN: Yeah, you see? Like that kind of remark. What's that supposed to mean? Oh, shit, Soolie, listen to me. I sound like a witch. I'm sorry. I really am sorry. I just, I don't know what to do about this. *(Phone by Susan rings. She picks up)* Hello? Yeah, he can come up. *(Hangs up)* I'm thirty-three. If I don't have it now . . . God, why is everything so fucking complicated? They ought to have a course in making up your mind. I'm sorry, but you see what I mean, don't you?

SELINA: Oh. Sure. You have a problem, that's all. It's O.K. You just have a problem.

SUSAN: I'm glad you think so.

SELINA: I don't really think anything, you know. All I think is I'm always in the middle with you two. Paul talks to me. You talk to me. Don't you ever talk to each other? I don't know what you should do. It's not my life. I mean I have enough of my own stuff to figure out and I don't go around asking people what I should do because they're my problems and they're not very interesting unless you're me. In which case, they're mostly just a pain in the ass. I'd like to move to New York, for instance. I'd like to work for Paul. I think I'm probably ready for it, although I think there must be a lot of editors around as good as me and that makes me wonder why you want me to move here. Is it because I'm good at my job or because you like me or because you and Paul don't know how to deal with each other and you need me as a middleman?

SUSAN: I didn't know you felt that way.

SELINA: You never asked. And I don't always feel that way either.

SUSAN: I think we better straighten this out.

SELINA: O.K. *(Doorbell rings)*
SUSAN: Shit. I'll be right back. *(Exits)*

(Selina pours more wine. Talking offstage, then enter Susan followed by Lawrence, talking.)

LAWRENCE: . . . and then in the middle they had this incredible column of balloons right up to the ceiling and out like branches, God, I love balloons. I decided that's what's been missing from my life. I'm going to have balloons in my life. I'm going to just walk around my apartment and kick balloons in front of me. Doesn't that sound fabulous? Just kicking balloons around in your own apartment. Except I'm going to only have one color—just white ones. Too many different colors would just get confusing and who needs more confusion? Hello. I'm Lawrence.
SUSAN: This is Selina.
LAWRENCE: Hi, Selina.
SELINA: Hello.
LAWRENCE: I love your turquoise. Where'd you get it, Arizona?
SELINA: Boston.
LAWRENCE: God, the Navahoes are everywhere. I always wanted a pendant like that. Isn't it funny how everyone's wearing turquoise nowadays? I never used to like it, but now everyone's wearing it and I'm beginning to see what they mean. There's nothing like a trend to change the way you feel about things.
SUSAN: If you want to see how the beds look, they're here.
LAWRENCE: The beds. What beds? Oh, the beds. Did they arrive already?
SUSAN: In the two end rooms. Why don't you have a look.
LAWRENCE: Was this a heavy conversation or something?
SUSAN: Yeah.
LAWRENCE: God, what a 4th of July. I've spent the whole day being rejected by everyone. Sylvia thinks I hate her because I was staring again. I swear I don't know what to do about it. I just can't help it. She's so glamorous for her age all she has to do is start talking to me and all I

can do is stare at her and for some reason that makes her think I don't like her. Maybe I stare wrong. Maybe I should learn a new way to stare. Do you have a mirror? I'll practice. Do you like the beds?

SUSAN: Oh, yeah. They're great.

LAWRENCE: Aren't they sensational? I was going to get one for myself, but then I'd have to redo the bedroom and I'm not in the mood. How long is this going to take?

SUSAN: We'll just be a few minutes.

LAWRENCE: All right. Call me when you're done. May I have some wine? *(Susan pours him a glass)* Maybe I'll watch some TV after I look at the beds. Do you have a *TV Guide?*

SUSAN: In the bedroom.

LAWRENCE: Where's Paul?

SUSAN: He had to catch a flight.

LAWRENCE: They all say that, don't they? Story of my life. *(The wine)* That's some champagne for later. *(The bag)* I stole it from Sylvia's party and whatever you do, don't tell her I came here. I said I was sick. God, I hope she doesn't call my place. I forgot to take the phone off the hook. It's just her parties are always the pits. She has fabulous decorations and terrible company. It's always the same thing. She just doesn't know who to invite. I mean D minus for people. This time it was all these horrible *On the Waterfront* types. You know the kind—leather jackets and keys hanging off their jeans. God, I can't wait till that style goes out. It reminds me of the janitor at my high school. And the silliest thing is I know she's doing it for me, but I don't know where she got the idea I was into leather. I hate it to death. Oh, and then she stopped me on the way out, Sylvia, did you ever notice how she does that? Waits till you're on the way out the door and then she hits you with some heavy dilemma? Some earth-shattering problem? Like this time it was, "should she have a face lift?" I mean, really. I just had to stand there and pretend to think about it when I knew she'd already made up her mind and all she wanted is for me to agree. That's all anybody ever wants. And then there I was staring at her again. Yes, I know, you're talking, I'm sorry. If you'd had the day I just had you'd understand. Don't be too long. *(Exits toward bedroom)*

SELINA: Who is he?

SUSAN: My boss. You know, on the magazine. He's helping us decorate. He found us the beds. Do you feel like talking?

SELINA: I don't have anything to say, really.

SUSAN: You think I should tell Paul?

SELINA: It's up to you.

SUSAN: I don't really feel like talking anymore. Maybe tomorrow. Are you angry?

SELINA: Why should I be angry?

SUSAN: Should I tell Lawrence to come back? Jesus, what do I keep asking you for?

PAUL *(Enters)*: I forgot my fucking ticket. I got all the way to the Midtown Tunnel and I realized I didn't have my ticket. I could've sworn I put it in my travel wallet. I put my wallet in my bag . . . Wait a minute. Oh no. I think I might've just done a very dumb thing.

SUSAN: What?

PAUL *(Opens jacket, looks, closes it quickly)*: I just did a very dumb thing. I have my ticket. My ticket is in my pocket.

SUSAN: Are you stoned?

PAUL: I was on my way to the airport. Of course I'm stoned.

SUSAN: You can still make it. It only takes half an hour.

PAUL: Yeah . . . but I think I don't want to. There seems to be something bigger than all of us telling me to stay.

SUSAN: You have a meeting, babe.

PAUL: Not 'til late tomorrow. I can make it if I catch an early flight and I remember my ticket. Remember that I have my ticket, that is.

LAWRENCE *(Reenters)*: Oh, good. I thought I heard something. How was California?

PAUL: Not bad. How was the party?

LAWRENCE: It was just on the verge of complete catastrophe when I left. Thank God you're here. They banished me to the bedroom with nothing good on TV.

SUSAN: So do you want to try to make the flight or stay and watch the fireworks?

PAUL: Is that champagne?

LAWRENCE: Chateau Sylvia.

PAUL: I'll stay and watch the fireworks.

LAWRENCE: Can I open it? *(Takes out the bottles, opening one)* Oh, dear, good old America. Two hundred and one years old and looking every minute of it. Actually, I think we should have stopped the whole show last year. I mean two hundred years is enough for any country, don't you think? There's just no way we can go anywhere but downhill after this. Hold your breath. *(Uncorks bottle. No pop. No fizz. Looks into bottle)* God, and I thought Sylvia was flat. *(Paul laughs. Lawrence laughs. Others join. They stop abruptly)* What are we laughing at?

PAUL: I don't know. *(They laugh again. Fade)*

Scene 7

Slide: 1978. Terrace of Paul and Susan's apartment. Deck chairs. Doors to apartment. Portable barbecue. Plants. Susan and Janice on deck chairs taking the sun. Janice smokes constantly and drinks a highball.

JANICE: I think it's just a question of respect. Mutual respect.

SUSAN: Yeah.

JANICE: Phil respects me. I respect him. I mean, that's it.

SUSAN: Yeah.

JANICE: Like with Russell, well, you never met him, but believe me . . . O.K. . . . a typical example of Russell. This time we were in Boston, but you'd gone to New York and I wanted to stop and see you. It was no big deal, real easy to change the tickets, but he wouldn't do it. You know why? Get this. I was too attached to the things of this world. That's what he said. O.K. So one time we were back in San Francisco and he saw this sports car and he bought it. I couldn't believe it. He wasn't even into cars, or if he was, I never knew about it. I never knew a lot of things about him, but when I said what about the things of this world, I mean, you can go buy a car, but I can't see a friend, you know what he says? He can buy the car because he isn't attached to it. He doesn't need it. Great. And the dumb thing is, I believed him. Like completely. No, not completely. No, that's right, that's what I was starting to say. *(Offers cigarette)* Want one?

SUSAN: No, I quit.

JANICE: Oh, yeah? When.

SUSAN: Six months ago.

JANICE: Wow. But, you know . . . I really do believe there's this part of you that knows better and all it takes is for one thing to happen. Like with Russell, we were meditating one day. Well, he was. I couldn't get into it, so I was just sort of pretending. I did that a lot. That's another thing. I used to wonder if he knew I was pretending, 'cause if he's supposed to be so spiritual he should be able to tell, right? But he never said anything. Anyway, this one time I was telling you about, I just started watching him, sort of squinting, and all of a sudden he like started changing shape in front of me and I could see the pores in his skin and all these little hairs all over his body. It's like he just turned evil right in front of me. I was even thinking later that maybe it was this really ironic thing happening. You know. Like the first time I finally had a mystical insight while I was meditating and what I saw was the guy that had got me into it in the first place was this really evil creep. Anyway, I just got up and walked out. He was still meditating. I never saw him again. It's weird how these things work out. Oh, by the way, my mother says hi. That's another great thing about being with Phil. I can go home again. I never wanted my folks to meet Russell. Phil and Paul really seem to be hitting it off. Phil usually takes a long time to like people. It's mostly he's just shy, I guess. I remember on our honeymoon we went to the Grand Canyon and he hardly talked to anyone at the hotel. I thought maybe he was angry. He's just shy. Do you like him? Sue. Susie? Susan.

SUSAN *(Waking)*: Huh? Sorry. What?

JANICE: Do you like Phil?

SUSAN: Who's Phil? Oh, Phil. Yeah. He seems like a nice guy.

JANICE: You guys seem real happy. Paul's in a great mood.

SUSAN: The film went well. They finished editing last month.

JANICE: I never realized he was so like, well, I never really knew him or anything, but he's really lively. Sometimes I'm not sure how to take him. *(Airplane flies over. They watch)*

SUSAN: Where is everybody?

JANICE: They're inside.

BEN *(Enters)*: How are the bathing beauties doing out here?

SUSAN: What's going on in there? *(Singing from inside. Enter Paul and Phil with birthday cake)*

PAUL AND PHIL: HAPPY BIRTHDAY TO YOU
HAPPY BIRTHDAY TO YOU . . .

SUSAN: Oh, no!!!

ALL: HAPPY BIRTHDAY, DEAR SUSAN
HAPPY BIRTHDAY TO YOUUUUU!!!!!!

SUSAN: I thought there was something fishy going on.

BEN: Admit it. Admit it. We got you. You weren't expecting it.

PAUL: Happy birthday . . . *(Sets down cake)*

BEN: O.K. Make a wish and blow out the candles.

SUSAN *(Thinks)*: Got it. *(Blows out candles)*

BEN: GERONIMO!!!!

SUSAN: Shhh, Ben, the neighbors.

BEN: Well invite 'em over, goddamn it. *(Yells down)* WE'RE HAVING A PARTY!!!

SUSAN: I'll get the plates. Everybody want? *(Yes. Goes in)*

BEN: And the champagne. Leave us never forget la champagne. *(Goes in)*

PHIL: Your brother's a real character.

PAUL: Oh yeah. He's a real character all right. Actually, what he really is is he's a helluva guy.

PHIL: He told me this great joke. I don't know if you know it. Why aren't there any ice cubes in Poland? Do you know that one?

PAUL: There aren't any ice cubes in Poland? I'm sure that's not true.

PHIL: No. No, it's a joke.

PAUL: I was in Warsaw last year and we had cocktails at this hotel and I'm sure they had ice cubes. Yes, yes, they definitely did. I remember . . . ice cubes.

PHIL: No, you're supposed to . . .

JANICE: He's putting you on, honey. *(Paul acknowledges this with good humor)*

PHIL *(Laughs quietly)*: You already heard it.

PAUL: He's my brother. We talk about everything. I'll tell you the problem I have with that joke, though. I'm supposed to say "Why" and you're supposed to say "The lady with the recipe died." O.K., but the thing is, Poland's been trading a lot with the West, so even if this lady had forgotten to write the recipe down, let's say, and then let's say she died. Well, there's all these other people in Poland who would've come into contact with Europeans who had the recipe. So the whole premise of the joke is too farfetched to be genuinely amusing.

PHIL: You guys are both crazy.

PAUL: Why are we both crazy?

PHIL: What?

PAUL: Oh, I thought that was the beginning of another joke. Hey, I'm just feeling good.

PHIL *(Laughs)*: Have you thought about that story idea at all?

PAUL: I have. I have thought about it.

PHIL: Do you think it could work? Tell me the truth.

PAUL: I think it could be very commercial.

PHIL: Seriously?

PAUL: Why not?

JANICE: Honey, what have you been bothering Paul about?

PHIL: I haven't been bothering him. I just asked him.

JANICE: Phil, nobody's going to want to make a movie about city planners. You think it's interesting because that's what you do. I told you not to bring it up . . .

PAUL: Now wait a minute. Wait a minute. I don't agree. I think if you handled it right there could be a big market for something like that. I'm telling you, people are sick and tired of violence and sex and glamour and fantasy. They want to see real life up on the screen.

PHIL: If I could write I'd do it myself, but I'm not really an artistic kind of person. I have it all up here. Like before I was just thinking about this one time when the computer broke down over at dispatch and all the buses got routed downtown to the city center. It was crazy. They were all lined up there bumper to bumper. People were yelling at each other. You should've seen it.

PAUL: Now that's what I'm saying. That's exactly the kind of thing that's missing from movies nowadays, scene like that. Buses all tangled up in the middle of town. *(Paul hugs Phil. Enter Susan with plates, followed by Ben with champagne)*

BEN: . . . but I already made reservations. It's all set.

SUSAN: Well, you'll have to ask them about it. They're the ones that have to catch a flight.

BEN: Janice and Phil, may I have your undivided attention for just one moment? A suggestion has been made by yours truly that we celebrate Susan's birthday with a disgustingly lavish dinner tonight at the Four Seasons compliments of. Now, Susan has very reasonably pointed out that you two have to leave tonight, but I say nuts to that and, furthermore, a certain company I work for happens to maintain a lovely suite of rooms at a very lovely hotel where you can stay after dinner and . . . And said company will provide you with a limousine to the airport tomorrow to meet any flight of your choosing. Now what do you say to that?

JANICE: Great!

BEN: Phil? Now think carefully before you say yes.

PHIL: Well, I'd really like to but . . .

JANICE: Honey, you don't have to be back at work on Monday . . .

PHIL: I was just thinking we shouldn't leave Jessie with my folks for another day. We've already taken advantage of them.

JANICE: Sweetie, they love taking care of her. They'll spoil her rotten.

PHIL: Well, I guess we could call.

JANICE: We'll stay.

PHIL: Never argue with a lady.

BEN: I'll drink to that. O.K. Now I suggest we open the champagne, cut the cake and embarrass the hell out of Susan by watching her open all her presents. All in favor say nothing. Motion passed.

PAUL: Ben, you're really great, you know that.

BEN: Aw, shucks, guy . . .

PAUL: No, really. I mean how many people would come all the way from England for a birthday? And this is the man who's broken every sales record in the history of Randle and Lane Securities, And, not only that, he's also managed to set up permanent offices in Spain, Greece, Italy, in East Germany. Where else, Ben? Have I missed any? Haven't you managed to break into a few other countries?

BEN: Let's get the presents.

JANICE: Phil, come on.

(Ben exits into apartment. Phil and Janice follow. Paul starts out.)

SUSAN: Paul . . .

PAUL: Huh?

SUSAN: Don't do that to Ben. He means well.

PAUL: I have to get the present.

SUSAN: Paul.

PAUL: What?

SUSAN: What's going on?

PAUL: Nothing *(Exits. Jet passes over. Susan watches)*

BEN *(Enters with two presents. Gives one to Susan)*: For you, my dear. Happy birthday.

SUSAN: What's that one?

BEN: Oh, just a little even-Steven, old family custom. Didn't Paul ever tell you about this? We always used to get a little even-Steven when the other one had a birthday. Dad had a theory it would prevent sibling rivalry. So much for *that* theory.

SUSAN: I'm sorry about the way he's behaving. I don't know what's going on. I really don't.

BEN: I'm used to it. *(Pause)* It's a watch.

SUSAN: Good thinking.

(Reenter Paul with Phil and Janice, bearing gifts.)

BEN: Ah, here it comes. O.K., guy, hand it over and face the music.

PAUL: Me?

BEN: You know what they say about presents—lovers first. Theirs are always the worst. Friends later. Theirs are always greater.

PAUL: Do they say that? I didn't know. Happy birthday. *(Gives Susan present)*

SUSAN *(Surprised by coolness)*: Thank you. *(Starts to open it)*

PAUL: I should explain this, by the way. I thought I'd get something really special this year and . . . there's these places midtown you never hear about. At least, I never did. They're shops, right, stores, like they sell things, but. Like where I found this thing. All they sell there is ancient Chinese treasures and you have to make an appointment to even get in the place. So . . . you're like the only customer. It's incredible. You get inside and you're in a different world. It's completely quiet. You can't hear any sounds from the street and all the stuff is under glass cases like a museum and the lady that shows you around says things like "Now here's an unusual little figurine . . . very rare T'ang Dynasty, perhaps you'd like me to take it out for you." I mean, that's what I call shopping. Do you like it? *(Susan holds up figurine of a horse. It has an opening in its back)*

SUSAN: It's beautiful.

PAUL: Isn't it nice? Genuine Ming Dynasty. There's only about twenty of them in the world. That's what the lady said. They were only for the royal family. That's why I thought it was a nice idea. What they'd do is if the Emperor had a son that died before he was old enough to rule they'd cremate the body and put the ashes in that hole in the back and then they'd bury the whole works. I guess that's why they're so rare. But listen to this. This is the great part. It's shaped like a horse because they had this belief that the horse would take the child's spirit on a ride where it'd see its whole life passing by . . . the life it would have had if it hadn't died. And that way it could go to its final resting place in peace. At least that's what the lady explained.

BEN: Jesus, guy, this must've set you back a few pennies.

PAUL: Oh, yeah. But like I said, I wanted to get something really special and I think I got a pretty good deal. They were asking ninety-seven thousand, but I got 'em down to ninety-three. Not bad.

BEN: A steal at twice the price. *(They're getting uneasy)*

PAUL: Still, I had to sell the business, all the editing machines, the office equipment, the lease on the building, and I had to cash in my stocks and take out all my savings, but I finally scraped it all together.

SUSAN: Paul . . . ?

PAUL: I just thought it was worth it. We need something in this apartment for all the ashes. The unborn embryos. Isn't that what they do after they take 'em out. Don't they burn 'em, or did you have one of those guys that just pops it in a baggie and into the trash can . . . ?

SUSAN: Would you leave us alone, please?

BEN: Hey, guy, what is this . . . ?

SUSAN: Just leave us alone. All of you. Please. *(Ben, Phil and Janice exit inside)*

PAUL: You mean you don't like it after all that?

SUSAN: Paul, is this for real?

PAUL: Is what for real?

SUSAN: This. *(The horse)*

PAUL: Oh, yes. *That's* for real . . . I thought you meant the embryo and I was going to ask you about that because it seems to have slipped your mind.

SUSAN: Is that what this is all about?

PAUL: I just thought it might be worth bringing up.

SUSAN: Who told you? Selina?

PAUL: Oh, is that what's important? Who told me? It wasn't you, that's for sure. And it's a pretty goddamn weird thing to find out about from someone else. That your wife had an abortion six months ago and didn't bother to tell you about it. I guess I must just be one of those naturally curious people because when I found out it made me want to know all kinds of things, Susan. Like just what the fuck has been going on in our life? All these wonderful little human dramas going on under my nose and I didn't know a thing about it. Was it mine?

SUSAN: Yes.

PAUL: Why didn't you tell me?

SUSAN: Paul, I don't know. I really don't know. I meant to. I wanted to.

PAUL: I see. Anything else, or is that sort of the full explanation?

SUSAN: I don't know anything else. I didn't mean not to tell you.

PAUL: That's very illuminating. That really makes me feel like this is something we can work out. I mean, what are we, Susan? Remind me because it's getting kind of vague in my mind. Are we married? Something like that? Is there some kind of unique relationship here? Something that might be worth looking into? Are you saying you didn't tell me because it isn't an interesting fact, or it's just not a very important thing for me to know about? Or it's an unpleasant topic of conversation or it's none of my business? I mean, what is this shit???

SUSAN: Stop it . . .

PAUL: SUSAN!!!!

BEN *(Appears on terrace)*: Hey, is everything . . . ?

PAUL: GET OUT!!!

BEN: I'm just inside if . . .

PAUL: GET THE FUCK OUT OF HERE!!!! *(Ben retreats. Quiet)* It hurts, Susan. It just hurts. All this silence between us. All this unknown stuff. You know how much I want a kid. You know that. I mean what've I been doing for the past three years? Running my ass off building up a business—working twelve hours a day? Am I supposed to have been doing that for the deep satisfaction it gave me? Do you think I'm a mental defective or something? I mean, at very worst I thought this was all some kind of weird test I was going through—some bizarre nest-building ritual to prove I was worthy of fertilizing your eggs. That was the only way I could look at it and still feel marginally sane. . . .

SUSAN: I don't believe this. Are you saying you did everything you did so I'd let you make a baby? Is that what you're saying? Because if it is . . . well, nice to know what you're keeping me around for. Thank you.

PAUL: Susan, you know that's not what I meant.

SUSAN: All I know is it's a pretty shitty thing to lay on me. Nobody forced you to do anything you didn't want to do. So what's this thing like it's all been some kind of t errible ordeal? Jesus, Paul, what's the matter with you? You are allowed to enjoy it, you know. There's no law that says you have to feel terrible about it. You earned it, for God sake. You deserve it. And I'm proud of you, babe. I really am. I just want to see you be happy with it.

PAUL: But why didn't you say anything?

SUSAN *(Quiet)*: Paul. I like what we have. I guess I just don't want anything to change it all.

PAUL: And telling me would have changed it all.

SUSAN: I don't know. Wouldn't it?

PAUL: Well, if it would, then what the hell is it we have that's so great?

SUSAN: Oh, so now we have nothing . . .

PAUL: Well, tell me, Susan, what do we have? Tell me what we have . . .

SUSAN: Everything you've done. Everything I've done. Everything we've got. It's all nothing? None of it means anything to you? My God, Paul, how you must be suffering.

PAUL: We really hate each other, don't we?

SUSAN: Babe, I don't hate you. I just don't understand why we always make everything so complicated for each other. Hasn't this been a good time? I mean, I was under the impression we were more or less happy. In fact, I was even thinking if Greg and Francine get divorced we'll be the longest couple of all our friends.

PAUL: Except for Doug and Maraya.

SUSAN: That doesn't count. They're not married. Shit!

PAUL: What?

SUSAN: I'm smoking. *(They smile)*

PAUL: I don't know what it is, Susan. I mean, yes, I want all this. Sometimes. Sometimes I'm really amazed it's me that's doing all this. There's been whole weeks when I went around thinking, "Hey, this is a pretty good deal. I'm happy." I mean, this is it, right? This must be it. I must be happy. But then one day I'll come home, I'll go in there and try to get comfortable, read or something, and for some reason I just can't concentrate. Try to watch TV, can't even manage that. So I start walking around the apartment and I see all the stuff we have. All this stuff. And I start thinking about what we do to get it. You pick up a little box and go click. I tape together pieces of film.

Presto. We have everything we want. We're so good at doing these things that make us able to have all this stuff, but we can't get it together to have one stupid little baby. Us. The two of us. Together. Doesn't that ever seem strange to you? You know, sort of intuitively wrong? Absurd. Something like that?

SUSAN: No, Paul. I'm sorry, it doesn't. The only thing I find strange is the way I keep feeling like I have to have a baby to be enough for you. I mean, what if I decide a baby isn't as important to me as a lot of other things? What happens if I decide that all I want is you? And our life together? And our work? I mean, couldn't that be enough? Paul. *(Pause)* Paul. Paul, answer me. Am I enough for you without a baby? *(Pause)* I see. And you wanted to know why I couldn't tell you.

PAUL: I don't know. I don't know. Why didn't you say something before this?

SUSAN: Maybe I didn't want to know what I just found out. Well, Paul, I'm sorry. I'm sorry you feel so badly about your accomplishments because I'm feeling pretty good about mine and I can't see any reason why I shouldn't. Doug starts doing well, you laugh about it. You think it's funny. You do well and suddenly it's wrong. I don't get it. You can't have it all ways, babe. We're not children anymore. You have what you have. If you want it, keep it and stop making excuses for it. And if you want to be a saint, go back and dig outhouses for the Nglele.

PAUL: Oh, boy.

SUSAN: What?

PAUL: We're in a lot of trouble, aren't we?

SUSAN: I guess we are.

PAUL: So now what?

SUSAN: I don't know. Should we be talking about this now?

PAUL: No. Let's go out and have a great time with Ben and Janice and Phil.

SUSAN: All right. We'll talk about it now. What are we going to do?

PAUL: I don't know.

SUSAN: Well, we're going to have to do something, aren't we?

PAUL: Like a divorce, you mean?

SUSAN: Is that what you want?

PAUL: Do you?

SUSAN: Well, I hadn't exactly been thinking about it a whole lot. Not today. Are you serious?

PAUL: Isn't that what's going on here? Can you think of anything else we could do?

SUSAN: Well, well, happy birthday.

PAUL: I meant it to hurt, Susan.

SUSAN: Yes. We'll call a lawyer in the morning.

PAUL: Lawyer? *(Pause)* O.K.

SUSAN: Fine.

PAUL: Jesus. *(Plane flies over. They look at each other. Blackout)*

Scene 8

Slide: 1979. The cabin, winter, snow outside. Early evening. Open potbelly stove with fire. Old couch with crochet-square afghan covering it. Paul and Susan wrapped in blankets, naked beneath. Paul sits on couch. Susan showing slides on wall from projector with a carousel. Slide of Doug and Maraya and three children standing proudly in front of construction firm's office building. Then the carousel is at an end leaving white square on wall.

PAUL: Wait a minute. Go back. Let me see the last one again. *(Susan backs up to Doug and Maraya and family)* Doug and Maraya. He shaved off his beard.

SUSAN: Yeah, a couple of months ago. That's his office. I used it for background on a job. *(Turns the lights on)* I think he's a little upset you haven't been in touch.

PAUL: It's the first time I've been back east.

SUSAN: You could've called. Written a letter.

PAUL: Hey.

SUSAN: What?

PAUL: This is real nice. I'd sort of forgotten. Well, I hadn't forgotten, but I hadn't remembered with total accuracy, if you know what I mean.

SUSAN: I think I know what you mean.

PAUL: So you actually went and bought this place.

SUSAN: Yeah, nostalgia. I got a good deal. The Pearsons let me have it cheap because we'd been married here. They're sentimental.

PAUL: Opportunist.

SUSAN: How come you haven't been in touch with anyone? Selina was asking about you. Gary and Linda. Even Lawrence. You hiding in San Francisco?

PAUL: No, I just . . . it didn't feel real until the divorce came through. I don't know. I just didn't want to think about all that.

SUSAN: Who's Edie?

PAUL: Edie? *(Susan exits into bedroom keeps talking)*

SUSAN *(Offstage)*: Yeah. I called you in San Francisco a couple months ago and someone called Edie answered the phone.

PAUL: Oh. She never said anything.

SUSAN *(Offstage)*: What?

PAUL: I said she never said anything.

SUSAN *(Offstage)*: I didn't tell her who I was.

PAUL: More secrets, huh?

SUSAN *(Offstage)*: Who is she?

PAUL: Just a woman I'm seeing.

SUSAN *(Offstage)*: Ah-hah. Seeing a woman called Edie, eh?

PAUL: She's nice. She has a kid.

SUSAN *(Offstage)*: Is it serious?

PAUL: I don't know. She's a photographer, speaking of making the same mistake twice. *(Susan enters, dressing. Paul puts wood in the stove)*

SUSAN: You're kidding.

PAUL: Not only that. She picked the same yellow tiles for her bathroom as you picked for ours.

SUSAN: She has good taste.

PAUL: Well, she picked me.

SUSAN: Are you happy?

PAUL: Happy? Why? I mean, yeah. I guess so. What about you?

SUSAN: Oh, I'm O.K. It's just . . . like this. Today, being with you again, I just started remembering how nice it was.

Sometimes. When it was nice. We should've married other people and had a long affair.

PAUL: It's a nice school where I'm teaching. Nice kids. Very bright. Rich, of course. I like it, though. I really do. I guess I'm happy.

SUSAN: Good.

PAUL: Hey.

SUSAN: Do you do that with Edie? Say "hey"?

PAUL: Come here.

SUSAN *(Watching him)*: I knew it'd happen like this. You'd just show up all of a sudden. Wouldn't phone. I'd've been able to say no if you phoned. It's funny how we can't seem to keep our hands off each other, even now.

PAUL: Come here.

SUSAN: Hang on a second. *(Exits again. Offstage)* How's Ben doing?

PAUL: Better. They did a cardiogram and discovered he'd had another heart attack three years before this one. Hadn't even known about it. Just cured himself.

SUSAN *(Offstage)*: Still drinking?

PAUL: Not for now. What are you doing in there?

SUSAN *(Offstage)*: Looking for my boots.

PAUL: What are you getting dressed for? Let's raid the icebox. It's almost time for . . . *(Watch)* Jesus, it's only five. I forgot how early it gets dark up here in the winter.

SUSAN *(Offstage)*: Go ahead. Help yourself. I think there's some chicken.

PAUL: Aren't you hungry? You always used to get hungry afterwards.

SUSAN *(Enters, dressed)*: How do I look?

PAUL: Terrible. Come here.

SUSAN: Why don't you get some food?

PAUL: Are you going somewhere?

SUSAN: Paul, I have a life. I can't just stop everything just because you show up unannounced. I'd made plans for dinner.

PAUL: Oh, you didn't say.

SUSAN: I wasn't really expecting anything like this to happen. It didn't leave much time for talking, did it?

PAUL: No, I guess not. Who's the lucky man?

SUSAN: You don't know him.

PAUL: What's his name?

SUSAN: Jerry.

PAUL: He's coming here?

SUSAN: Don't worry. I'll go out to the car.

PAUL: Can I come? Sorry. Can I wait for you?

SUSAN: I don't think that'd be a very good idea.

PAUL: You're coming back with him?

SUSAN: We usually do.

PAUL: You see him a lot, huh?

SUSAN: He has a place near here. It's convenient. He lives in New York. He's an illustrator. He's 5'11", 165 pounds, vegetarian, blue eyes. Anything else you'd like to know?

PAUL: He sound fabulous.

SUSAN: He's all right. Actually, he's very nice.

PAUL: Nice. Funny, that's what I said about Edie. Maybe we should introduce them. When'll I see you again?

SUSAN: When'll you be back east?

PAUL: Depends. I might come back real soon if you made me a good offer. Another dirty weekend in New Hampshire.

SUSAN: I don't think we should do this again.

PAUL: Why not?

SUSAN: Well . . . we're being unfaithful. I don't know, Paul. I guess you just don't get over nine years so easily. I don't.

PAUL: No. *(Car noise outside)*

SUSAN: Jesus, he's early. What time is it? *(Paul has a watch)*

PAUL: Ten past.

SUSAN: Damn. Do I look O.K.? Sorry. Listen, when you go, just throw a few logs on the fire and make sure the damper's turned down. 'Bye, Paul. *(Susan takes winter coat and starts out door. Stops. Yells outside . . .)* HANG ON, JERRY, I'LL BE RIGHT OUT. I . . . I FORGOT MY BAG. *(Susan comes back into room. She and Paul embrace, kiss, hold each other. Then it's over)* 'Bye, babe.

PAUL: 'Bye. *(Susan goes. Paul watches car from window. When it's gone he sits, turns on projector, watches slides. Fade)*

End of Play

Michael Weller has written over forty dramatic works, including the plays *Moonchildren, Fishing, Split, Loose Ends, Ghost on Fire, Spoils of War, Lake No Bottom, Help!, Buying Time, Momentum, What the Night Is For* and *Dogbrain* (a play for young audiences) and the films *Hair, Lost Angels* and *Ragtime*. His plays have been produced at Arena Stage, New York Shakespeare Festival/Public Theater, Second Stage Theatre, Ensemble Studio Theatre, Circle in the Square, Ensemble Theatre of Cincinnati, Mixed Blood Theatre Company, Stage One: The Louisville Children's Theatre and Seattle Repertory Theatre.

His new comedy *The Heart of Art* and his award-winning play *Ghost on Fire* will both be produced in 1998. His screenplay of Paul Watkin's novel *In the Blue Light of African Dreams* is being produced by Zanuck/Brown and Cruise/Wagner Productions and he is currently at work on an original screenplay for Talking Wall Pictures.

One of Mr. Weller's most satisfying professional experiences has been working with apprentice playwrights when his plays premiere in not-for-profit theatres around the country. Several have gone on to wide acclaim, including Sally Nemeth, Heather McDonald, Christopher Kyle and Joe McDonough.

Mr. Weller is a member of the Dramatists Guild of America and lives in New York City with his wife and two children.